Essays on Shakespeare

Essays on Shakespeare

WILLIAM EMPSON

EDITED BY DAVID B. PIRIE

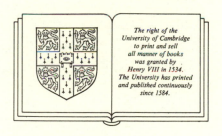

The right of the
University of Cambridge
to print and sell
all manner of books
was granted by
Henry VIII in 1534.
The University has printed
and published continuously
since 1584.

CAMBRIDGE UNIVERSITY PRESS

Cambridge
London New York New Rochelle
Melbourne Sydney

Published by the Press Syndicate of the University of Cambridge
The Pitt Building, Trumpington Street, Cambridge CB2 1RP
32 East 57th Street, New York, NY 10022, USA
10 Stamford Road, Oakleigh, Melbourne 3166, Australia

First published 1986

Printed in Great Britain at
the University Press, Cambridge

British Library cataloguing in publication data

Empson, William
Essays on Shakespeare.
1. Shakespeare, William – Criticism
and interpretation
I. Title II. Pirie, David B.
822.3'3   PR2976

Library of Congress Cataloguing in Publication Data

Empson, William, 1906–
Essays on Shakespeare.
Bibliography: p.
1. Shakespeare, William, 1564–1616 – Criticism and
interpretation – Addresses, essays, lectures.
I. Pirie, David. II. Title.
PR2976.E554   1986   822.3'3   85–29977

ISBN 0 521 25577 5 hard covers
ISBN 0 521 31150 0 paperback

WD

Contents

Preface

In November 1982, Sir William Empson signed a contract with
Cambridge University Press agreeing to "write, or compile from
his previous writing" two volumes of critical essays. The first was
to concentrate on Shakespeare while the second would consist of
articles on other Elizabethan and Jacobean writers.

Empson discussed his more detailed plans for each volume in
letters to his publisher. The correspondence about the project
began as early as August 1981 and carried on until a few months
before Empson's death in April 1984. He wanted to have some
wholly new pieces ready for inclusion in each of the two books.
However, from the outset, he had planned that each volume
would consist mainly of essays which had already appeared in
journals. Some of these previously published but hitherto
uncollected essays would simply be reprinted; but most would be
substantially revised.

Empson had done an enormous amount of work towards both
volumes; and the Shakespeare book, which he had aimed to
finish first, was almost complete when he died. Lady Empson
and Cambridge University Press have agreed that both volumes
should be published; provided, of course, that they contain only
those essays where Empson's surviving papers give decisive
guidance as to which version he himself intended to publish.

Thanks to Lady Empson's great kindness in allowing me
unrestricted access to the relevant manuscripts and typescripts, I
have been able to establish reliable texts of all but one of the
seven essays that Empson had planned to include in this first
volume.

The exception is an essay on *A Midsummer Night's Dream*.
This was to have been one of the two new articles in the volume
and would have made a substantial work of about 20,000 words.
It does survive in numerous alternative versions; but I have had
reluctantly to conclude that Empson had not produced in any of

these drafts a complete text that he judged ready for publication. I have therefore included instead a short piece on the same play, "Fairy flight in *A Midsummer Night's Dream*", which Empson did choose to publish in 1979. This article offers many of the propositions which Empson was exploring at so much greater length in the unfinished essay. All the other essays in this volume are those that Empson himself had decided to include.

To edit Empson would be an impertinence. Even the addition of a more detailed reference than he chose to supply when citing some other critic's work might alter the pace that he had designed for his own prose. However, where the essays do explicitly mention the views of other scholars and critics, the reader may wish to find the works that Empson seems to have in mind, so I have compiled and placed at the end of the volume a list of the books and articles to which he alludes. There will, of course, have been numerous other works that Empson consulted when he was writing and revising the essays so my list must not be mistaken for a full bibliography. In addition, I have corrected a few inaccuracies in the quotations from Shakespeare.

D.B.P.

University of Manchester

Sources
and acknowledgements

"The Globe Theatre" is published for the first time. "Falstaff" is a substantially revised version of "Falstaff and Mr. Dover Wilson" which first appeared in *The Kenyon Review* 15, no. 2 (Spring 1953). Copyright 1953 by Kenyon College. Reprinted by permission of *The Kenyon Review*. "*Macbeth*" is a substantially revised version of "Dover Wilson on *Macbeth*" which first appeared in *The Kenyon Review* 14, no. 1 (Winter 1952). Copyright 1952 by Kenyon College. Reprinted by permission of *The Kenyon Review*. "*Hamlet*" is a substantially revised and expanded version of "*Hamlet* When New" which first appeared in the *Sewanee Review* 61 (Winter and Spring 1953). "The narrative poems" was first published as the Introduction to *Shakespeare's Narrative Poems*, edited by William Burto, Signet Classics, New American Library, 1968. "Fairy flight in *A Midsummer Night's Dream*", a review of *A Midsummer Night's Dream* edited for the Arden Shakespeare series by Harold Brooks (Methuen, 1979), was first published in *The London Review of Books*, 25 October 1979. "Hunt the symbol" was first published in *The Times Literary Supplement*, 23 April 1964.

1   The narrative poems

The poems of Shakespeare have great ability and moments of genius, but we need not labour to praise them, since we must rejoice that he went back to the theatre – recognising perhaps that they were in some way inadequate for him. Nonetheless, they saved his career at the one crucial time, and they record (though mainly in the *Sonnets*) an experience so formative that the plays echo it for the rest of his life. No other playwright known to us worked regularly for the public theatres both before and after their long shutdown because of the plague in 1592–4, after which new companies of actors had to be formed; to survive it was an achievement. At this time a patron was essential for him, whereas afterwards (apart from one graceful kindness) he seems to avoid writing for patrons. His early life is obscure but two facts stand out like rocks: he dedicated to the Earl of Southampton (b. October 1573) both *Venus and Adonis* (1593) and *The Rape of Lucrece* (1594), sounding much more intimate on the second occasion. Our first record of Shakespeare as a member of the Lord Chamberlain's Company, in which he stayed for the rest of his working life – indeed our first record of it performing at a London theatre – is dated just after the Earl's coming of age. The Earl became liable to a heavy fine for rejecting a marriage arranged during his minority, so perhaps did not pay very much, but would help to get the company launched. By writing for a patron, Shakespeare met the crisis in an accepted manner, as a modern author might apply for "relief"; the playwright Marlowe, born in the same year, was also at this time writing a mythological narrative poem, though it happened to be interrupted by his murder; maybe they pretended to one another that this was a tiresome chore. Shakespeare's metre had been made the fashionable one for the purpose by Lodge in 1589; and may I at once refer anybody who wants further information of this scholarly kind to the excellent New Cambridge edition of the

1

Poems by J. C. Maxwell (1966). I want in this essay to concentrate on what may be called the human or experiential reality of the poems, presenting such evidence as I have about that with decent care.

Taking this line of approach, it is a startling initial fact that *Venus and Adonis*, his first publication, appears in the Stationers' Register as licensed by the Archbishop of Canterbury in person. The poem soon made its impact, and libidinous undergraduates are said to have slept with it under their pillows. To have bearded and won over the "little black husband" of Elizabeth, a particularly grim member of her Court, argues that the Bard was in great nerve and good spirits. Shakespeare was not yet thirty, and few of the people who had enjoyed his plays would remember his name, but that is a time when authors need to make contacts. One can glean a little from the Register itself about the conditions of his problem. The *Dictionary of National Biography* reports that John Whitgift (1530–1604) accepted the theories of Calvin throughout his career, sometimes to the annoyance of the Queen, but denied their application to Church Government, so that he was free to persecute Calvinists as well as Papists, bringing them ruin by repeated fines; at this work he showed "brutal insolence in examining prisoners, and invariably argued for the severest penalties". Having a private fortune, he maintained a troop in his own livery, and this was what arrested Essex and his followers during their attempt at rebellion. Soon after his appointment in 1583 he secured a tightening-up of the licensing system: for example, the ballads on separate sheets had now to be approved; and, unlike his predecessor, he would license a few books under his own name every year. Nearly all of them were pamphlets on current theological controversies, for which his decision would anyway be needed, but he also showed a creditable interest in the advancement of learning; for example, he licensed books purporting to teach the Welsh language and the history of China. The Bishop of London, who was another established licensing authority, also adopted the custom of giving his own name to a few books each year; most of them dealt with political news from Western Europe. He worked closely with the Archbishop but seems to have had no literary leanings, though he had of course social ones.

Thus in February 1591, the Archbishop and the Bishop together licensed the rather perfunctory translation of the *Orlando Furioso* by Sir John Harrington. The Queen (so people said at the time) had found her maids of honour giggling over his translation of a sexy canto, and had ordered him to go and stay in his country house till he had translated the whole epic. Both his parents had been with her during her imprisonment in the Tower, when she was almost without hope, and she had made him her godson. It was agreed that the English badly needed raising to the cultural level of the Italians somehow, and yet admittedly, on the moral side, such a poem needed thorough sanctification by the Church of England. Thus the occasion had every claim upon the assistance of the hierarchy. I count about 180 entries in the Register for 1590, 40 of them by the Bishop and 8 by the Archbishop; these proportions are fairly steady for the next few years. In 1592 the Archbishop licenses a book of love poems, though in Latin – the *Amintae Gaudia* of Thomas Watson (1557?–92). Watson was a classical scholar of good family, and he had just died; he had assisted the poverty of better poets, and his verses were sure not to excite desire. The Archbishop entered the fatal year 1593 by licensing Hooker's *Ecclesiastical Polity* and on 9 April he licensed Churchyard's *Challenge*. The book is a final miscellany by a sturdy, loyal old chap, then about seventy-three, who died soon after; it calls the Queen a phoenix on several occasions. Nobody could blame the Archbishop, but he was perhaps starting to go a little out of his way, as Churchyard had no social claims. Within three weeks he had licensed the indecent *Venus and Adonis*. There is no immediate sign of trouble; it is the only year he reaches double figures, ending in September with Nashe – *Christ's Tears over Jerusalem* and *The Unfortunate Traveller* (Nashe had defended the Anglican hierarchy in comic pamphlets, and the first of these books is a work of penitence). But in the following year, 1594, only one publication is licensed by the Archbishop himself: "The Table of Ten Commandments, with the Pictures of Moses and Aaron". A poster, no doubt, for display in all churches; the Queen felt she had to let him keep up appearances so far. In the following year he appears to be forgiven, signing for works of theological controversy at a merry pace, but never again does he license anything even appearing to be a work of literature.

When the poem became notorious, somebody would look it up in the Register hoping to find an irregularity; and, when the truth got about, the Queen evidently told the Archbishop that he must stop making a fool of himself for at least a year. We may be sure he said, as a number of modern critics would say, that these randy students were the ones who had got the poem wrong; probably he could also claim that the author had told him so. A letter from Southampton would be needed for Shakespeare to get an interview, but it would cut little ice with the Archbishop, and Shakespeare would then have to rely on his own eloquence. The apology of Chettle shows that he was socially adroit.[1] He would be found to share the anxieties of the Archbishop about the petulant Earl, regarding him with grave pity. His own little poem, designed as a warning for the young man, carried a peculiarly high and severe moral allegory; and might he perhaps illustrate the point by quotation? (He would read from the final curse of Venus, saying that all loves on earth will in future be upset by parents arranging marriages and suchlike.) Whitgift had almost certainly ruined Shakespeare's father, whether the father was a Papist or a Puritan; it gives a welcome feeling of reality to see an author of revenge plays actually taking a quiet civil revenge. I doubt whether he felt this as a duty, but it might seem an excuse for letting himself be pushed forward by the giggling Southampton. He would enjoy the scene chiefly as a test of skill.

C. S. Lewis found the poem disgusting, mainly because Venus sweats, and J. C. Maxwell writes very sensibly here (his edition, p. xii): Shakespeare, he finds, is "exploiting . . . the sheer comedy of sexuality" in lines 230–40, where we meet the "sweet bottom-grass" of the erotic landscape. This explanation is rather too disinfectant; there is a joke, sure enough, based on evasion of a censorship, but a young man who felt prepared to take this Venus on would find the description positively exciting. We recognise Venus as divine because she is free not merely from bodily shame but even from social precaution; that Adonis is snubbing her just cannot enter her mind. But also the modern conventions about sweat are sharply different from the Elizabethan ones. Many love poems of the time regard the sweat of a lady as somehow a proof of her elegance and refinement; the smell is not recommended as an excitement for our lower nature, the only way it could be praised in a modern novel. In this book we find the sweat of the chaste Lucrece while she is peacefully asleep singled

---

[1] Chettle had published the dying pamphlet of Greene, which contained various libels on authors – some of them justified, says Chettle (December 1592); but he has now met Shakespeare and found "his demeanour no less excellent than the quality he professes. Besides, divers of worship have reported his uprightness of dealing, which argues his honesty, and his facetious grace in writing, which approves his art."

out for praise; one hand is

> On the green coverlet; whose perfect white
> Showed like an April daisy on the grass,
> With pearly sweat resembling dew of night.   (lines 394–6)

I do not know that any poet before Andrew Marvell praised the smell of the sweat of male farmhands, but I expect someone did. Spenser would have blamed Lewis here for being "nice", meaning squeamish and proud of it, an unsoldierly trait. And indeed the impressiveness, the final solidity, of *Venus and Adonis* does turn upon not being "nice", partly from its firm show of acquaintance with country sport, partly from not even caring whether you find the details funny or not. And then, in his own mind, the story would have some bearing on his marriage to a woman of twenty-six when he was eighteen. No doubt it all took a bit of nerve.

At the end of the poem (line 1,166) the corpse of Adonis is "melted like a vapour" and a flower springs up from his blood; Venus plucks it, saying that it smells like Adonis, though not as nice, and that the sap dripping from the break is like the tears that he shed too readily:

> . . . this was thy father's guise –
>   . . .
> For every little grief to wet his eyes;
> To grow unto himself was his desire,
> And so 'tis thine; but know, it is as good
> To wither in my breast as in his blood.   (lines 1,177–82)

The earlier Sonnets frequently blame the man addressed for trying to live to himself like a flower, and for resisting a marriage; the personal application was easy enough to recognise. But people in the know were meant to regard this as only incidental to the structure. The poem recounts a Myth of Origin, like "how the Elephant got its Trunk", a form that scholars, both in Shakespeare's time and our own, revere to a rather surprising degree. (The genuinely ancient examples are believed to have been designed to support the practice of some already existing ritual or custom.) Shakespeare meant his poem to be classically respectable, unlike the plays which he could make a living from, and the motto on his title page boasts of it; but he is not hampered by the form, spurred by it rather. The terrible prophecy of Venus, at the end, at least seems to tell a general truth and thereby give the

poem a universal "significance". Also, I have come to think, he
extracted from the Myth of Origin a new literary device, very
important in the seventeenth century, though hardly ever
employed by himself in its pure form except for *The Phoenix and
the Turtle*.

The central trope of John Donne, the only bit of metaphysics
in Metaphysical Poetry, runs as follows: A ruler or mistress or
saint is being praised, for Justice, Beauty, Holiness, or what not,
and this is done by saying "You are the Platonic Idea, in person,
of Justice or what not"; in the same way, Venus had always been
Love walking about in person. Elizabeth Drury has to hold this
position in the *Anniversaries*, or they are mere nonsense. Only
Jesus Christ (an individual who was also the Logos) had ever
deserved such praise, but the literary acceptance of classical
deities meant that it could be used without feeling blasphemous.
It has become an arid formula when Donne writes to the
Countess of Bedford:

> Your (or You) Virtue two vast uses serves;
> It ransoms one sex, and one Court preserves.

The two words in parenthesis have to mean "or perhaps Virtue *is*
you", but probably poor Donne is just hammering out the
formula to try and get some of his wife's grocery bills paid. When
I was a student, people thought that he had imported this trick
from Spain, but Edward Wilson kindly tells me that there is at
least no prominent use of it in sixteenth-century Spanish poetry.
Some recent critic has named the trick "inverted Platonism", and
it certainly needs to be distinguished from Platonism. It is rather
silly, though there were some splendid uses of it, so perhaps I will
not seem too patriotic when claiming it as a home product.

No one will be surprised that Shakespeare could see the
dramatic or "quibbling" possibilities of his story, as when saying
of Venus:

> She's Love, she loves, and yet she is not loved.   (line 610)

or when the irritated Adonis, like C. S. Lewis, says that what she
calls love is really "sweating Lust" (line 794). But Venus at line 12
is already saying it about Adonis, who is merely human – at any
rate, till after he is dead. In the full "metaphysical" trope, it is
standard to say that the death of the individual entails a universal
absence of the abstraction – after Punctuality Smith has died,
nobody can ever catch a train again. But why should this be true

of Adonis, unless because Venus will go off in a huff? Her presentiment of his death, she says, cannot be true because the consequences of it would be too awful:

> "O Jove," quoth she, "how much a fool was I
> To be of such a weak and silly mind
> To wail his death who lives, and must not die
> Till mutual overthrow of mortal kind!
>   For he being dead, with him is beauty slain,
>   And, beauty dead, black chaos comes again."

(lines 1,015–20)

She already expects the race of man to destroy itself; and the last two hundred lines of the poem, after she has found him dead, are loaded with her despairing insistence that there is no love left in the world. The conception is not a minor decoration in the poem.

Shakespeare did not need to invent it here because he had already used it superbly in *Titus Andronicus* (V.ii), published in 1594 to help launch the Company but probably written about 1590. The Empress Tamora, who has done great wrong to Titus, believes him to be in consequence so mad that he can be tricked into facilitating the murder of his surviving son Lucius. She therefore visits him disguised as Revenge-in-Person, bringing her two sons disguised as Rape and Murder. An Elizabethan spectator was of course thoroughly accustomed to allegorical pageants and charades; he too could if necessary have disguised himself as Revenge. Titus cannot help behaving queerly, but uses this weakness to further his revenge, like Hieronymo in *The Spanish Tragedy* of Kyd, and the eventual Hamlet of Shakespeare. He plays up to her with eerie glee and magnificent rhetoric:

> (To Demetrius) Look round about the wicked streets of
>   Rome,
>   And when thou find'st a man that's like
>   thyself,
>   Good Murder, stab him; he's a murderer.

After a good deal of this, she is so certain he is mad that he can easily deceive her into eating her two sons, disguised as a pie. It is wild but not irrelevant, indeed flatly true, because the practical trouble with revenge is that it does not finish, but produces blood feuds. Shakespeare is always prepared to think, "Why are we interested in the story?" and then say the reason why on the stage. The poem about Venus offered a very different opportunity for the technique, but one can see that his mind would take to it readily. I do not know that anybody else was already using it so early.

We need not doubt that Shakespeare considered the end of the poem dignified, and half believed what he told the Archbishop. But the dedication of it already envisages that a "graver labour" will come next, so there was no change of plan before setting out on *The Rape of Lucrece*. This too is a Myth of Origin; to insist upon it, the death of Lucrece causes an absurd change in human blood (line 1,750). A hero did not need to be a god before such things could happen; one could easily have a historical Myth of Origin (for example, *Macbeth* is about how the Scots, thanks to the Stuarts, took to civilised hereditary rule instead of tribal warfare). The story of Lucrece was an exciting and dangerous example because it explained how Rome threw off her kings and thus acquired an almost superhuman virtue; though somewhat obscurely, this gave its justifying importance to the heroine's choice of suicide. Both the Bible (I Sam. 12:12–25) and the classics (in practice, Plutarch) disapproved of royalty; the institution could only be defended as a necessity for our fallen natures. Also Brutus had a mysterious importance for a patriot and a dramatist. No other great period of drama, anywhere in the world, had so much interest in madmen as the Elizabethan one. This apparently derived from the Hamlet of Kyd, whose story came from a twelfth-century historian of Denmark, "the Saxon who knew Latin". But the story had classical authority from Livy's brief remarks on Lucius Junius Brutus, who pretended imbecility in order to be safe till he could take revenge; indeed, Saxo has been suspected of imitating Livy to provide elegance for his savage material, so that Hamlet, whose basic trouble in the fairy tale was that he could not tell a lie, was truthful as ever when he said "I am more an antique Roman than a Dane." The Brutus who killed Caesar was his bastard, as Shakespeare remarks in *Henry VI, Part Two* (IV.i), though he kept it out of *Caesar*; and a more antique Brutus, a parricide as usual, had been the first to civilise Britain; hence the name. Now, it was Brutus who plucked the dagger from Lucrece's body and championed the expulsion of the kings. He had pretended imbecility up to that very moment . . .

> Burying in Lucrece' wound his folly's show.
> He with the Romans was esteemèd so
> As seely jeering idiots are with kings,
> For sportive words and utt'ring foolish things;

But now he lays that shallow habit by
Wherein deep policy did him disguise . . .   (lines 1,810–15)

The Romans take an oath, and the last line of the poem says that the Tarquins were banished forever.

J. C. Maxwell says in his note:

It is curious that Shakespeare makes no mention here (though the Argument concludes with it) of the historical importance of this, as involving the abolition of the monarchy (unless "everlasting" glances at it); this tells heavily against the view . . . that the popularity of the poem owed much to its bearing on political issues.

It is curious that the scholars of our age, though geared up as never before, are unable to imagine living under a censorship or making an effort to avoid trouble with Thought Police; these unpleasant features of current experience were also familiar in most historical periods, so that the disability must regularly prevent scholars from understanding what they read.

Southampton, who seemed fated to irritate the Queen, might well be inclined to cool thoughts about royalty; and Shakespeare would be wise to hesitate as to how far one might go. Though never very republican, you would think, he was certainly interested in Brutus; he had already, in *Titus Andronicus*, written better than any other Elizabethan the part of the half-genuine madman. Yet both themes are subdued to the decorum of his poem.

The resulting work is hard to read straight through, but one should realise that Shakespeare has made it static by deliberate choice. Francis Berry pointed out in *The Shakespeare Inset* that, although both these poems contain a high proportion of dialogue, the reader does not remember them so, because all the harangues might just as well be soliloquies. Indeed the silent colloquy between Lucrece and the low-class messenger, blushing together at cross-purposes (line 1,339), stands out because it is as near as we get to any contact between two minds. In a play the audience wants the story to go forward, but here the Bard could practise rhetoric like five-finger exercises on the piano. Also, the rhetoric works mainly by calling up parallel cases, so that here again the figure of myth becomes a sort of generalisation. Even this perhaps hardly excuses the long stretch of looking at tapestries of the Fall of Troy, which one may suspect was written later as a substitute for dangerous thoughts about royalty; Lucrece when appealing to Tarquin flatters his assumptions by recalling the virtues of royalty, and the highly formal structure of the work demands that she should recognise the inadequacy of such ideals after her appeal has failed. It would be sensible to have an unpublished version suited to the patron, who contributed a great deal more than the buyers would; and besides, it would give the welcome feeling of conspiracy. But anyhow the poem needs here a feeling of grim delay – she has already decided upon suicide, but has to wait for the arrival of the proper witnesses.

Whether she was right to kill herself has long been discussed, and Shakespeare was probably not so absurd as we think to let her review the Christian objection to suicide – its origins are hard to trace. St Augustine, caddish as usual, had written "if adulterous, why praised? if chaste, why killed?"; and one might suspect that the romantic rhetoric of Shakespeare is used only to evade this old dilemma. But he is interested in the details of the case, and probably had in mind a solution, though he did not care to express it grossly. Livy already has Tarquin force her by an inherently social threat; if she rejects him, he will stab both her and a male servant in the same bed and claim afterwards that he had been righteously indignant at finding them there (line 670). It is assumed that her reputation has a political importance for her aristocratic family, which she puts before everything else; he gags her with her bedclothes, but not because she is expected to resist. Immediately after the rape, and till her death, she speaks of herself as guilty, and Shakespeare concurs. However, just before she stabs herself the assembled lords protest that she is still innocent, and she does not deny this, but brushes it aside as unimportant beside a social consequence:

> "No, no!" quoth she, "no dame hereafter living
> By my excuse shall claim excuse's giving."   (lines 1,714–15)

Coleridge in a famous passage derided Beaumont and Fletcher because the ladies in their plays regard chastity as a costly trinket which they are liable to mislay, and it is not obvious why Shakespeare is different here. When Tarquin slinks from her bed, he says, "She bears the load of lust he left behind"; "She desperate with her nails her flesh doth tear"; she "there remains a hopeless castaway" (lines 734, 739, 744). Perhaps, he reflects, the instability of women is an excuse for her: they have "waxen minds . . . Then call them not the authors of their ill" (lines 1,240–4). Just before killing herself, she speaks to her husband and the

assembled lords of her "gross blood" and its "accessory yield-
ings" (lines 1,655, 1,658); one could hardly ask her to be much
plainer. She was no virgin, having several children; and it is a
basic fact about the young Shakespeare that he considers young
men in general overwhelmingly desirable to women, let alone
brave young lords. Thus she took an involuntary pleasure in the
rape, though she would have resisted it in any way possible; that
is why she felt guilty, and why some of her blood turned black,
making a precedent for all future corrupted blood (line 1,750).
The reader perhaps is also guilty, having taken a sexual pleasure
in these descriptions of sexual wrong – as much at least as the
"homely villain" who wondered how she was making him blush.
But we are not told that she would have killed herself for this
private shame; she considers the suicide useful for public
reasons. St Augustine would conclude that she deserved death
for enjoying the rape and Hell for her suicide afterwards; but the
dramatist is sure that all her reactions, in this tricky situation, do
her the greatest credit and are enough to explain the permanent
majesty of Rome.

The Passionate Pilgrim (1599) is a cheat, by a pirate who is very
appreciative of the work of Shakespeare. It starts with two
genuine sonnets (138 and 144 in Sonnets) each of them implying
plenty of story and giving a smart crack at the end; and the third
item, a sonnet extracted from Love's Labour's Lost, follows
quite naturally. Paging ahead in the bookshop, one found poems
that might easily be Shakespeare's, though most of them are now
generally considered not to be; it would be sensible to buy at
once. What we learn from this is that Shakespeare had become
news, a personality exciting curiosity, and there are other signs of
it. In the previous year, for the first time, a play had been printed
with his name on the title page ("Love's Labour's Lost, as it was
presented before her Highness this last Christmas"), and the
absurd Palladis Tamia by Meres had at least treated his work as
deserving scholarly attention. The Shakespeare Allusion Book
finds many more references to Falstaff than to any other character (Hamlet comes second, with the others far behind him). Thus
in 1598 his reputation so to speak came to the boil; this was why
his public was willing to trust him through his tragic period,
though they did not like it so much.

The editor would have printed more sonnets if he could, and
yet the ones chosen are well suited to his purpose – how could
that happen? Dover Wilson in his Introduction to the Sonnets of

Shakespeare thought that the Dark Woman (he will not call her a lady) had allowed a publisher two specimens with a view to raising the price of her whole collection. But this ignores the state of the market; she would have succeeded in publishing her collection and would not have needed to offer bait. I think that a visitor was left to wait in a room where a cabinet had been left unlocked – rather carelessly, but the secret poems were about five years old; he saw at once that they would sell, but did not know how much time was available. Thumbing through the notebook (the poems cannot have been on separate sheets, or he could have taken more without being noticed), he chose two with saucy last couplets for hurried copying. In one of the variants, the 1609 edition has a simple misprint, but as a rule it has slightly the better text – either because the thief miscopied or because Shakespeare had second thoughts. I think that one of these cases allows us to decide the alternative:

> I smiling credit her false-speaking tongue,
> Outfacing faults in love with love's ill rest.

In 1609 the second line has become:

> On both sides thus is simple truth supprest.

J. C. Maxwell gives an admirable gloss for the pirate version: "With (the help of) the ill-grounded sense of security that is characteristic of love", and plainly this is more like Shakespeare. But it is rather out of place; the poem has very little to do with his private experience or sensibility, commenting with sad good-humour on almost universal departures from truth. The duller line is more good-mannered in a way, and he would not give his first draft of a sonnet to his "private friends" (as Meres wrote), or even, one would think, to the Dark Lady. Poets of our own time have been known to add in the desired obscurity when they rewrite, but Shakespeare is more likely to have removed it. So probably he was the one who left the cabinet unlocked.

This publication also refutes the Herbert Theory of the Sonnets, for a reason that its supporters have been too high-minded to observe. William Herbert, later Earl of Pembroke, became eighteen in April 1598, and was hardly allowed to come to London earlier, as he was a sickly lad, addicted to headaches (Dover Wilson, *op. cit.*, p. 66); though later, I don't deny, an honest man and a useful patron, who deserved to have the First Folio dedicated to him in 1623. But this would mean that the sonnet about letting Shakespeare's boy patron borrow his mistress, when the pirate got it into print, would be hot news. The Elizabethans would call the incident thorough toad-eating, and it would be sure to get mentioned in some of the letters of gossip. I am not saying that Shakespeare would not have done it, though I think it was outside his mode of life at this date, but that he could not have hushed it up, in these circumstances. Consider what moral Ben Jonson would find to say (whereas, in 1594, moral Ben Jonson had not yet poked his nose above the boards). The first soliloquy of Prince Hal, assuring the audience that he will betray Falstaff, has close verbal echoes of the first of the pathetic sonnets ("Full many a glorious morning") trying to defend the patron for a betrayal of Shakespeare. But this does not mean that they were written at the same time; the implications would be horrible. The joke of Falstaff largely turns on the repeated bite of his self-defence, and Shakespeare may well be drawing a good deal upon his own humiliations when the servant of a patron, in his twenties. But he would need to use these memories in the assurance of secrecy, feeling them distant, feeling that they could be laughed over.

The reader should be warned of a slight change of idiom in the couplet:

> The truth I shall not know, but live in doubt
> Till my bad angel fire my good one out.

The Variorum edition gives a list of references to periodicals, mainly Victorian, and till I looked them up I imagined they proved that the Dark Lady is accused of having gonorrhea. They merely show that the phrase *fire out* was then used as we use *fire*, to mean "dismiss a person from a job"; it did not then, as now, inevitably suggest firing something from a gun. Shakespeare need only be saying: "I will not know whether the Dark Lady has seduced the Patron till she gets bored and dismisses him; then no doubt both will come round to me with indignant stories." We may be sure he did realise that an explosive insult was in the background, because he had a complex verbal awareness, as when he left his wife his second-best bed; but if the Dark Lady had really caught the disease we would hear more about it in his personal poems. A laboured epigram by Edward Guilpin, published in 1598, is I think simply a crude imitation of Shakespeare's joke here; he must have been one of the "private friends" who were allowed (says Meres) to read some of the "sugared Sonnets". It would be pretty sad to believe that Shakespeare copied the merry thought from Guilpin as soon as he read his book, and had it stolen at once.

One has to try to make sense of these dates; it is fundamental to the understanding of Shakespeare's development, I think, that the relations with a patron come in 1592–5, when a patron was needed. Leslie Hotson, indeed, has put the *Sonnets* five years earlier, in an entertaining recent book that proposed a new addressee for them (*Mr. W. H.*, 1964); he laughs at the scholars for viewing Shakespeare as Little Dopey, shambling along in the rear of Marlowe and the rest, "a remarkably late developer". But his development really is unusual; usually the lyrical power comes earlier than the constructive one. Reading through the plays in the generally accepted order – *The Comedy of Errors*, the three parts of *Henry VI*, *The Taming of the Shrew*, *Titus Andronicus* – you get hardly a breath of poetry so far, though plenty of vigorous rhetoric, and a clear mind at work making the best of the plots. A little poetry comes in with *Richard III*, so that he was just beginning to be a poet, aged twenty-seven or so, when the plague forced him to rely on it for survival. After two years, when the theatres open again, he seems essentially a poetic dramatist. Another contrast, though more trivial, is perhaps more striking. Bernard Shaw remarked that Shakespeare must have suffered torture if he ever read over his comedies after he had grown up – assuming, I think, that any adult feels an obscure personal shame when he hears another man boast of being a gentleman. Probably the boasting of lads together is much the same in all classes, but it is true that an entry of three young lords, swanking by making jokes that are assumed to be top-class, occurs in all his comedies between 1594 and 1598, whereas the characters in the early comedies are mostly traders, and the lords in *Henry VI* simply murderers. One might perhaps blame Shakespeare for choosing to write about aristocrats, but not, having chosen to, for doing some fieldwork on how they actually talked. It is not what is now called snobbery, because he could not pretend to be anything but the servant of his Earl. Probably he would be allowed to hand around drinks at a party given by the Earl for young men of standing – listening with all his ears, though, as one gathers from the plays, much more free to make jokes himself than a modern servant is. In private he seems to have scolded his lord unreasonably, as privileged servants often do. C. S. Lewis, in *English Literature in the Sixteenth Century*

(1954), spoke of "the self-abnegation, the 'naughting'," of the sonnets, more like a parent than a lover: "In certain senses of the word 'love', Shakespeare is not so much our best as our only love-poet" (p. 505). This is noble, but it is perhaps only the other side of a feeling that the gratitude is over-strained. And yet, a number of the sonnets thank the patron because

> thou . . . dost advance
> As far as learning my rude ignorance.   (Sonnet 78)

The actual teaching of the Earl can hardly have been more than a few social tips, but as a window upon the great world Shakespeare had been feeling the need of him badly. The feelings seem better grounded if you realise that the childish patron was giving far more than he knew. And, unless you redate the plays as a whole, remembering that the evidence is quite an elaborate structure, there is only one plausible time for fitting in this bit of education.

A Lover's Complaint was printed at the end of the sonnets in 1609, but many critics have denied that Shakespeare wrote it – chiefly on grounds of vocabulary and imagery, but also by calling lines bad when they are simply dramatic, imagined as by another speaker (e.g. lines 106–11). Much of it, he would consider, had needed correcting before it was published, as indeed do many of the sonnets themselves; he forces the words into his rhyme scheme and general intention so hurriedly that our textual notes sometimes only amount to lame excuses (e.g. around line 235). But at least Kenneth Muir has now proved Shakespeare's authorship, by "clusters" (*William Shakespeare 1564–1964*, ed. E. A. Bloom); the principle is that if an author happens to use one word of a cluster his mind drags in most of the others soon after, and this process is not conscious or noticeable enough for an admirer to imitate it, nor is it affected, as imagery in general can be, by a change of subject matter or recent experience. I think the poem is evidently by Shakespeare on psychological grounds, and a kind of echo of the sonnets (this of course is why they were kept together, and eventually pirated together); but I am confronted by an agreement among the scholars (Maxwell's edition, p. xxxv) that it must have been written after 1600. Similar arguments have been used to maintain that the sonnets themselves were written late; the explanation, I think, is that Shakespeare often first tried out a novelty of style in his private poetry. I only ask for two years; the poem was written in 1598, with tranquillity, looking back with tender humour at his relations with Southampton, and just after killing off Falstaff. There would be no intention of publication; perhaps he wrote it in the evenings of a solitary journey. It would at any rate be a change, after seeing himself as Falstaff, to become the traditional forsaken damsel (forsaken, because by 1596 the Earl had become absorbed in his dangerous life; we need not look for a specific ground of quarrel, though we may expect that Shakespeare did, at the time). Shakespeare, like other authors, often used poetry to scold himself out of a bad state of mind, and took for granted that no one would realise he was doing it. He knew it was a delusion that the Earl had betrayed him, and writing about Falstaff had aggravated the sentiment, so he wrote a parody. Or perhaps he merely felt it was delightful to carry the belief to a wild extreme. These conjectures have the merit of explaining why the poem was written at all, though (fairly clearly) not intended for publication. Most people find that working for a repertory company is exhausting in itself, especially if they have part responsibility for the management; a man who also gives the company two masterpieces a year, as regular as clockwork, with a good deal of reading behind them, is not looking around for something to do. It is thus in order to suppose an internal reason for undertaking this quite lengthy bit of work, since there is no external one.

The first ten verses set the scene, and the rest is all spoken by the ruined girl; as many critics have remarked, the best and most Shakespearean lines express reproach:

> Thus merely with the garment of a Grace,
> The naked and concealèd fiend he covered . . .   (lines 316–17)

> O father, what a hell of witchcraft lies
> In the small orb of one particular tear!   (lines 288–9)

All the same, the girl firmly asserts in the last words of the poem that she would have him ruin her again if she got the chance:

> O, all that borrowed motion, seeming owed,
> Would yet again betray the fore-betrayed
> And new-pervert a reconcilèd maid!   (lines 327–9)

No other author would do this; one man would bewail the seduction and another treat it jovially, but not both at once. Indeed, rather few male poets seem convinced that young men in general are irresistible to women. A reader of novels will rightly feel baffled at not knowing the social arrangements of this

village, where many people write sonnets expounding the suit-
ability of the rich jewels that they are presenting to the young
man (line 210); is it in Arcadia or Warwickshire? is he the son of
a labourer, or the heir to a hundred acres, say?

> He had the dialect and different skill,
> Catching all passions in his craft of will,
>
> That he did in the general bosom reign
> Of young, of old, and sexes both enchanted,
> To dwell with them in thoughts, or to remain
> In personal duty, following where he haunted. (lines 125–30)

The magical picture only applies to one person, who had been
already an Earl when still a child; no wonder, after puzzling their
heads, they decided that he was the one who was clever, and not
just his horse (lines 114–19). In all the undramatic poems Shakespeare is deliberately holding back the power to be funny, which
was considered when he wrote *A Lover's Complaint* to be much
his greatest power; but he knew a joke when he saw one, even if
he had just written it down himself. But perhaps when I say
"funny" I would be more intelligible to young people (who have
such grim ideas now of what makes a joke) if I said "charming".
The chief merit of A. L. Rowse's account, on the other hand
(*William Shakespeare*, 1964), was its powerful presentation of
Southampton as a typical neurotic invert, intolerably disagreeable, who could only regard the Queen as a personal rival. Under
James, after he had unexpectedly won back his life, he played a
considerable part in founding the English colonies in America,
and the only picture that conveys his charm shows him as an elder
statesman. (It is in C. C. Stopes's *Life*, p. 449.) But we have a
glimpse of him when twenty in the Valentine of the *Two Gentlemen of Verona*. This figure is bustling along, with a rope ladder
hidden under his cloak, to abduct the daughter of the Duke of
Milan, but the Duke accosts him and asks his advice – how is one
to abduct a lady who is kept locked up in a high bedroom? Why,
with a rope ladder, of course, equipped with grappling irons but
light enough to carry under one's cloak; Valentine feels he is
cleverly secret because he just manages to restrain himself from
offering to share the use of his rope ladder with the outraged
father, but so far from that, he and his cloak are farcically transparent. The brash informative practicality of this does not feel to
me neurotic at all, and I expect that many of his servants were in
love with him when he was twenty, not only Shakespeare. Plainly

he seemed very young to Shakespeare, who was not only ten years older but had had a harder time. The Bard could not be considered low; as heir to an ex-mayor of Stratford he would become entitled to gentility. But the social ladder was long and steep, and the expense of the clothes the Earl wore all the time would alone be enough to make him seem legendary – though he did not seem another breed from common men, the title being a recent creation.

A grave change in the whole tone of Shakespeare's writing arrives at the time of *Hamlet* (1600), the first major tragedy, and here it would be fussy to suppose that he was even remembering his relations with the patron. Critics since A. C. Bradley have pretty well agreed that "sex-horror" is prominent all through the tragic period (perhaps burning itself out in the unfinished *Timon of Athens*, before *Antony and Cleopatra*). I do not understand this change, though I expect there is a simple answer if we knew it. The reason why *The Lover's Complaint* must have been written before it is simply that otherwise it would have been much grimmer. The change I think is prominent even in the parallels to *Hamlet* which give Kenneth Muir his main evidence; *The Lover's Complaint* is regularly less fierce than the echoes of it which convey the doom of Ophelia. We have no nondramatic poems to guide us after the tragic period has set in.

Only one remains to be considered, and it is short; but it has come to seem the only very good poem in the book, exquisite, baffling, and exalted: *The Phoenix and the Turtle*.[2] It is much better, I think, if viewed less portentously than has become usual. The occasion for Shakespeare's agreeing to write this bit of praise, in late 1598 or early 1599, was a humane and domestic one, though socially rather smart. I have no impulse to deny that vast and fundamental meanings derive or arise from the poem, such as were adumbrated when C. S. Lewis said that reading it

---

[2] There has been a recent move in favour of saying *The Phoenix and Turtle* instead of *The Phoenix and the Turtle*. It is true that the title pages of Chester speak of "The Phoenix and Turtle", and Shakespeare's poem as first printed has no title. But his way of regarding this pair has long been recognised as slightly different from Chester's. A social column will report the presence at a party of "The Earl and Countess of X" because they are expected to go together, and that is how Chester feels about his Phoenix and Turtle, but Shakespeare, whatever else he feels, always regards their co-presence with a touch of surprise. A critic may write about a poem: "The familiar lion and unicorn serve to emphasize the wholly conventional character of the imagery", but they become "the lion and *the* unicorn" when they are fighting for the

was like entering the secret origins of creation, or at least of the creation of the heroines of Shakespeare's plays. But it does not tell Queen Elizabeth to produce an heir by the Earl of Essex, nor even mutter about the marital secrets of the Countess of Bedford. If Shakespeare had been prone to say things like that, he would not have stayed afloat for at all long upon the smoking waters of the Court. It may be hoped that such theories are going out of fashion, but what we are regularly told now, though it sounds more modest, is quite as damaging to the poem. J. C. Maxwell takes it for granted when he remarks that Shakespeare's poem "contradicts the personal allegory of Chester's poem", so that "our interpretation must be from within the poem itself". He seems to feel that this makes it pure. But Shakespeare would have been abominably rude if he had behaved like that, after agreeing to take part in the social event of offering a volume of congratulation to Sir John Salisbury. The whole book was about the birth of a new phoenix from the ashes of the old one, a story that every reader had been taught at school, and here it was somehow in praise of Salisbury's marriage; but Shakespeare is presumed to say: "No, of course, the new Phoenix wasn't born. When you burned the old one you simply killed it, as anybody could have told you you would." But, even if he had tried to offer this rudeness, it would not get printed. The immense indulgences nowadays offered to the avant-garde are not in question here. Salisbury was a forthright and decisive man, brought up to advance the glory of his house, and we know he made Ben Jonson rewrite one of the poems for his book; he would no more have allowed Shakespeare to palm off on him a subjective poem than a seditious one.

Verses by Shakespeare, Marston, Chapman, and Jonson, and also by an anonymous poet who seems to be Jonson again (probably one of his team had backed out from fear of ridicule) are added at the end of a long allegorical poem, *Love's Martyr*, by

---

crown. Shakespeare's poem really is a bit like "The Walrus and the Carpenter", and cannot be properly appreciated unless that is seen. Looking now for evidence to support the traditional preference (though it is apparently no older than a Boston edition of 1805), I find the poem grants it repeatedly:

Phoenix and *the* turtle fled . . . *this* turtle and his queen . . . *the* turtle saw his right . . . it made this threne, To the phoenix and *the* dove . . . And *the* turtle's loyal breast To eternity doth rest.

In effect, *The Phoenix and the Turtle* emerges as a habitual rhythm of Shakespeare's poem, and an illogical pedantry ought not to be allowed to destroy so natural a title.

Robert Chester (unregistered, 1601); a separate title page assures us that these too are "never before extant, and (now first) consecrated to the love and merit of the thrice-noble knight, Sir John Salisbury." The book appeared at the height of the War of the Theatres, when several of the contributors were quarrelling, and soon after the execution of Essex, when it was very dangerous to print a riddle that might arouse the suspicions of the Queen. Surely it is natural to expect that the poems were written earlier.

The introduction to an edition by Carleton Brown (1914) of *Poems by Sir John Salusbury and Robert Chester* (Early English Text Society, 113) is a mine of information and entertainment about these characters, and ought I think to have settled the question. Salisbury (we may use the ordinary spelling because Chester's book does) was squire of Lleweny in north Wales, and had married in 1586 at the age of twenty an illegitimate but recognised daughter of the King of Man (or Earl of Derby); some verses written for the wedding already call her a royal bird. In 1595 he came to London as a law student and was made squire of the body to the Queen; he was her cousin, and a determined Anglican (having got the estate when his Papist brother was executed for the Babington Plot), and had a standing quarrel in Denbighshire with supporters of the Essex faction. This last would be no help until the execution of Essex, early in 1601, but in June of that year he was knighted by the Queen herself. By October he is back home being elected to Parliament as Knight of the Shire, with scandalous disorders, so he must have moved fast. Clearly, the poem was hurried out to celebrate the knighthood, unregistered to save time and because the Queen would not suspect a man she was rewarding for his loyalty; but the writing would have been done beforehand, to wait for the occasion. A line from Jonson's "Epode" here is quoted in *England's Parnassus* (1600) showing that at least some of these poems were ready about two years before publication. Also an autograph copy of Jonson's "Enthusiastic Ode" survives, inscribed to the Countess of Bedford. The squire would show round all the poems at Court, as soon as they were ready; and the ever-helpful Countess might be expected to want her own copy of Jonson's contribution, as it was not yet to be available in print. In this poem he was evidently struggling to be as jolly about the Phoenix as the Turtle demanded. Clumsy as Jonson was, he would not have given it to the Countess as direct praise of her own charms; or at least, she would not have kept it, if he had.

In 1597 the squire had printed some poems at the end of *Sinetes Passion* by Robert Parry, who calls him "the Patron"; they make very elaborate anagrams (in easy singing lines) on the names of three adored ladies, one of them his wife's sister. While very pugnacious, he was what a later age called "a martyr to the fair", attentive to the ladies, so it had seemed all right at the time of the wedding to make him a sacrifice as Turtle beside the semi-royal bride as Phoenix. In 1598 he would be a very useful patron for the young Ben Jonson, who was in desperate need of one, and he seems to have told Jonson to whip up a chorus of London poets. Shakespeare's company was giving Jonson a production, and it would be consistent to help him here too – assuming that Shakespeare had no objections to the general plan. So far from that, Shakespeare was amused or charmed both by the squire and his poet – as is clear once you admit that he wrote his tribute, not while Hamlet was saying he couldn't bear to think what his mum did in bed, but while Henry the Fifth was saying:

> Though it appear a little out of fashion
> There is much care and valour in this Welshman.

Shakespeare made it part of his business to keep an eye on these pushful Welsh cousins of the Queen, and he recommended them to his audiences without hiding their absurdity.

Chester, says Brown, was probably the resident chaplain in the big house at Lleweny, anyway a dependent who praised the family by an allegory at the time of the grand wedding. Later he was induced to add a lot of tedious padding (Nature takes the Phoenix on a grand tour), but the basic allegory is quite short and readable, though radically absurd. A marriage does indeed require mutual accommodation, and love may genuinely receive "a mystical reinforcement" on the birth of a child; but to praise a grand marriage by calling it a martyrdom is a gaffe, all the more absurd because sure to be suspected of being true. Chester evidently came to feel this during the years while he was adding the encyclopedia verses, and when at last he had to tell the London poets what the whole thing meant, so that they could reinforce it, he said it meant "married chastity". This idea had not been prominent when he began, though the intention was already high and pure. When Nature at last leads the Phoenix to the Turtle, she asks whether he has been chaste, and, on being reassured, explains that for her to produce issue requires burning alive; both birds at once collect twigs, so there is no long period of married chastity. (This of course is *why* you sometimes see birds carrying about twigs.) The main poem by Ben Jonson puzzles about his set theme, in a plain-man way; it seems a new idea to him. Trying to isolate the ideal, he appears to describe a man who spares his wife the act of sex in order not to offend her delicacy. We should welcome any sign of readiness among men of that age to treat their wives more considerately, especially if it meant spacing out the childbirths; but the refined thoughts expressed by Jonson here are remote from his tastes and convictions as otherwise known. He is not a hypocrite, because he is writing to a set theme; but his modern admirers should not praise him for his nobility. Rather out of the side of his mouth, he lets drop that one need not praise a husband who chose this course merely to hide impotence:

> We do not number here
> Such spirits as are only continent
> Because lust's means are spent.

Oddly enough Shakespeare manages to work the same reflection into his mood of total praise; the reproduction of the Phoenix, he surmises, has only failed because of the married chastity of the couple:

> . . . 'Twas not their infirmity.

Various modern critics have explained that Shakespeare could not bear the thought of reproduction when he wrote the poem; but nobody has yet ascribed quite so much delicacy to Ben Jonson.

The Mutual Flame by G. Wilson Knight (1955) shows that the Phoenix legend had often been used to symbolise a love denied bodily consummation, because that would be adulterous or homosexual or politically disruptive, so that the love is driven to more spiritual courses. He suggests that the poem may be about the squire's love for his wife's sister, which would at least avoid absurdity. One should remember here an epigram of C. S. Lewis, that Spenser was the first poet to have the nerve to say it is convenient for a man to be in love with his own wife. There had been a change of feeling since the Middle Ages, a thing so general that poor Chester, in the backwoods, around 1587, was running

Spenser close for the priority. Salisbury of course really did consider himself ready for heroic self-sacrifice whenever that
became necessary; the idea was basic to his status, and had to be
expressed firmly in his book; but otherwise he wanted the book
to be as jolly as possible, and his pride in his wife had better be
expressed in a firmly sexy manner – that was a point where he
could take over from his chaplain. His marriage had produced
four children in the first four years, six in the next ten (no twins),
and one of his bastards had been baptised in the parish church in
1597. No wonder Jonson argued about what Chester could have
meant. The Phoenix herself will not have come to London, with
all those ailing children, but a few vigorous comments survive
from her and she apparently lived to be seventy-five.[3] Shakespeare might genuinely have supposed it to be an ideal though
perhaps barbaric marriage.

The Wilson Knight thesis does have a secondary truth; what
keeps the long absurd poem sweet is Chester's love for his
master. This kind of love was avowable and not usually
tormented, but when Chester comes to present himself as the
Pelican, who gazes upon the burning, he positively claims a share
in the honours of sacrifice; both the Phoenix and the Turtle
become the "young ones" of this Pelican and feed their "hungry
fancies" on her breast. He has been under-rated, I think; so long
as he is praising his dear lion (the coat-of-arms of Salisbury was
a white lion) he has any amount of limpid depth. And why should
not his absurdity (though he fears it) express something
profound? If anything seems wrong with his poem, he says as he
lumbers toward the end, abandoning for a moment the disguise
of the Pelican,

> tis lameness of the mind
> That had no better skill; yet let it pass,
> For burdenous loads are set upon an ass.

This is the royal generosity of the Shakespearean clown, and
Shakespeare was quite right to salute it.

---

[3] Brown, *op. cit.*, p. xxvi. Chester's poem says that the Phoenix had been anxious
before meeting the Turtle, being of ripe age and fearing to have no offspring.
No doubt it was often a tricky business to find a good enough marriage for the
bastard daughter of an Earl. I expect she was twenty-five when the elder
brother of young John was hanged, so that he inherited the estate and became
free to marry her in what would be considered the nick of time. It does not
mean that she was the Queen, who would be sixty-five.

Once the general tone has been grasped, of slightly fuddled good-humour, the dramatic placing of the piece by Shakespeare can be seen as reasonably good. The two first additional poems are subscribed "Vatum Chorus" (all the poets) and praise the virtues of Salisbury only, not his wife or family; then two poems subscribed "Ignoto" (Unknown, by the starving but invincible Ben Jonson again of course), without pretending not to know the Phoenix legend (which would be too absurd) manage to direct our attention onto the sacrifice of the old Phoenix, not presenting it as repaid by the birth of a new one. Such is the purpose of the phrasing:

> One Phoenix born, another Phoenix burn.

The build-up is only rough, but it is an intentional preparation for what Shakespeare is going to do. Shakespeare then presents himself as one of the spectators after the burning, among the non-predatory birds who are the voice of Reason, and they fall into despair because the result of the experiment is delayed. I gather from J. C. Maxwell's edition that it was traditional to allow a period of dramatic suspense. Shakespeare ingeniously fits in the set theme of "married chastity" as an excuse for the failure of the experiment. But what follows his noble resignation, what holds the opposite page, is the astonishment of a birth from the ashes. It begins:

> O twas a moving epicidium!
> Can Fire? Can Time? Can blackest Fate consume
> So rare Creation? No, tis thwart to sense;
> Corruption quakes to touch such excellence.

The recent scholarly edition of Marston's *Poems* (1961, ed. Davenport) says firmly that this word *epicidium* (poem about death) means the poem by Shakespeare just concluded. Marston snatches a moment to compliment Shakespeare, as he bounds onto the stage to describe the event in an entirely different literary style; and his only objection is that the forecast in Shakespeare's poem has, astoundingly, turned out wrong:

> Let me stand numbed with wonder; never came
> So strong amazement on astonished eye
> As this, this measureless pure rarity.

I consider that very good poetry. The subsequent poems all deal with Salisbury's domestic life, wife or child being mentioned every time, so that Shakespeare's poem acts as a watershed. Anyhow, he could not have intended to spoil the show because of his neuroses; that would be quite outside his habits and training. He was acting as a good trouper when he left the climax to Marston, and he seems to have remembered Marston's bit long afterwards for the last scene of *The Winter's Tale*.

Having thus restored the poem to decency, one may consider its use of "inverted Platonism". It says that, because these two ideal lovers are dead, there will never be real lovers again, anywhere:

> Truth may seem, but cannot be;
> Beauty brag, but 'tis not she;
> Truth and Beauty buried be.

However, the next and final verse abandons this high extremity of nonsense:

> To this urn let those repair
> That are either true or fair;
> For these dead birds sigh a prayer.

I suppose the reason why Shakespeare can afford to be lax about it in this curious way, which allows him a graceful ending to the poem, is that he is working in an accepted mode. All the poets in the book seem in command of the trick, even Robert Chester; he uses it when the Pelican rejoices that the Turtle chose to burn alive, though the Phoenix tried to spare him (the experience turned out to be a pleasure, according to the Pelican's eye-witness account). Otherwise, he says:

> Love had been murdered in the infancy;
> Without these two, no love at all can be.

It is clear then that Chester was writing another Myth of Origin. But can he have had the whole machine ready in 1587, a homely author, remotely secluded? This seemed to me a great puzzle, and I am glad to have it removed by W. H. Matchett's book on the poem (1965). He explains that Chester added the Pelican section, at the end of his first draft, when the squire took him to London to negotiate with the poets (the squire would not himself have demanded to be praised for married chastity). In a way, Chester must have known the idea from the start because it is inherent in this use of myth, but he had become uneasy about the absurdity of his whole plan; so that it would be a great relief when the smart poets, though they did laugh at him as he had expected, told him that his absurdity had become the height of fashion. He was inspired to add what is the most eloquent and personal section of the whole work.

Matchett has a very welcome energy of logic and research; what other critics limply assume, he follows up.[4] I hope his book will drive out of people's minds the main idea which he champions, that Shakespeare was writing about the loves of Elizabeth and Essex; when he says that Shakespeare refers to the Queen as already dead in order to rebuke her for not having followed his previous advice, whereas in fact the exasperated and appalling old woman had become dangerous to anybody who had to approach her, surely this is enough to act as a purge. But I think he is right (for instance) in saying that Jonson became frightened on hearing that the poems would appear during 1601, when they were likely to be supposed to be about Essex; he made some baffling remarks in his plays of that year, hoping to offset the publication. Matchett also gets his teeth into "inverted Platonism", as one might expect, and it is a great comfort to find a critic who is prepared to attend to the words. Somehow he contrives to denounce Marston and not Shakespeare for using this trope:

Against Shakespeare's materialistic basis for negative judgment, he asserts a pseudo-Platonic basis for positive judgment. As an exposition of Platonic abstractions, Marston's poem is an awkward melange; as a compliment to an allegorized individual – claiming that this person is himself the Idea upon which all else depends – his poem further degrades the very idealism it pretends to express.

Marston says he had been wondering why all the young girls were so ugly and stupid nowadays till he saw the new Phoenix, and then he realised that Nature had just been saving up, so as to give her everything. The eldest Salisbury child, a daughter, would be about twelve when this was written for her, and it seems well enough calculated for her age-group; she would think it rather fun. If anything, I should call it Science Fiction not Platonism; it does not deserve to be rebuked as false philosophy, because it scarcely even pretends to be philosophy. But somebody else

---

[4] He remarks that a scribe may write the name of the author after copying a poem without intending a signature, and this would destroy a good deal of the edifice of Carleton Brown. But if you wrote a name with set formal flourishes, surely that implied it was your signature.

deserves the rebuke; why do modern critics invariably write down that the trope is neoplatonic? Its effects, very various, are nearly always broader and more imaginative than would be gathered from this docketing.

Elizabethan jokes are notoriously confusing, but it would be wrong to think that the Welsh squire was being fooled by the city slickers. He wanted his book as jolly as was compatible with having it sustain the glory of his house, and he rejected the first draft of Ben Jonson's "Invocation"; at least, there is no other reason why this much more solemn version in Jonson's handwriting should have got kept among the Salisbury papers. And he must rather have strained the goodwill of his chaplain when he inserted his own "Cantos" at the end of the allegory, celebrating his delight in the beauty of the Phoenix in a very unsacrificial manner (only the first is announced as written by the Turtle, but they all have his very recognisable facility and ingenuity, and the printer might well get confused among the stage directions and acknowledgements). The celebration of his knighthood positively required family jollity; indeed, one can understand that Shakespeare, though willing to assist, felt he would avoid strain if he joined them only in their darkest hour. Even so, what he was joining was a kind of domestic game.

An important idea is at work in such love poetry, though admittedly one that was ridiculous in the eyes of the world; it forbade a husband to claim marital rights through his legal superiority, and such is the point of Shakespeare's ninth verse. We know that Chapman thought the affair funny, though in a grave pedantic manner, because he headed his piece (which praised the knight who has learned his virtues by serving his lady) "Peristeros, or the male Turtle". He has had to invent a masculine form for the word, since the Greeks considered all doves female; however monogamous they may be, the creatures do not know which sex they are, but try out the alternatives (Sir Julian Huxley, in *Essays of a Biologist*, reports this of various water birds). A female Phoenix had been invented by the Renaissance to gratify a taste for Amazons – till then its secret sex had been "known to God alone"; but a Turtle wearing the trousers does seem to have been a real novelty, not only for a classicist. It proved the grandeur of the Lion, as his poet almost says in the *Epistle Dedicatory*, that he was safe from ridicule even when presented as a Turtle. The Latin "Tur tur" no doubt gave to the cooing of the pets of Venus, in the minds of the poets, a deeper note of sultry passion; to make them into symbols of chastity thus put an extra strain upon the gravity of the reader – it had been the charm of the silly creatures that no frustration attended their single-minded desires. Shakespeare's poem is a wide valley brimful of an unspecified sorrow, but one should also feel, before hearing any explanation, the gaiety inherent in its effects of sound. As the anthem of the birds reaches its severest exultation their tweeting modulates into the arch baby-talk of a dandling nurse; as we soar heavenward between the Co-supremes, we mysteriously almost graze the Cow that jumped over the Moon;

> To themselves yet either neither,
> Simple were so well compounded.

It does seem rather odd, in a way, that he went straight on from this to his great tragic period.

2   Falstaff

The theory that Shakespeare made Falstaff appear in his first draft of *Henry V*, so that our present text of that play is much revised and thereby confused, seems to be accepted now by most of the competent authorities; indeed to be regarded as the most positive result of Dover Wilson's very detailed work on the Falstaff trilogy, and therefore as the main support for a narrow view of Falstaff in general. I want in this essay to ask the reader to look at the whole position again. Whether Shakespeare changed his mind about *Henry V* is perhaps not very important, but it gives a definite point to start from; and I think it is time someone pointed out how very weak the evidence for this theory is.

To be sure, the evidence offered is imposingly various; from the Epilogue of *II Henry IV*, from some historical possibilities about censorship, and from the text of *Henry V* itself; but I think it breaks down all round. The relevant part of the Epilogue says:

One word more, I beseech you. If you be not too much cloyed with fat meat, our humble author will continue the story, with Sir John in it, and make you merry with fair Katherine of France; where (for anything I know) Falstaff shall die of a sweat, unless 'a be already killed with your hard opinions; for Oldcastle died a martyr, and this is not the man.

"For anything I know" and "if you want it" are a good deal more doubtful than what we are accustomed to nowadays in the way of advance publicity. Among Elizabethans it is not unique (e.g. the end of *Selimus*, for which the proffered Second Part seems not to have been wanted); but we need not suppose that Shakespeare was really feeling hesitant about whether these very popular plays were worth continuing. It seems likely that the Company, when it was forced to stop calling the buffoon of these plays Oldcastle, also had to promise to apologise before the public audience; some graceful bits of chat were therefore arranged, so as to drop in the apology with an air of casualness. In any case, the speaker disclaims knowing what the author will do, beyond the broad fact that the next part of the familiar story is being considered for a play; and the Company might not want to give away the secrets of the next production, even if Shakespeare had decided on them. Dover Wilson makes the valuable point that the Quarto order for the text of this epilogue shows it is two of them jammed together; the Folio editor merely altered the order to make the combination speakable. The first was spoken by someone responsible for the performance, perhaps the author, probably at Court, and the second by a dancer before he began his jig or what not; the second therefore need not be taken very seriously, and only the second includes this little advertisement. Dover Wilson says he cannot believe that the "jesting" apology about Oldcastle was "spoken on the stage while the matter was still dangerous", but I cannot see what he deduces from that; it seems to be a matter of months rather than years. As to the main point, I think Falstaff *is* quite prominently "in the play", though not in the cast, and indeed I think the new king's hard opinion, which Falstaff does die of, *is* a kind of "public opinion", so that there is no inconsistency at all. Of course this would be "stretching a point" if anyone gave it as an official explanation, but it is the kind of thing the Elizabethan mind would put up with, and the whole trick of this advertisement is to tease the audience by ostentatiously refusing to satisfy their curiosity. Shakespeare could have let it be spoken if he had already decided to kill Falstaff; it is as likely that he hadn't yet started on the new effort (one would expect he dallied till he knew he had to work fast); but either way it is no proof that he wrote out two whole versions.

Dover Wilson's argument in his edition of *Henry V* (1947) was that there was nobody to act Falstaff because Kemp had suddenly left the Company. I gather that this line of effort has now been abandoned. There was a Court performance of *I Henry IV* in 1600 (described as a private one, for the Flemish Ambassador), after Kemp is supposed to have gone, and the recent attempts to decide which actor took which part do not give it to him anyway. Kemp was a low comedian (a fine chap too), whereas one of the points you needed to make clear about Falstaff was that he was a scandalous gentleman; it doesn't seem Kemp's part at all. Besides, they would have to have some kind of understudy system. The argument has now moved to a more aristocratic ground, and we are told that Falstaff was removed from

Agincourt because the descendants of "Fastolfe" influenced the censor. He was not suppressed altogether; the Ambassador could hardly be shown a play recently banned for libel, and Part II was printed in 1600, and indeed *The Merry Wives* (on this view) was brought out as an alternative to showing him at Agincourt. Dover Wilson suggests that the Company hid its embarrassment by *inventing* a story that the Queen asked to see him in love, and that Shakespeare could gratify her in three weeks. This was "convenient" for them, he thinks. I do not believe it could be done. Falstaff was a very prominent object, much the most successful Shakespeare character before Hamlet; some of this would be likely to leak out. The legend that the Queen commissioned *The Merry Wives* is recorded late and not worth much; it is evidence that the terrifying old woman had laughed at Falstaff, and that her moods were watched and remembered, but not much more. As negative evidence, however, it seems to me very strong; if she had allowed her underlings to suppress Falstaff, even in part, no "publicity" arrangement would be likely to get away with the opposite story. Besides, the "embarrassed" Company would just as soon have the truth leak out. And what about the treatment of a much more real Fastolfe in *Henry VI*? And why not deal with the new name firmly, as had been done to the previous name Oldcastle? All the same, peculiar things do happen, and the descendants of Fastolfe might have been just strong enough to keep him out of Agincourt, and to hush the suppression up, though not strong enough to suppress him elsewhere. If we found confusions in the text of *Henry V* which needed a very special explanation this theory might be plausible. But surely it is very gratuitous if we find none.

The textual arguments for revision, in Dover Wilson's edition, are as follows.

I. Pistol says at V.i.85 that he hears his Doll is dead of syphilis, so he has lost his rendezvous. I agree that the author ought to have put "Nell", and the actor had better say it, because the other word confuses us with another character. But the modern Damon Runyan slang happens to have been Elizabethan slang too; the slip was an easy one for the author to make. And I think there was an extra reason for making it here. The ladies were last mentioned in Act II; we learned that Pistol had married Mrs Quickly (Nell) and heard his express contempt for Tearsheet (Doll) as in hospital for syphilis; he had always skirmished with Doll (when on the stage with her) and had now become keen to stand by Nell, whose position was clearly more hopeful. There can be no point in assuming he has changed over without warning the audience. But we need not be surprised that Mrs Quickly got the disease too, and there is a deserved irony if Pistol, who talked brutally about Doll's trouble at the beginning of the play, finds at the end that the same applies to his Nell. Now, if Shakespeare meant this, both women were in his mind, and that is the kind of case where a hurried writer puts down the wrong word. It comes in the Quarto, supposed to be pirated by actors, not only in the Folio, but that need only be another of the depressing bits of evidence that Shakespeare never corrected the acting text.

Such is what I would make of it, but Dover Wilson deduces that the whole speech, and much else of the part of Pistol, was written for Falstaff, to whom Doll was last seen attached. Before erecting this mountain of conjecture I think he might have answered the note here in the Arden edition, which points out four other places where the text goes wrong over proper names; one of them calls the King of England "brother Ireland" (V.ii.2), and compared to that (which Dover Wilson believes to be a mistake in writing by Shakespeare, who must have been thinking about Essex, he says) I do not think a reasonable man need feel very solemn about these two dolls.

I also feel that, even if Shakespeare did first write this flabby blank verse for Falstaff and not for the now miserably deflated Pistol, we need not call in the machinery of censorship to explain why he changed his mind; if his first thoughts were so bad we had better keep to his second ones and be thankful. Maybe he did toy with the idea of taking Falstaff to Agincourt – he would feel the natural strength of any easy temptation – but we have no proof here that he wrote a whole draft of it.

II.   The prologue to the second Act ends:

> . . . the scene
> Is now transported, gentles, to Southampton;
> There is the playhouse now, there must you sit:
> And thence to France shall we convey you safe
> And bring you back, charming the narrow seas
> To give you gentle pass; for if we may
> We'll not offend one stomach with our play.
> But, till the King come forth and not till then,
> Unto Southampton do we shift our scene.

The next four scenes are in London, Southampton, London, and

France, with the London ones describing first the illness and then the death of Falstaff. The final rhymed couplet, which follows another, whereas the prologues to the other four Acts all end with one rhymed couplet, seems a rather slack attempt to clear up a muddle and only succeeds in adding a contradiction (the Arden edition remarks, with psychological but perhaps not literal accuracy, that "the negative notion, being uppermost in his mind, thrusts itself in prematurely"). Dover Wilson deduces that the scenes about the death of Falstaff were added later. But he and the other people who hold this theory assume that comic scenes about Falstaff always existed in the play and had to be put somewhere, however different the first draft of them may have been. To prove that their position has been altered does nothing to prove that their content has been altered. It is rather curious, I think, that this simple fallacy is so convincing at first blush. You might perhaps argue that the dying Falstaff could not leave London, whereas the swashbuckling Falstaff could be shown in Southampton; but it would be almost necessary to start him off in London, if only for a farewell to the ladies. The first Act is just under four hundred lines long, and the average for the other four Acts, all a good bit longer, is just under six hundred. The technique of five "epic" prologues was new to Shakespeare, and obviously difficult to combine with his usual unbroken one; and all the Acts contain comic material except the first. Surely he might have tried to polish off Falstaff in Act I, and then found that the balance had gone wrong, as I think it would, and then corrected the second prologue rather casually. It seems to me equally possible that he had not thought of the solemn prologues as anything to do with the comedians, and had always intended a short banging first Act, and then pushed another couplet onto the prologue to Act II, of a baffling kind, merely because the Company objected that it didn't apply to them.

III.   The first two arguments point out real confusions, but the third (for which Dover Wilson gives credit elsewhere) only marks a lack of understanding in the critics. The long scene IV.i, they say, must contain a huge interpolation. The King says he wants a council of lords at his tent, so they must come there "anon", but first he wants to think alone (this is at line 31); then he has three successive conversations in disguise with his troops; then a long soliloquy about how they don't understand his difficulties, because they have been saying that the King had no right to invade France and drag them into this hopeless situation (we must remember that they all expect death, and that the King has behaved well in refusing a separate escape); then Erpingham, who took the message before, comes back and says the lords are seeking him through the camp, and the King says they must be called back but adds graciously that he will be there before the messenger (this is about line 300); then all he does is to walk out to the audience and start off on another soliloquy – he is at last ready for his solitary prayer, and it is not at all hurried. A number of critics beside Dover Wilson have found this "awkward", therefore a mark of interpolation. The lords would find it awkward but the audience didn't; they thought it as clear as a bell. The sequence merely drives home the repeated argument of the previous plays that Henry had learned to be a good king by his experience of low life. Henry thought nothing of keeping the lords waiting while he talked to the troops; talking to the troops would even keep him from his prayers, but talking to experts on strategy never would. I do not believe that this very strong dramatic effect was an accidental result of enforced revision; I should be more inclined to call it playing to the gallery; and when Dover Wilson cannot see it he throws himself under serious suspicion, as an interpreter of Falstaff as well as of King Hal, because he is missing the whole popular story about the King he claims to rehabilitate.

Some other arguments for revision given by J. H. Walter in his article "With Sir John In It" (*MLR* July 1946) should perhaps be recognised here, but they seem to me unimportant. Fluellen doesn't use "p" for "b" in talking to Pistol (III.vi) but does so to Gower just afterwards, therefore the Pistol incident was added later (but he is on his dignity in talking to Pistol); we are promised "a little touch of Harry in the night" but don't get any of the fighting we expect, only morale-building (this seems to me an absurd objection; there was assumed to be much excitement in getting a stray contact with what Pistol calls "the lovely bully", and the morale for next day was more important than any skirmishing could be); in F though not in Q a comic capture by Pistol is impossibly made the first action of the battle (but if put later it breaks the dramatic sequence); Fluellen at the beginning of Act V "relates to Gower an entirely fresh motive for his annoyance; it has no connection with Pistol's insults in III.vi" (Shakespeare always multiplies motives, and Pistol could be trusted to do the same; besides, Fluellen might not care to repeat the insults); at the end of this scene, in the "My Doll" speech, "Pistol's charac-

teristic verse is completely absent" (of course it is; he is deflated
and in soliloquy; is this Falstaff's characteristic verse, then?) and
says he is old though, unlike Falstaff, he is not (he feels old); the
Dauphin comes to the battle against his father's express orders
(another detail to make his father look weak); there seems an
intention to bring Henry and the Dauphin into opposition, but as
it comes to nothing the Master of the Revels may have cut a
degrading representation of royalty (then Shakespeare may have
avoided going to such lengths as might have induced the Master
of the Revels to make a cut); Fluellen was present when Williams
told Henry about the glove, so ought to have recognised Williams
later (but he is too excitable; the plot is not meant to be deep),
and there is no reason why Henry should tell both separately to
go and look for Gower (but it is only to make sure they meet and
have an absurd quarrel; this bit of rough fooling, ending with
tossing away some gold, is entirely "in character" with the Henry
of the Falstaff scenes, and was very much needed to show him as
the same man in his stern grandeur). I don't much like the play,
and do not mean to praise it by defending the text; but the fashion
for finding "joins" in the text has I think been carried to
absurd lengths, though by people who agree with Dover Wilson
rather than by himself, and I hope this tedious paragraph has
proved it.

There is of course a reason why we find this struggle made to
prove that Falstaff was meant to go to Agincourt. Dover Wilson,
as I understand, was working on his edition of the Falstaff plays
during the Second World War, and felt a natural irritation at any
intellectualist fuss against a broad issue of patriotism. He felt that
Henry V is a very good patriotic play, and the man Henry V is the
ideal king, and Falstaff is a ridiculously bad man, and if you can't
face that you had better wince away from the whole subject.
Then when he came to carry out this programme he decided that
the Victorian critics had put us all wrong about Falstaff by
making a fuss about the report of Falstaff's death, at the beginning of *Henry V*; this had made them sentimentalise Falstaff. If
it could be proved, then, that this description was only thrown in
as a "job", to cheat the audience and hide a bit of truckling to
high officials, then we need no longer smear false sentiment over
him and (what is more) the modern royalist is safe in revering Hal
as the ideal king. I agree that there has been some false sentiment
about Falstaff, and it is a good thing to have the sturdy point of
view of Dover Wilson tested out by a man who understands so

well what tests it must pass. But he can't make it stand up; he is only flying from one extreme position to another; indeed, after stating his sentiment crudely, as I have just tried to do, I feel I can retort it back on him. When Dover Wilson winces away from recognising the positive merits of Falstaff, he is blinding himself to the breadth and depth of these plays, a thing which was recognised with great enthusiasm by their rough popular audiences at the time. What is really hard is to stretch one's mind all around Falstaff; he was felt to be a very rich joke, and one must never forget that in the course of argufying about him.

In trying to weaken the story of his death, Dover Wilson descends to such arguments as that "neither ague nor 'sweat' has anything to do with a broken heart", whereas when Henry IV dies the critic is eager to explain that apoplexy was not always due to over-eating but sometimes (as here) to cares of state. He jeers at the bad language in which Nym and Pistol, unsentimental characters one would think, echo the plain statement by Mrs Quickly, "the king has killed his heart", at which he dare not jeer. To be sure, their language is funny, and after Mrs Quickly's great description of his death they only say "Shall we shog?" like fleas. But they understand what has happened; the excuse for Hal made by Nym, "The King is a good king, but it must be as it may; he passes some humours and careers", is stuffed full of the obvious coarse sentiment about Hal which seems unable to enter Dover Wilson's mind. The idea is that he is like a race-horse in training; you must expect him to throw a rider. The hero is expected to kill his tutor, in fact it proves that the tutor had the real magical skill to produce a hero; we are to be reminded later that Alexander also killed his friend. It is no use for Dover Wilson to "play down" the death of Falstaff, because it was once for all "written up", and indeed he is in a logical dilemma there; how could the passage do what he supposes, swing over an audience resentful at being cheated, if they would only think it ridiculous? We can all imagine them taking it rather casually; it is Dover Wilson who needs to argue that they cried when Mrs Quickly brought out her comical remarks, as I daresay they did.

His attitude to the death, I think, could almost be called mean, which is very surprising from him, but one must realise that this comes from a conviction that the story demands reverence; that any idea of Shakespeare as "stating the case for Falstaff" should be met with indignation:

Shakespeare plays no tricks with his public; he did not, like Euripides, dramatize the stories of his race and religion in order to subvert the traditional ideals those stories were first framed to set forth. Prince Hal is the prodigal, and his repentance is to be taken seriously; it is to be admired and commended . . .

and so forth. It seems to me that, in this generous impulse of defence, he is rather underrating the traditional ideals of his race and religion. They do not force you to ascribe every grace and virtue to this rather calculating type of prodigal, merely because he defeated the French. So far from that, if you take the series as a whole (and here we are greatly indebted to E. M. W. Tillyard, another of these rather royalist critics), the main point of the story is that he was doomed because he was a usurper; France had to be lost again, and much worse civil wars had to break out, till at last the legitimate line was restored. The insistence on this is fierce in *Richard II* and both parts of *Henry IV*. Henry V has a very inspiriting kind of merit, and I think Shakespeare meant us to love him, though in an open-eyed manner; but the idea that Shakespeare presents him as an ideal king seems to me to show a certain lack of moral delicacy, which need not be described as a recall to the higher morality of an earlier world. And then again, it may be said that the audience were not thinking of such things; the intention of the series was a simple and patriotic one, whether "high" or not. But I should say that the popular story about the prodigal was itself complex (and by the way "Renaissance" not "medieval"), so that the whole of this defence for Hal is off the point – he did not need it. Of course I don't deny that there was plenty of patriotism about the thing, and that Shakespeare took that seriously, but it left room for other sentiments.

   I think indeed that the whole Falstaff series needs to be looked at in terms of Dramatic Ambiguity, before one can understand what was happening in the contemporary audience; and I think that if this is done the various problems about Falstaff and Prince Hal, so long discussed, are in essence solved. Nor would this approach seem strange to Dover Wilson, who has done the most interesting recent work on the subject. Most of this essay has the air of an attack on him, but my complaints are supposed to show cases where he has slipped back into taking sides between two viewpoints instead of letting both be real. Slipped back, because on at least one occasion he uses explicitly and firmly the principle

I want to recommend; and perhaps I will look more plausible if I begin with that illustration of it.

The question whether Falstaff is a coward may be said to have started the whole snowball of modern Shakespearean criticism; it was the chief topic of Morgann's essay nearly two hundred years ago, the first time a psychological paradox was dug out of a Shakespeare text. Dover Wilson, discussing the plot about the robbery in the first three scenes where we meet Falstaff, says that the question whether Falstaff sees through the plot against him, and if so at what point he sees through it – for instance, whether he runs away from the Prince on purpose or only tells increasingly grotesque lies to him afterwards on purpose – is *meant* to be a puzzle, one that the audience are challenged to exercise their wits over; and that this had an important practical effect (it is not a matter of deep intellectual subtlety of course) because you would pay to see the play again with your curiosity undiminished. The whole joke of the great rogue is that *you* can't see through him, any more than the Prince could. I think that Dover Wilson's analysis of the text here is the final word about the question, because he shows that you aren't meant to find anything more; the dramatic effect simply *is* the doubt, and very satisfying too. Dover Wilson is a rich mine of interesting points, and it seems rather parasitic of me to keep on repeating them as weapons against him; but it seems important to urge that the method he has established here should be tried out on adjoining cases.

However, I recognise that this approach is liable to become tiresomely intellectualistic; a man who takes it into his head that he is too smart to look for the answer, on one of these points, because he knows the author means to cheat him, is likely to miss getting any real experience from the play. Besides, the actor and producer have to work out their own "conception" of Falstaff, in each case, and are sometimes felt to have produced an interesting or "original" one; it would be fatuous for the theoretical critic to say that they are merely deluding themselves, because there isn't any such thing. I do not mean that; the dramatic ambiguity is the source of these new interpretations, the reason why you can go on finding new ones, the reason why the effect is so rich. And of course there must be a basic theme which the contradictions of the play are dramatising, which some interpretations handle better than others; after planting my citadel on the high ground of the Absolute Void, I still feel at liberty to fight on the plains against Dover Wilson at various points of his detailed interpretation. But this way of putting it is still too glib. The basic argument of Dover Wilson is that the plays ought to be taken to mean what the first audiences made of them (and they took not merely a moral but a very practical view of the importance of social order and a good king). I agree with all of that, and merely answer that the reaction of an audience is not such a simple object as he presumed. No doubt he succeeds in isolating what the first audiences would find obvious; but we may still believe that other forces had to be at work behind Falstaff, both in the author and the audience which he understood, to make this figure as Titanic as we agree to find him; nor need we plunge for them deep into the Unconscious. The Falstaff plays were an enormous hit, appealing to a great variety of people, not all of them very high-minded, one would think. Obviously a certain amount of "tact" was needed, of a straightforward kind, to swing the whole of this audience into accepting the different stages of the plot. To bring out examples of this tact as evidence of the author's single intention, or of a single judgement which he wanted to impose on the audience, seems to me naive. So far from that, I think that on several occasions he was riding remarkably near the edge; a bit breathtaking it may have been, to certain members of the first audiences.

One cannot help feeling some doubt when Dover Wilson insists that Hal was never a "sinner", only a bit wild; especially when it becomes rather doubtful, as he goes on, what even the wildness may have consisted in. Not sex, we gather; it seems only old men like Falstaff go wrong like that. The same applies to drunkenness. Even the bishops in *Henry V*, Dover Wilson maintains, do not say that he has been converted, only that he has begun working hard (actually they say more); and even his father in reproaching him only speaks of sins in others which his wildness might encourage. Robbery, the reader is now to decide, he could not possibly have committed; to suppose that he even envisaged such a thing is to misread the whole play.

It is true that the early scenes of *I Henry IV* can be read as Dover Wilson does. I ought to admit this the more prominently because I said in my book *Pastoral* that "we hear no more" about the Prince's claim that he will repay the stolen money, which we do (III.iii.177). But after correcting this mistake I claim all the more that the dramatic effect is inherently ambiguous. Dover Wilson points out that we ought to consider the order of events on the stage, how the thing is planned to impress you; I warmly agree, but he only uses this rule for his own purpose. It is plain, surely, that we are put in doubt whether the Prince is a thief or not, at any rate in the early scenes; if you got a strong enough impression from those scenes that he was one, you would only regard the later return of the money as a last-minute escape from a major scandal (it has become possible for him because civil war has given him a well-paid appointment). No doubt, if you felt sure from the start that he couldn't really be one, the return of the money would act as laughing the whole thing off; but even so, the dramatist has put you through a bit of uncertainty about what he will ask you to believe. So to speak, an escape from a scandal is what happens to the audience, whether it happened to the Prince or not; and a dramatic structure of this kind assumes that at least some of the audience do not know the answer beforehand (in the old *Famous Victories*, for that matter, he simply *is* shown as stealing). It is therefore ridiculous, I submit, for a critic to argue heatedly that he has discovered the answer by a subtle analysis of the text. Such a critic, however, could of course turn round on me and say I am wrong to suppose it is "this kind of dramatic structure"; so far from that, he would say, he has shown the modern actor and producer how to make the play intelligible and coherent even to a fresh audience from the beginning. I therefore need to join in his labours, instead of calling them ridiculous; I need to show that the text is so arranged that the uncertainty can still not be dispelled even after the most careful study.

Among the first words of Falstaff, who is then alone with the Prince, he says "when thou art King, let not us that are squires of the night's body be called thieves of the day's beauty" and so on, and *us* is quite positively accepted by the Prince in his reply (whether for a joke or not) as including himself: "the fortune of us that are the moon's men doth ebb and flow like the sea" and so on. Of course I am not pretending that this proves he is a thief; I give it as an example of the way the dramatist starts by making us think he *may* be a thief. The next point, as the jokes turn over, is a grave appeal from Falstaff: "Do not thou, when thou art King, hang a thief." Falstaff gets much of his fun out of a parody of moral advice, especially in these earlier scenes, and the point here must be that the Prince has no right to hang a thief because he is one himself. His reply (a very sufficient one) is that Falstaff will do it. Falstaff then inverts the obvious by upbraiding the Prince for leading him astray; he threatens to reform, and the Prince's answer is, "Where shall we take a purse tomorrow,

Jack?" Falstaff accepts this as if they are old partners in robbery, and is only concerned to defend his courage – "Zounds, where thou wilt, lad, I'll make one, an I do not, call me villain and baffle me." Poins now enters and announces a scheme for robbery, and when the Prince is asked if he will join he speaks as if the idea was absurdly outside his way of life – "Who, I rob? I a thief? Not I, by my faith." Falstaff has already assumed that the Prince knows this plan is being prepared ("Poins! Now we shall know if Gadshill have set a match"), and Poins is the Prince's own gentleman-in-waiting; however, Dover Wilson naturally makes the most of this brief retort:

The proposal that the prince is to take part in the highway robbery is received at first with something like indignation, even with a touch of haughtiness, and only consented to when Poins intimates, by nods and winks behind Falstaff's back, that he is planning to make a practical joke of it.

The nods and winks are invented by the critic, of course (and printed in his text of the play), but they seem plausible enough; indeed the line, "Well, then, once in my days I'll be a madcap", reads like a rather coarse attempt to keep the respectable part of the audience from being too shocked. They are welcome to decide that the Prince is not really a thief after all. The point I want to make is that another part of the audience is still quite free to think he is one; indeed, this pretence of innocence followed immediately by acceptance (followed by further riddles) is just the way Falstaff talks himself. Poins then arranges the plot against Falstaff with the Prince, and finally the Prince makes his famous soliloquy, claiming that his present behaviour is the best way to get himself admired later on. I do not think that the words suggest he is doing nothing worse than play practical jokes on low characters. To be sure, the "base contagious clouds", the "foul and ugly mists", only *seem* to strangle the sun; you can still think the Prince innocent here; and he only describes his own behaviour as "loose". But then we hear about a reformation of a fault, and about an offence which must apparently be redeemed (though literally it is only time which must be redeemed). It seems to me that the balance is still being kept; you can decide with relief that surely after this he can't be a thief, or you can feel, if you prefer, he has practically admitted that for the present he is one. In one way, the doubt about the Prince doesn't matter, because the whole life he was sharing is displayed to us; but in another way, if a censorious man wants to claim this is a punishable libel against royalty, he will find that the text remains on a razor edge and never crosses it. This being what Shakespeare was clever enough to do, it is usual to "prove" that he must get off on one side or the other.

The more usual question about this soliloquy is whether it shows the Prince as "callous and hypocritical", determined to betray his friends. Naturally Dover Wilson argues that it does not, because "it was a convention to convey information to the audience about the general drift of the play, much as a prologue did", and in any case at this stage of the play "we ought not to be feeling that Falstaff deserves any consideration whatever". I think this carries the "sequence" principle rather too far, if only because most people would know the "general drift" before they came; but I don't deny, of course, that the placing of this soliloquy is meant to establish Hal as the future hero as firmly as possible. Even so, I do not see that it does anything (whether regarded as a "convention" or not) to evade the obvious moral reflection, obvious not only to the more moralising part of the audience but to all of it, that this kind of man made a very unreliable friend. Surely the Elizabethans could follow this simple duality of feeling without getting mixed; it is inevitable that if you enjoy Falstaff you feel a grudge against the eventual swing-over of Hal, even though you agree that the broad plot couldn't be different. The real problems about the rejection do not arise here; we have no reason to presume it will come as a painful shock to his present friends (though "falsify men's hopes" may be a secret mark of the author's plan). I think a fair amount can be deduced about Shakespeare's own feelings for this kind of condescending patron, but in any case it was a commonplace of his period that the friendships of great men very often were unreliable. The whole thing seems to me in the sunlight, and for that matter the fundamental machinery seems rather crude, and perhaps it had to be to carry such a powerful conflict of judgement. There does not seem much for critics to disagree about.

Dover Wilson, however, feels that there is, because he wants to build up Hal as a high-minded creature of delicate sensibility. A brief scene with Poins (*II Henry IV*, II.ii) is made important for this purpose. We are told about Hal that:

The kind of reserve that springs from absence of self-regard is in point of fact one of his principal characteristics, and such a feature is difficult

to represent in dialogue . . . We have no right to assume that Hal is heart-
less because he does not, like Richard II, wear his heart on his sleeve
. . . Why not . . . give him a friend like Horatio to reveal himself? . . .
Shakespeare gives him Poins, and the discovery of the worthlessness of
this friend is the subject of one of the most moving and revealing scenes
in which the Prince figures. In view of all this, to assert as Bradley does
that Hal is incapable of tenderness or affection except towards members
of his own family is surely a quite unwarranted assumption.

Hal begins this scene by treating Poins with insolence, as one of
the butts for his habit of contempt, and Poins answers (they have
just got back from Wales as part of the civil war):

How ill it follows, after you have laboured so hard, you should talk so
idly! Tell me, how many good young princes would do so, their fathers
being so sick as yours at this time is?

I can't see that this is an offensive retort; he is expected to keep
his end up, and there is not even an obvious insinuation that the
Prince wants his father dead – he may be being advised to recover
favour. No doubt it could be acted with an offensive leer, but the
usual tone in these scenes is merely a rough jeering. The Prince,
however, becomes offended and says that his heart bleeds
inwardly at his father's illness, but that he can't show it because
he keeps bad company such as Poins. It seems a fair answer to
this challenge when Poins says he would indeed think the Prince
a hypocrite to show sorrow at the prospect of inheriting,
"because you have been so lewd, and so much engraffed to
Falstaff". "And to thee", says the gay Prince with his usual
brutality. Now of course I agree that the scene is meant to tell the
audience that Hal is starting to repent of his bad habits; it could
not be more straightforward. It could be acted with a moody
sorrow, but I don't think it need be; the main fact is that he
is physically tired. But why are we supposed to think that he is
"failed" by his friend in a pathetic manner, or shows affection to
anyone not a member of his own family? The whole truth of this
little scene, in its surly way, is to be so bare; it does nothing to put
Poins in the wrong, and indeed lets him show a fair amount of
dignity and good-humour; the Prince's feelings are dragging him
away from his old companions, and no new fault of theirs needs
to be shown. Surely Poins has much more difficulty than Hal in
expressing delicate sentiments here; if he tried to condole with
the Prince he would be rebuffed more harshly than ever. A

production which made the Prince disillusioned at not getting sympathy would have to cut most of the words.

A more important argument of Dover Wilson for Hal is that it is extremely generous of him to let Falstaff get all the credit for killing Hotspur, especially because if Hal claimed his due he might become more acceptable to his father. Besides, he had promised his father he would kill Hotspur, and most men would feel their honour made the claim necessary. We are also told that the sudden fame thus acquired by the previously unknown Falstaff goes to his head and is the cause of the gradual nemesis which gathers throughout Part II. This seems to me a valuable idea, unlike the special pleading about the Poins scene, which would mislead an actor. The trouble about the death of Hotspur, it seems to me, is that the story is deliberately left ambiguous, and we should not allow a learned argument to impose a one-sided answer. The lyrical language of Dover Wilson about the native magnanimity and high courtesy of the Prince, "which would seem of the very essence of nobility to the Elizabethans", really does I think bring out part of the intended stage effect at the end of the First Part, though the text is silent. The question is whether it is meant to go on reverberating all through the Second Part. To do the right thing at a dramatic moment is very different from going on telling an absurd and inconvenient lie indefinitely. Dover Wilson's view of the matter, I think, really would be picked on by spectators who preferred it that way, but other spectators could find quite different pointers. I do not want, therefore, to refute his view but to show that it is only one alternative, and I thus give myself an easy task.

The claim of Falstaff to have killed Hotspur is made to Prince Henry in the presence of Prince John, who says, "This is the strangest tale that e'er I heard." Prince Henry says:

> This is the strangest fellow, brother John.
> Come, bring your luggage nobly on your back.
> For my part, if a lie may do thee grace,
> I'll gild it with the happiest terms I have.

In Dover Wilson's edition, of course, "aside to Falstaff" has to introduce the last two lines. But I don't see Hal nipping about the stage to avoid being overheard by John, whom he despises; his business here is to stand midcentre and utter fine sentiments loud and bold. Just what lie was told, and what John made of it, we don't hear. It seems to me that the Second Part begins by throwing a lot of confusion into the matter, and that Dover Wilson merely selects points that suit him. At the start of the play three messengers come to the rebel Northumberland; the first with good news – the Prince has been killed outright and "(his) brawn,[1] the hulk Sir John" taken prisoner by Hotspur. Five other people are mentioned, but it is assumed that Falstaff was worth attention before he was believed to have killed Hotspur, and that even Hotspur has done well to capture him. The second messenger says that Hotspur is dead, the third that he was killed by the Prince. Dover Wilson admits this shows that the facts of his death "had been observed by at least one man", but adds that no other witness is quoted. But nobody at all, in the Second Part, says that Falstaff killed Hotspur. The King himself appears not to know that the Prince did it, says Dover Wilson; but the King has other things to talk about whenever we see him, and never implies that Hal can't fight. "The Lord Chief Justice grudgingly praises Falstaff's day's service at Shrewsbury", says Dover Wilson, so he must think Falstaff killed Hotspur. He says that day's service "hath a little gilded over your night's exploits at Gad's Hill", which hardly fits a personal triumph over the chief enemy hero. Certainly people think he fought well somehow (perhaps because he got his troop killed to keep their pay); the joke of this is driven home in the Second Part when Coleville surrenders to him on merely hearing his name. But even Coleville does not say, what would be so natural an excuse, that he is surrendering to the man who killed Hotspur. What is more, Falstaff himself does not once say it, and he is not prone to hide his claims. Surely the solution of this puzzle is clear; Shakespeare is deliberately *not* telling us the answer, so that an ingenious argument which forces an answer out of the text only misrepresents his intention.

Consider how difficult it is for a dramatist, especially with a mass audience, to run a second play on the mere assumption that everybody in the audience knows the first one. On Dover Wilson's view, they are assumed to know that all the characters in the Second Part hold a wrong belief derived from the First Part, although the Second Part begins by letting a man express

---

[1] *Brawn* suggests the wild boar, a strong and savage creature, honourable to hunt, though the fatted hog is not quite out of view. A similar ambivalence can be felt I think in the incessant metaphors of heavy meat-eating around Falstaff compared to "one halfpennyworth of bread to this intolerable deal of sack", where it is asssumed (already in Part I) that the drunkard has no appetite.

the right belief and never once lets anybody express the wrong belief. This is incredible. But if some of the audience are expected to *wonder* how the Prince's bit of chivalry worked out, their interest is not rebuffed; they may observe like Dover Wilson that Falstaff is getting above himself. In the main the theme is simply dropped; perhaps because some of the audience would not like the Prince to be so deeply in cahoots with Falstaff, perhaps because Shakespeare did not care to make the Prince so generous, but chiefly because it would only clutter up the new play, which had other material. The puzzle is not beyond resolution; it is natural to guess (if you worry about it) that the Prince waited till the truth came out and then said that Falstaff had been useful to him at the time – thus the claim of Falstaff did not appear a mere lie after the Prince had gilded it in his happiest terms, but had to be modified. This would have been the only sensible lie for the Prince to tell, and indeed Dover Wilson hints at it when he says people thought Falstaff had "slain, *or helped to slay*" Hotspur, which has no source in the text. You may now feel that I have made a lot of unnecessary fuss, when it turns out that I agree with Dover Wilson; but I think that his treatment ignores the dramatic set-up and the variety of views possible in the audience.

The next step in his argument is that Falstaff only becomes "a person of consideration in the army" because of the Prince's lies (whatever they were) about the Battle of Shrewsbury; "in Part I he is Jack Falstaff with his familiars; in Part II he is Sir John with all Europe". This is why he over-reaches himself; the final effect of the Prince's generosity at the end of Part I is that he is forced to reject Falstaff at the end of Part II. Now, on the general principle that one should accept all theories, however contradictory, which add to the total effect, this must certainly be accepted; it pulls the whole sequence together. But it must not be carried so far as to make Falstaff "nobody" at the beginning, because that would spoil another effect, equally important for many of the audience. Falstaff is the first major joke by the English against their class system; he is a picture of how badly you can behave, and still get away with it, if you are a gentleman – a mere common rogue would not have been nearly so funny. As to the question of fact, of course, we are told he is a knight the first time he appears, and it is natural to presume he got knighted through influence; Shallow eventually lets drop that he started his career as page to the Duke of Norfolk. This is rather confusing now, as suggesting a social climb; but in those days to plant the boy in a great house-hold gave him a good start in life, rather like the modern public school. The Stage History section of Dover Wilson's edition has some interesting hints, from both the eighteenth and twentieth centuries, to show that he has always been expected to be a gentleman; the dissentient voice is from a nineteenth-century American actor, who wrote a pamphlet claiming that he was right *not* to make the old brute a gentleman. Rather in the same way, I remember some American critic complaining that Evelyn Waugh shows an offensive snobbery about Captain Grimes, since he despises him merely for not being a real gentleman. So far from that, the whole joke about Grimes is that he is an undeniable public school man, and therefore his invariably appalling behaviour must always be retrieved by the other characters, though it always comes as a great shock to them. This English family joke, as from inside an accepted class system, may well not appeal to Americans, but in the case of Falstaff I think English critics have rather tended to wince away from it too.

Maintaining that he was nobody till after the Battle of Shrewsbury, Dover Wilson has to explain his presence at the council of commanders just before it, and says it was simply because Shakespeare needed him on the stage. This lame argu-ment would not apply to the Elizabethan stage. At the actual council he only makes one unneeded joke; he is needed for talk with the Prince afterwards, in what our texts call the same scene, but the back curtain will already have closed on the royal coat-of-arms and so forth; Falstaff could simply walk onto the apron. He is at the council because that adds to the joke about him, or rather because some of the audience will think so. However, it is clear anyhow that the Prince brought him; the battle itself gives a more striking case of this line of argument from Dover Wilson. A. C. Bradley had argued that Falstaff shows courage by hanging around in the battle till the Prince kills Hotspur, and the reply has to be: "To establish his false claim to the slaying of Hotspur he must be brought into the thick of the fight." Surely this makes Shakespeare a much less resourceful dramatist than he is; even I could think of a funny device to trick the great coward into his great opportunity, after he had imagined he had found a safe place. Shakespeare does not "have to" give false impressions; and what we do gather from Falstaff is that he regards a battle as a major occasion for misusing his social position (e.g. "God be thanked for these rebels; they offend none but the virtuous"). I don't deny that those spectators who would resent the social satire are given an opportunity to evade it, and take him as the "cowardly swashbuckler" of the Latin tradition; but they aren't given very much. Over the crux at the start of the Second Part, I think, the indignant special pleading of Dover Wilson reaches actual absurdity:

> The special mention of [Falstaff's] capture in the false report of the battle that first reaches the ears of Northumberland . . . are all accounted for by the indecent stab which the dastard gives the corpse of Hotspur as it lies stricken on the bleeding field.

To be sure, Falstaff "goes a bit too far" when he does that; it is his role. (By the way, the reason why we feel it so strongly is that the rebels have been made to look rather better than the royal family.) But really, how are we to imagine that the sight of Falstaff stabbing a recumbent Hotspur (in another play) made a messenger report that Hotspur was safe and Falstaff captured? No doubt almost any confusion can happen to a real messenger, but how can a dramatist expect his successive audiences to invent the extraordinary subtle confusion imputed here? The fact is, surely, that these pointers represent Falstaff as already a prominent figure, though an embarrassingly scandalous one; they could easily be ignored by members of the audience who were using a different line of assumption, but they would give great assurance to members who started with this one.

The interesting thing here, I think, is that Dover Wilson is partly right; but in the next case I think he is simply wrong. Nobody, whichever way he took up Falstaff, was meant to think him too abject a coward even to be able to bluster. Dover Wilson refuses to let him drive Pistol out of the inn; chiefly, I suppose, because his theory needs Falstaff to be degenerating in Part II. At II.iv.187 Doll wants Pistol thrown out, so Falstaff says "Quoit him down, Bardolph", and Bardolph says "Come, get you downstairs", but Pistol still makes a threatening harangue; Falstaff then asks for his rapier (197) and himself says "Get you downstairs", while Doll says "I pray thee, Jack, do not draw"; then the Hostess makes a fuss about "naked weapons", then Doll says "Jack, be quiet, the rascal's gone. Ah, you whoreson little valiant villain, you", then the Hostess says "Are you not hurt i'the groin? Methought a' made a shrewd thrust at your belly"; Falstaff says to Bardolph, who must return, "Have you turned him out of doors?" and Bardolph says "Yea, sir, the rascal's drunk. You have hurt him, sir, in the shoulder"; Falstaff says "A rascal, to brave me!" and Doll in the course of a fond speech says he is as valorous as Hector of Troy. It is unusual to have to copy out so much text to answer a commentator. This is the textual evidence on which Dover Wilson decides that Falstaff dared not fight Pistol at all, and he actually prints as part of the play two stage directions saying that Bardolph has got to do all the work. It must be about the most farcical struggle against the obvious intentions of an author that a modern scholarly editor has ever put up.

This view of Falstaff is supported by a theory about Doll, rather obscure to me: "We have, I think, to look forward to 19th-century French literature to find a match for this study of mingled sentimentality and brutal insentience, characteristic of the prostitute class." I thought at first, not going further afield than *The Beggar's Opera*, that this meant some criminal plot for gain; but the audience could not know of it (this is the first we hear of Pistol), and I suppose it means that both she and Mrs Quickly like watching two men fight. The argument, therefore, is that she jeers at Falstaff for shirking the fight she had encouraged, so this proves he didn't fight. After Pistol has gone he boasts, "the rogue fled from me like quicksilver" and she answers (on his knee) "I'faith, and thou followedst him like a church." Dover Wilson has to push "aside" into the text before this remark and "sits on his knee" afterwards, before he can let it go on with her praise of his courage. She does not hide her remarks from him anywhere else. I take it she means that he followed like a massive worthy object, though too fat to do it fast; to find sadism here seems to me wilful. The same trick is used against Mrs Quickly in *Henry V*, II.i.36, over the textual crux "if he be not hewn now", which Dover Wilson refuses to change to "drawn" – "as Nym draws Q screams to her bridegroom to cut the villain down, lest the worst befall". But this frank blood-thirst is not at all in her style, and if it was she could hardly keep her house open. It seems that this picture of the ladies is drawn from the sombre vignette at the end of the Second Part, just before the rejection, when they are dragged across the front stage by beadles because "the man is dead that you and Pistol beat among you". Dover Wilson is breaking his own rules about the order of scenes, if he makes this imply that they were in a plot with Pistol at his first appearance.[2]

---

[2] I see that in his edition of the *Merry Wives* (1921) Dover Wilson was already assuming (with joviality, as at correct though spirited behaviour) that Henry V

What we do gather before his entry is that they are afraid he may kill somebody in the house, and know they will get into trouble if he does. He starts threatening death as soon as he comes, whether as a bawdy joke or not ("I will discharge upon her, Sir John, with two bullets"). Also Doll had just begun a pathetic farewell to Falstaff, who is going to the wars; she is cross at their being interrupted. Also she came on for this scene already elegantly unwell from too much drink. I need to list the reasons for her anger, because Dover Wilson comments on the line "Sweet knight, I kiss thy neaf" that Pistol "is ready to go quietly, but Doll will have thrown him out" – that is, she insists on having a fight. It is hard for Mrs Quickly to turn her own customers out, and Doll will be helping her to avoid serious danger if she can scare the bully away permanently; this, if anything, is what is underlined by the beadle scene, though by the time of *Henry V*, as we needn't be surprised, Pistol has become a valuable protector. Such is what I would call her motive, if I looked for one, but she may well simply be too drunk and cross to realise that he is already going quietly. Either way there is no need to drag in sadism.

Dover Wilson has still another argument from this scene to prove Falstaff's increasing degeneration. After Pistol has been thrown out the Prince arrives and eavesdrops on Falstaff, who is making some rather justified remarks against him, so that Falstaff again has to find a quick excuse; he says he dispraised the Prince before the wicked, that the wicked might not fall in love with him. "He now whines and cringes on a new note, while he is forced to have recourse to defaming Doll in turn, a shift which is neither witty nor attractive." To be sure, the words "corrupt blood" may imply that she has syphilis; it is only the editor's stage direction which makes him point at her, but the idea does give her a professional reason for displaying anger. He has long been saying he has it himself, so there doesn't seem any great betrayal in saying that she has it too (he does imply it, more gently a few

had ordered the women to be thrown into jail the moment he got hold of power, before Pistol could get back from telling Falstaff that Henry IV was dead. I should have thought that this could only be invented by someone who hated Hal bitterly. The dramatic point of the scene, surely, is that the ordinary processes of law are going firmly on. Pistol rushed off to Falstaff because he had got into trouble, and both he and the women assume wrongly that Falstaff can clear it up. We are not asked to suppose that the new King is indulging immediate private malice against these humble characters.

lines later. In the next play she has to retire to hospital.) I imagine
that the point of the joke is to insinuate that the Prince has it; thus
it is too late to save him from the wicked, and too late for him to
think he can cure himself by saying he has reformed. Falstaff
needs to forestall being laughed at, as an ugly old man found
making love. So he welcomes the Prince among his fellow-
sufferers. The badinage in these circles is always a bit rough, and
I don't deny that it is hard to know how you are expected to take
it. But in this case we have an immediate pointer from an "aside"
by Poins, who as usual is in a plot with the Prince against Falstaff.
(By the way, this shows what nonsense it is to suppose that the
Prince made a sudden pathetic discovery of the worthlessness of
Poins only two scenes before, a decisive step in his life, we are to
believe; they are on just the same footing as ever.) Poins says,
"My lord, he will drive you out of your revenge, and turn all to a
merriment, if you take not the heat." How could this be said if
Falstaff was only whining and cringing, or even if he were picking
a serious quarrel with the ladies? At the end of the scene, when
he is called off to the war as an important officer (a dozen cap-
tains are knocking at every tavern door for Sir John Falstaff,
sweating with eagerness – so says Peto, and Bardolph corrobor-
ates about the dozen; and however much the editor insists that
this is only "a summons for neglect of duty" it still treats Falstaff
as worth a lot of trouble in an emergency), both the women speak
with heart-breaking pathos about how much they love him, and
the text requires Doll to shed tears. If we critics are to call this a
"calculated degradation", I do not know what we expect our own
old age to be like. The truth is, surely, that we never see the old
brute more triumphant; doomed you might already feel him, but
not degraded.

However, I do not want simply to defend Falstaff against the
reproaches of the virtuous, represented by Dover Wilson; it was
always an unrewarding occupation, and even the most patient
treatment of detail, in such a case, has often failed to convince a
jury. I think, indeed, that Dover Wilson's points are well worth
examining, being of great interest in themselves; but, what is
more, I think many of them are thrown in with a broadminded
indifference as to whether they fit his thesis or not. Some of them
seem to me rather too hot on my side of the question, and this
may serve to remind us of what is so easily forgotten in a controversy, that the final truth may be complex. For example, he
has a fine remark on Mrs Quickly's description of Falstaff's

death. She says she felt his feet, and then his knees, and so upward and upward, and all as cold as any stone. The only comment that would occur to me is that this dramatist can continue unflinchingly to insert bawdy jokes while both the speaker and the audience are meant to be almost in tears. Dover Wilson, taking a more scholarly view, remarks that the detail is drawn from the death of Socrates; the symptoms are those of the gradual death from hemlock. But whatever can he have intended by this parallel? Surely it has to imply that Falstaff like Socrates was a wise teacher killed by a false accusation of corrupting young men; his patient heroism under injustice, and how right the young men were to love him, are what we have to reflect on. I hope that somebody pointed out this parallel to Shakespeare; he did, I believe, feel enough magic about Falstaff for it to have given him a mixed but keen pleasure; but that seems as far as speculation can reasonably go. To make it an intentional irony really would be like Verrall on Euripides, and it would blow Dover Wilson's picture of Falstaff into smithereens. And yet, though it seems natural to talk like this, I am not certain; the idea that Falstaff was a good tutor *somehow* was a quite public part of the play, and might conceivably have been fitted out with a learned reference. He has a similar eerie flash of imagination about a stage direction in *Henry V*, where the heroes of Agincourt are described as "poor troops". He rightly complains that modern editions omit the epithet, an important guide to the producer; the story would be mere boasting if it did not emphasise that their victory was a hairbreadth escape after being gruelled. But then he goes on: "Did the 'scarecrows' that Falstaff led to Shrewsbury return to the stage?" It seems rather likely, for the convenience of a repertory company, that they did; but what can it mean, if we suppose it to mean anything? What is recalled is the most unbeatable of all Falstaff's retorts to Henry – "they'll fit a pit as well as better; tush, man, mortal men, mortal men". Falstaff has just boasted that he took bribes to accept such bad recruits ("I have misused the King's press damnably" – and the audience would not think him a coward here, but that it took a lot of nerve to be so wicked) and he boasts later that he got them killed to keep their pay (it is before his success has "degraded" him) but this makes his reply all the more crashing, as from one murderer to another: "that is all you Norman lords want, in your squabbles between cousins over your loot, which you make an excuse to murder the English people". This very strong joke

could be implied in *Henry IV*, as part of a vague protest against
civil war, but to recall it over Henry's hereditary claim to France
would surely be reckless; besides, the mere return of those stage
figures could not carry so much weight. But I believe that
thoughts of that kind were somewhere in the ambiance of the
play, however firmly they were being rebutted; it is conceivable
that Dover Wilson here is being wiser than either of us know.

One gets rather the same effect, I think, from his remarks
about killing the prisoners at Agincourt, though here he is
making a sturdy defence, not a bold conjecture. The position is
that the King comes out in IV.vi, "with prisoners", and says his
side has done well but must be careful; a pathetic anecdote is
told; then an alarum sounds, and the King immediately (without
enquiry) says:

> The French have reinforced their scattered men:
> Then every soldier kill his prisoners!
> Give the word through.

Dover Wilson insists that this has been misunderstood because
the stage direction "with prisoners" has regularly been omitted –
it should be made clear on the stage that there are more prisoners
than captors. But this needed to be said, not shown; the chief
effect of bringing the prisoners onto the stage could only be to
make the audience in cold blood see the defenceless men killed
– indeed, that is clearly the reason why the editors left it out. He
goes on to argue, convincingly I think, that this incident was used
in the chronicles Shakespeare drew from as an example of
Henry's power to recognise a necessity at once, and that the
French chroniclers do not blame him for it, though Holinshed is
apologetic. But we are concerned with the effect on an audience,
and here the very next words, which are from Fluellen to Gower,
say:

Kill the boys and the luggage! tis expressly against the law of arms, tis as
arrant a piece of knavery, mark you now, as can be offert.

Gower remarks that *because* the Frenchmen escaping from the
battle have killed unarmed boys in the King's tent *therefore* the
King "most worthily hath caused every soldier to cut his prisoner's throat. O, tis a gallant king." These experts of course have
just walked on for a new scene, and do not know, as we do, that
it was Henry who started killing unarmed men, not the French.
"Shakespeare, who might have omitted it", says Dover Wilson,

"offers no apologies, but sets the device in a framework of circumstances which makes it seem natural and inevitable." This seems to me comic; the framework not only does nothing to make us think the killing of helpless people necessary but condemns it fiercely. (Even Dover Wilson reflects that it might be rather a waste of time, under a sudden counter-attack, if one hadn't got machine-guns.) Fluellen goes on to compare Henry in detail to Alexander the Big, mispronouncing it as PIG, and the final parallel is that as Alexander killed his friend Cleitus "in his ales and his angers" so Henry – well, he only turned Falstaff away, and wasn't drunk at the time. We have already seen Nym taking the same view – one must expect a hero to be ungrateful and violent; but this is a remarkable time to recall it. Henry soon comes back saying he is angry and again demanding that prisoners be killed; and even Dr Johnson, the patron saint of Dover Wilson's criticism, found it absurd that a man who had just killed all his prisoners should express anger by trying to kill them again. The Quarto of 1600, described by Dover Wilson as "a 'reported' version, probably supplied by traitor-actors, of performances – perhaps in a shortened form for provincial audiences – of the play as acted by Shakespeare's company", not only gives the whole prisoner sequence but adds a delighted "coupla gorge" from the coward Pistol, as he prepares to join in this really safe and agreeable form of warfare. He was already practising the phrase (almost his only acquirement in the French language) before he left London, so that it is firmly associated with his particularly sordid point of view; and if we are to believe that he is shown starting the massacre the play does everything it can to make the audience nauseated by such actions, even before it has them denounced by Fluellen. I do not see that Dover Wilson makes out his case at all (the question of course is not about the historical behaviour of the Prince, for whom the opinion of the French chroniclers is a weighty support, but about an effect on the Elizabethan stage). If we accept the text we must think (1) that Shakespeare's disgust against Henry explodes here, (2) that Henry's treatment of Falstaff is recalled as part of a denunciation of his brutality and deceitfulness in general, and (3) that Shakespeare, in his contempt for his brutal audience, assumes that nobody will realise what he is doing. I agree with Dover Wilson that this vehement picture is improbable; I want the conflict of forces in the play to be real, but not secret and explosive in this way.

Surely there is an easy escape from the dilemma, which must have been suggested before. Shakespeare first followed the chroniclers about Henry's decision, without making any accusations against the French; then he felt this made Henry look too brutal and "got round it", just as he contradicted the statement of Holinshed that Henry sacked Harfleur. Instead of saying that Henry started killing unarmed men he said the French did; this propaganda device is familiar nowadays – you do not simply ignore the story against your side, in case it is floating in the minds of your hearers, but contrive to plant it on the other side. This required adding both Fluellen's remarks and Henry's speech about being angry, but cutting only the single line "Then every soldier kill his prisoners." We have then to suppose that the Company ignored the omission mark, not seeing the point of it, and that the actor of Pistol added his usual gag. We are making them pretty stupid, and assuming that Shakespeare didn't much bother over what they did with his texts; but Dover Wilson is among those who have made a strong case for thinking so. Now, after making the incident more reasonable in this way, I still think that Shakespeare must have been in a mixed frame of mind when he wrote this comic speech of Fluellen, as part of a plan to make Henry appear milder than he was. Saving Henry's face was getting to be rather an effort, surely. I do not mean that Shakespeare was secretly opposed to his work, still less that he was trying to insinuate a criticism of Henry for the wiser few; I think he felt it a duty to get into the right mood for the thing, and could manage it, but found he had to watch himself, and go back and correct himself – any author who has done propaganda knows this frame of mind. Such at least is what I would make of it, but I am not certain that the view of Dover Wilson, so much more startling than he realises, is not the true one.

Where the possibilities are so complicated, I think, a critic needs to hold on to the basic material, the *donnée*, as Dover Wilson advises. But one also needs to realise that this story of a prodigal who became a hero was already very rich when Shakespeare took it over or "cashed in on it"; it was the most popular part of the History series and carried a variety of implications, all the more because it was taken easily as a joke. To re-plan the trilogy on the basis of leaving some of them out, and that is really what Dover Wilson is up to, is sure to mislead; also I find it odd of him to claim that a historical point of view is what makes him treat Falstaff as medieval rather than Renaissance. Of course this does not make me deny that the medieval elements are still there. Falstaff is in part simply a "Vice", that is, an energetic symbol of impulses which most people have to repress, who gives pleasure by at once releasing and externalising them. His plausibility is amusing, and his incidental satire on the world can be accepted as true, but what he stands for is recognised as wrong, and he must be punished in the end. Also (as a minor version of this type) he is in part the "cowardly swashbuckler", of the Latin play rather than the Miracle Play, whose absurdity and eventual exposure are to comfort the audience for their frequent anxiety and humiliation from "swashbucklers". As part of the historical series, he stands for the social disorder which is sure to be produced by a line of usurpers, therefore he is a parallel to the rebel leaders though very unlike them; the good king must shake him off in the end as part of his work of reuniting the country. Also I think there is a more timeless element about him, neither tied to his period in the story nor easily called Renaissance or medieval, though it seems to start with Shakespeare; he is the scandalous upper-class man whose behaviour embarrasses his class and thereby pleases the lower class in the audience, as an "exposure"; the faint echoes of upper-class complaints about him, as in the change of his name, are I think evidence that this was felt.[3] For these last two functions, cowardice is not the vice chiefly required of him. But surely we have no reason to doubt that there were other forces at work behind the popularity of the myth, which can more directly be called Renaissance; something to do with greater trust in the natural man or pleasure in contemplating him, which would join on to what so many critics have said about "the comic idealization of freedom". I think it needs putting in more specific terms, but I don't see that Dover Wilson can be plausible in denying it altogether.

The most important "Renaissance" aspects of Falstaff, I think, can be most quickly described as nationalism and Machiavellianism; both of them make him a positively good tutor for a prince,

---

[3] The objection by one family to the name Oldcastle is merely natural. But there is evidence from stage directions that Falstaff's gang once had several members bearing such prominent names that they all had to be suppressed (e.g. Dover Wilson's *II Hen. IV*, note on II.ii). If this is true, Shakespeare was showing a good deal of nerve; it looks as if he felt in such a strong position with the censor that he threw in extra names merely to let the censor take them out before the real bargaining started. I don't quite believe in this picture, but his position must have been fairly strong to carry the Company through their performance of *Richard II* for the Essex rebels.

as he regularly claims to be, so that it is not surprising that he produced a good king or that his rejection, though necessary, could be presented as somehow tragic. The Machiavellian view (no more tied to that author then than it is now, but more novel and shocking than it is now) is mainly the familiar one that a young man is better for "sowing his wild oats", especially if he is being trained to "handle men". The sort of ruler you can trust, you being one of the ruled, the sort that can understand his people and lead them to glory, is one who has learned the world by experience, especially rather low experience; he knows the tricks, he can allow for human failings, and somehow between the two he can gauge the spirit of a situation or a period. The idea is not simply that Falstaff is debauched and tricky, though that in itself made him give Hal experience, and hardly any price was too high to pay for getting a good ruler, but that he had the breadth of mind and of social understanding which the Magnanimous Man needs to acquire. This is very unmedieval, seems a lower-class rather than an upper-class line of thought and is, of course, militantly anti-Puritan, as we can assume the groundlings tended to be, and Falstaff can be regarded as a parody of it rather than a coarse acceptance of it by Shakespeare, but surely it is obviously present; indeed I imagine that previous critics have thought it too obvious to be worth writing down – there was no need to, till Dover Wilson began preaching at us about his Medieval Vice and his Ideal King. After rejecting Falstaff Henry continues to show the popular touch and so forth that Falstaff taught him; indeed, *Henry V* limits itself rather rigidly to describing the good effects of this training, for example in his treatment of the troops and of the Princess.

In looking for the basic legend about King Hal, before Shakespeare took it over and invented Falstaff to illustrate it, we are fortunate to have *The Famous Victories of Henry V*, published in 1596 but probably a good deal older. It is a vigorous and worthy object (too often recalled with contempt, I think); very much "in the school" of Shakespeare, even if the school taught Shakespeare and not he it, especially in the power to make homely but heart-piercing jokes. There is no single line in Shakespeare about Henry as strong and funny, granting that the Prince is somehow loved, as "I dare not say he is a thief, but he is one of those taking fellows". Maybe it is a kind of luck for the author that the pun on "taking" is still obvious, but it is a kind of luck he has often; the style is very direct. However, there is no great need here to praise it; the question is what Shakespeare accepted and what he altered.

Here we come to the main point, which I fear I have approached too slowly. Henry V was considered the first national King of England, the first who wasn't really a Norman, speaking French, and modern historians agree in so far as he was the first King of England to use the English language for his official correspondence – as would easily be learned by anyone in a position to look up the documents. The only dates one seems to need are that Agincourt was in 1415 and Chaucer died in 1400; we may imagine that the real Henry only accepted something which had happened, but the legend gave him the credit for it. Obviously, they thought, he refused to do his French lessons; he must have hung about the pubs with somebody like Falstaff, and decided, very properly, not to learn anything except what he learned there. That is why you get so much fuss about the French language in *HenryV*, whereas the plays usually ignore any language problem. The basic point of Henry's first soliloquy, saying that he will be more admired later because he is despised now, is not a cynical calculation to betray his friends but a modestly phrased reassurance that he is learning how to be a national king. All this made a much more serious defence of Falstaff, in the mind of a realistic spectator, than any romantic idea that he had improved the Prince by showing him low life; to have made the monarchy national was a decisively important thing, however absurdly bad Falstaff was otherwise, however much he needed to be rejected;[4] and, for that matter, the story does not need us to suppose that Henry was very good to start with, either. The whole trilogy about Falstaff and the Prince, I think, becomes painfully confusing, because your sympathies are torn between two bad characters, unless you regard it as showing how a useful development occurred; then it can be enjoyed freely.

Some critics have suggested that Shakespeare privately loved Falstaff but, like the Prince, betrayed him in public or when

---

[4] The fact that Oldcastle was a Lollard, therefore a forerunner of the National Church, indeed a "martyr", might come into the earlier stages of the growth of the legend – Henry while his father lived made a friend of Oldcastle, and this could be regarded as "national" behaviour. But it must have come to seem remote from the popular story, because Shakespeare cannot have wanted to run up against it, and his apology gives a convincing impression of surprise at finding the knight was a Puritan.

taking an official view of affairs; no doubt that feeling was somehow present, for many of the audience as well as for Shakespeare; but even from a political angle Falstaff stood for something valuable – I do not deny that it seemed absurd to say so, but one felt there was "something in it". Nor was this sentiment at all furtive, because it fitted so naturally into the official Tudor propaganda. That the Tudors were the first really national dynasty was a regular plank in their propaganda. Henry fitted in, apart from using the English language, because like them he was partly Welsh, and the claim is made for him several times in *Henry V*. The Tudors were supporting their doubtful right to the throne (as Tillyard pointed out in *Shakespeare's History Plays*) by a claim that their Welsh ancestors were the real British line, with magical virtues about them, involving Brutus and King David of Jerusalem himself, and anyhow older than the Saxon invaders let alone the Norman ones. I suspect that the Elizabethans did not take this line of talk as solemnly as they sometimes pretended, and it is mixed up here with a more rational desire to forget old quarrels so that the island can be united; but antiquarian arguments were serious to them – for that matter, the scholarly rediscovery of how to read Anglo-Saxon legal documents was one of the things that cut off Charles I's head. I suspect that Shakespeare was giving the Government, as well as the popular audience, a great deal of what they wanted, so much that they would put up with some things they didn't want (it is hard to see why else the Company escaped after the performance of *Richard II* for the Essex rebels); perhaps his apparent subservience to the Tudor Myth, which anyhow came from a genuine horror of civil war, worked out as giving him more freedom. In any case, it was not mere rhetoric at the beginning of *I Henry VI*, when the characters were bemoaning the death of Henry V, to make them say:

England ne'er had a King until his time.

This was an idea that the audience had already taken into its head. He held a position rather like that of John the Baptist; he was the forerunner of the Tudors. I realise that this is a bit remote from the needs of a modern producer, because he cannot get it across to his audience, but it does I think remove the suggestion of false sentiment against which Dover Wilson very understandably revolted.

One tends now to think of the wooing scene of Henry with

Katherine, at the end of *Henry V*, as a sickeningly obvious bit of film dialogue; the good young millionaire democrat can immediately melt the fastidious aristocratic foreign beauty by the universal power of his virile or earth-touching mode of approach. Dr Johnson and Voltaire did not find it sickeningly obvious but implausibly low; Henry could not have been such a hayseed, they thought, even if Katherine could have liked it. Shakespeare did not invent the incident; there is a shorter and less aggressive version of it in *The Famous Victories*, and one might argue that his epilogue to *II Henry IV* promises the audience that the expected scene will be treated fully. I suspect that all later examples of it are derived from the Hal Legend, so that it is a specific invention, like matches; but at the start it had to have a positive point, not merely its later rather mysterious background of democracy or something. It was a kind of hyperbole to suppose that the Norman Prince could not talk his own language to his Norman bride (instead of making the end of the play flabby, as Dr Johnson thought); and he was rationally admired for the incapacity because it proved he had changed his allegiance. There is also an idea that only his wild oats, or only Falstaff, could have taught him this; but the main idea is the patriotic one. Also, even here, the audience is not expected simply to "identify" themselves with Hal; his boasts about what a fine fighter his son by Katherine will be are bound to strike a chill, because everybody knew that Henry VI was going to be the final disaster for his usurping line. Dover Wilson points out in his notes that there is "an irony" here, but does not seem to consider what an irony is used for. Even in his triumph Hal could only be a forerunner of the real British Tudors.

We tend to forget that the rising power of England, in Shakespeare's time, was still rather embarrassed to have been so long ruled by an invading dynasty who spoke French; but that is only because the English are good at forgetting such things. *Henry V* itself has one or two memories of the Norman Conquest which have been neglected; I only noticed them myself when looking over the text after seeing the British wartime version of the play, to find where the cuts stood out. One would expect that the rougher propaganda of earlier days had left in some damaging admissions, but that the national hero had at any rate been patriotic all right. But when Henry is answering the French Ambassador who brought the insulting tennis balls something much odder turns up. He boasts that he will conquer and rule

France, his proper heritage as a Norman, and in answering the Dauphin's jeer at his life he says he naturally lived like a beast when he had only England to live in:

> We never valued this poor seat of England,

but he will live in an entirely different way when he has got hold of the much more valuable bit of property called France. Critics, so far as they attend to this, placidly call it irony; and no doubt a contemporary of Shakespeare could take it that way too. Nor is it then flat, because a patriot should always regard his country as weak but heroic, certain to win but only certain because of its virtues. But surely it would be a natural reflection to many in the first audiences that a feudal lord really did think of a country like this, without any irony. Surely it is odd, when the dramatist clearly wants to make the hero patriotic, that he gives the audience such a very strong and plausible case where he isn't. It seems to me riding very near the edge, in that audience, to make the ever-popular Hal say (may I repeat what Dover Wilson's Ideal King said),

> We never valued this poor seat of England.

Of course I willingly agree that the answer is merely the familiar one of dramatic suspense; this remark comes early in the play, and by the end of it we have got Hal being almost shamingly homey; if he can't talk French, he obviously can't move as a feudal lord from London to Paris. Also it is rather an odd kind of dramatic suspense, because the audience already knew that Henry wasn't this kind of feudal lord; it was only a kind of playing at saying the tactless thing. But it would be very noticeable to the audience, and the author did not mean it to be thrown away at once by the nods and winks at the audience which Dover Wilson is so fond of inserting in his stage directions. That Hal turned out to be the first "English" king, unlike his ancestors, was to be presented with drama, and the dramatist gives it a certain violence (though of a kind which could be explained away) by recalling the doubt which would have appeared real to a fifteenth-century audience, and perhaps did not appear very unreal to a sixteenth-century one either.

You cannot call it far-fetched of me, in looking at this play, to argue that the English were conscious of having been ruled by the French, because the Dauphin is made to say it very firmly about the English lords:

Shall a few sprays of us,
The emptying of our fathers' luxury,
Our scions, put in wild and savage stock,
Spirt up so suddenly into the clouds,
And overlook their grafters?

The Duke of Bourbon follows with the line

Normans, but bastard Normans, Norman bastards,

a comment on the English aristocracy which has more carrying power in the theatre than on the printed page. Soon after, the Dauphin reports that "our madams" say the cross-breeding has made the English lords more virile than the French ones. It is all rather coarse propaganda, but there is no doubt what it means. One must remember that Queen Elizabeth herself was felt to have done a fair amount to exclude the older aristocracy from power, and surround herself by lords of her own creation.

The answer of the play to the surprise of the Dauphin is that the British islands were becoming united and therefore strong; the idea is not simply that the English were determined to enslave the French, because of a very obscure argument about the rules of succession among Norman conquerors. This "jingo" aspect of a superficially rather coarse play (rightly described by the Germans around 1914 as "good war reading") is a bit embarrassing, and I think it is mostly removed if you remember a political background which is not part of the text. The English had been in doubt during the sixteenth century whether to have military adventures in Europe or to compete with Spain in adventures for new worlds. Elizabeth's father had made a fool of himself in Europe, which could not be said publicly, but Elizabeth herself had quietly and penuriously shown a preference for new worlds; it would not appear recklessly unpatriotic, even in *Henry V*, to insinuate that there was something to be said for her policy. Indeed, this was the only possible line of expansion; if the English had kept France, a modern reader is likely to reflect, they would soon have been ruled from Paris; and for that matter if they had kept America (later) they would soon have been ruled from Washington – the two great losses secured national independence. I am not saying that Shakespeare was wise about this controversy, or even right (he seems remarkably little interested in new worlds, apart from some good jokes against them in *The Tempest*; however, in the *Merchant of Venice* he can see the romance of making London a world trading centre like Venice all right); only that this was the context of political controversy in which he was building up his enormously popular stage machine. After all, the only claim of Hal to France is that he is a Norman not an Englishman, and almost the only thing he is praised for is learning to be an Englishman not a Norman. Shakespeare, I think, felt that one ought to be patriotic and yet that one needn't pull a long face about not ruling France; the international angle was all right somehow, though one had better keep on the fence a bit, whereas the danger of civil war at home wasn't. In the middle of his play of conquest, therefore, he can cheerfully let Hal admit to God that he has no right to conquest, and only beg for the escape of these particular devoted troops (who have been questioning the rights of the war):

> Not today, O Lord,
> No, not today, think not upon the fault
> My father made in compassing this crown,

This is the most genuine thing Henry ever says (some critic argues that even now he was trying to cheat God over the deal, if you look into the facts about his offer of chantries, but that is off the point I think); and we are to regard it as accepted by God, therefore successful in saving these troops; but it does not, of course, remove the doom from Hal himself or from his usurping lineage, or even perhaps from the Norman-English claim to rule France, and he never prays for any such enormous thing. I would not want to sentimentalise the Prince, but "Not today, O Lord" really is a noble prayer when you realise how harshly limited he knows it to be; he is hardly praying for anybody except the individual troops he has just been talking to. (Naturally it was cut from the wartime film production.) And by being genuine there (as I understand the feeling) he gets not only what he asked but a magical extra gift, never known to himself but worth celebrating for ever, as he says the battle itself will be; not the conquest of France but the gradual unification of his own islands. They still had to go through a terrible slow mill, because God grinds down small; the Wars of the Roses had still to come after his early death; but Hal deserved his moment of triumph because he had shown the right way or at any rate seen things in their right proportions, before his time. That is the "religious" or "patriotic" feeling about Hal (one can hardly say which), and I feel it myself; it is a real enough thing, though grand claims need not be made for it. On this view, of course, the play isn't interested in conquering France, but in showing a good leader getting troops from different parts of the islands to work together in a tight corner and a foreign place. You may feel that this is an absurd amount of whitewashing of the play's motive, and I don't deny that the obvious appeal was the simple drum-and-trumpet one; what I maintain is that there was a controversy about these questions of foreign policy, and the play had to satisfy the less simple-minded spectators too. For that matter, Shakespeare had made Henry's father talk with almost comic cynicism about how he would use foreign aggression, or a crusade, or something, to avoid civil war; and the one thing in politics that Shakespeare really did regard seriously was civil war. I am not imputing to him an idea which could not have come into his head.

I ought now to say something about the introductory scenes of the play which give the reasons for the war, though I can say little. The clergy first make clear that the war is to their own interest and then recite Henry's technical claim to the French throne at great length. (Modern historians, as I understand, consider that Henry had no decent reason for attacking France, except possibly the one that Shakespeare made his father give.) The wartime film handled this, rather ingeniously, by keeping us in the play-house at the beginning and turning this recitation into farce, guying old-world techniques rather than anything else. It is hard to imagine how the first audiences took it; one must remember they were well accustomed to hearing sermons. Dover Wilson's attempts to save the face of the clergy do not seem to me worth a reply, but he is right in insisting that the recitation did not seem dull, as it does now; not, however, as he thinks, because everybody took it for granted. I imagine that Shakespeare was rather ostentatiously not making up anyone's mind for them.

Assuming then that the legend about Hal and the value of his tavern life had this rather massive background. I want now to say something about the interior of Falstaff; that is, not anything which was kept secret from the first audiences, but how it was that Shakespeare's incarnation of the legend could be felt intuitively as a very real character, whom one was curious to know more about; as evidently happened. The eighteenth-century Morgann, if I may avoid appearing too "modern" at this point, has some piercing remarks about the interior of a stage character in general, and how the impression of it is built up; but is mainly concerned to say about Falstaff (after using this idea to explain how we feel he isn't a coward though he appears one) that his deeper interior is more sordid than we are encouraged to recognise, though we still somehow know it. This interior of Falstaff, rather hard to get at for most of us, is also sharply lit up by some remarks of Dr Johnson; and one could wish that Dover Wilson, who is rightly fond of pointing out that later critics have not had the firm good sense of Johnson, had profited by his master here. It is not surprising that Johnson speaks with confidence about this sort of life, because he had observed it; he could say without absurdity that he regretted not having met Falstaff. Also he himself was a man of startling appearance; a pugnaciously and robustly amusing talker, who regularly conquered but never won anything that mattered, a hero of taverns, fretted by remorse (which Falstaff makes much play with if nothing more), starved of love, unwilling to be alone. He has several comments such as that "a man feels in himself the pain of deformity"; "however, like this merry knight, he may make sport of it among those whom it is his interest to please". If we compare this with the struggles of Dover Wilson to prove that Falstaff was a Medieval Vice, with no interior at all, surely the truth of Johnson stands out like a rock. The picture of him as driven on by an obscure personal shame, of an amoral sort, has several advantages, I think. Wyndham Lewis has written well about his incessant trick of "charm", his insistence on presenting himself as a deliciously lovable old bag of guts, helpless but able to make a powerful appeal to the chivalry of the protector; one needs to add that this curious view of him made a sharp contrast to his actual wickedness – that was the joke; but both sides of it are really present. He clamours for love, and I do not see why Dover Wilson should ignore it. I made a mistake in my *Pastoral* from assuming that this line of talk was concentrated upon the Prince; in *I Henry IV*, II.ii – "If the rascal have not given me medicines to make me love him, I'll be hanged; it could not be else – I have drunk medicines", it must be Poins, not the Prince, who is supposed to have administered the love-philtre. Poins has just told the audience (though not Falstaff) that he stole the horse whose loss creates all this amorous tumult (because Falstaff is too fat to walk) and Falstaff was shouting for Poins; to be sure, the Prince is the only person yet spoken to by Falstaff in this scene, and the Prince's usual claim to innocence has put him under suspicion – the actor could drag the words round to apply to the Prince, as I first thought, and Falstaff can hardly know which of them stole it.

But even Falstaff could hardly say of the Prince, "I have forsworn his company hourly any day these two and twenty years, and yet I am bewitched by the rogue's company." The historical Hal was about sixteen here; the stage one might be regarded as twenty-two, so that Falstaff had forsworn his company since he was born, but this would be rather pointlessly absurd, and the natural view is that it applies to his (presumably older and steadier) gentleman-in-waiting. It is a rather startling cry, and comes early while the character of Falstaff is being defined to the audience; I take it the idea is that he regularly expresses love towards the young men who rob for him, and that this is a powerful means of leading them astray – it is a proud thing to become the favourite of such an expert teacher. For that matter Fagin in *Oliver Twist* is always expressing love to flatter the Artful Dodger and suchlike; even a member of the audience who hated Falstaff from the beginning would recognise that this bit of the machine had to be there, as a normal thing. It doesn't make very much difference whether Falstaff said it about Hal or Poins. The only thing that still puzzles me here is the recurrence of the number twenty-two, which probably means some private association of Shakespeare's. When the Prince says he has repaid the money gained by robbery he adds that he has procured Falstaff a charge of foot (they can all get their faces straight, now that civil war has loosened the purse-strings) and Falstaff says: "I would it had been of horse. Where shall I find one that can steal well? O for a fine thief, of the age of two and twenty or thereabouts. I am heinously unprovided." The numbers regularly have a magical claim; consider the repeated thousand pounds; these twenty-two years of the young thief seem to me like the laborious number-magic in *Hamlet*, designed to prove that the First Gravedigger was appointed on the day of Hamlet's birth and has been waiting there ever since for an arrival never before seen but now due. I don't suppose the number twenty-two was meant to tell the audience anything.

Returning to Falstaff's heart, I think there is a quick answer to the idea that the old brute had no heart, and therefore could not have died of breaking it. If he had had no heart he would have had no power, not even to get a drink, and he had a dangerous amount of power. I am not anxious to present Falstaff's heart as a very attractive object; you might say that it had better be called his vanity, but we are none of us sure how we would emerge from a thorough analysis on those lines; the point is that everybody felt

it obvious that he had got one – otherwise he would not be plausible even in attracting his young thieves, let alone his insanely
devoted "hostess". I daresay that the wincing away from the
obvious (or from Wyndham Lewis's account) which I seem to
find in recent critics is due to distaste for homosexuality, which is
regarded nowadays in more practical terms than the Victorian
ones; the idea of Falstaff making love to the Prince, they may
feel, really has to be resisted. But surely Johnson gives us the
right perspective here; Falstaff felt in himself the pain of a
deformity which the audience could always see; no amount of
expression of love from Falstaff to his young thieves would excite
suspicion on that topic from the audiences, not because the audiences were innocent about it, but because they could assume that
any coming thief (let alone the Prince) would be too vain to yield
to such deformity. I agree that a doubt here could not have been
allowed, but there was no need to guard against it. A resistance
to it should not prevent us from noticing that Falstaff is rather
noisily shocked if young men do not love him. It is as well to take
an example from near the end of Part II, where on Dover
Wilson's account there should be practically nothing left in him
but degeneration. He complains about Prince John (IV.ii.85),
"this same young sober-blooded boy doth not love me, nor a man
cannot make him laugh", and goes on in a fairly long speech to
claim that he has taught Prince Hal better humanity. This is easily
thought ridiculous because it is almost entirely a praise of drink,
but the mere length presumes dramatic effect; and drink was presumed to teach both sympathy and courage (it is the culmination
of these two ideas in a "heart", of course, which make it rather
baffling to discuss what kind of heart Falstaff has); and we have
just seen Prince John perform a disgusting act of cowardly
treachery. This detail of structure, I think, is enough to prove
that at least the popular side of the audience was assumed to
agree with Falstaff. Indeed, if you compare Hal to his brother
and his father, whom the plays describe so very unflinchingly, it
is surely obvious that to love Falstaff was a liberal education for
him.

It is hard to defend this strange figure without doing it too
much. May I remind the patient reader that I am still doing what
this essay started to do, trying to show that Falstaff from his first
conception was not intended to arrive at Agincourt, because the
Prince was intended to reach that triumph over his broken heart.
The real case for rejecting Falstaff at the end of Part II is that he

was dangerously strong, indeed almost a rebel leader; Dover
Wilson makes many good points here, and he need not throw the
drama away by pretending that the bogey was always ridiculous.
He is quite right in insisting that the Prince did not appear
malicious in the rejection, and did only what was necessary;
because Falstaff's expectations were enormous (and were recklessly expressed, by the way, to persons who could shame him
afterwards); the terrible sentence "the laws of England are at my
commandment, . . . and woe to my Lord Chief Justice" meant
something so practical to the audience that they may actually
have stopped cracking nuts to hear what happened next. The
small capital would be entered by the mob for a coronation, and
how much of it Falstaff could raise would be a reasonable subject
for doubt; he could become "protector" of the young King; once
you admit that he is both an aristocrat and a mob leader he is a
familiar very dangerous type. The "special pleading" of Dover
Wilson here, that the King only gave him honour by sending him
to the Fleet Prison, a place where lords were put in temporary
custody while waiting for enquiry before the Privy Council and
such like, instead of treating him as a common criminal, seems to
me off the point; he really was important enough for the Fleet
Prison, both in the eyes of the imaginary fifteenth-century and
the real sixteenth-century audience. Dover Wilson argues,
rightly I think, that Henry shows a good deal of forbearance in his
conditions to Falstaff, so far as one can interpret them; but one
must remember that the King and the dramatist both had to show
forbearance, for just about the same reasons, and facing a similar
mob. I do not mean that either of them privately wanted to be
hard on the old man, only that they both had to get through a
public event. As to why Shakespeare's play had a casual
Epilogue, for some performances, saying "maybe Jack will bob
up again some time", it is not hard to imagine that he might need
to send his audience away in a good temper by having that said.
So much so, indeed, that it is not evidence of his real intentions;
maybe he had suddenly become so important that he had to lie
like a Foreign Office. In the same way, Henry had to get rid of
Falstaff with unquestionable firmness but without any suspicion
that he had behaved with malice, because a rising in favour of
Falstaff was just what he needed to avoid. A bit of political
understanding, I think, is enough to make this problem
transparent.

However, to say that the rejection has to be done firmly if done

in public is not to say that it need be done so at all. The real case
against Hal, in the reasonable view of A. C. Bradley, is that he
was dishonest in not warning Falstaff beforehand that he would
have to reject him after coronation, and still more in pretending
on that occasion that Falstaff had misled him. Their separation,
says Bradley, might have been shown in a private scene rich in
humour and only touched with pathos; a remark which shows
how very different he would like the characters to be. Dover
Wilson answers that *Falstaff* makes a public rejection necessary;
the Prince "first tries to avoid the encounter, begging the Lord
Chief Justice to say for him what must be said. But Falstaff will
not allow it . . . Though under observation (the Prince) falters
and finds it difficult to keep up", etc.; and the Prince could not
have warned Falstaff at a convenient time, because "Shakespeare has been busy since Shrewsbury manoeuvring the former
friends into different universes between which conversation is
impossible". One is often baffled by a peculiar circularity in the
arguments of Dover Wilson. This may be an adequate defence
for Hal, though his claim that he was misled still looks unnecess-
arily shifty; but it cannot also be a defence for the dramatist;
indeed, I think it brings into a just prominence the fact that
Shakespeare wanted, and arranged, to end his play with this
rather unnerving bang. By the way, Dr Johnson called it, so far
from a bang, "a lame and impotent conclusion", and poor Dover
Wilson has to argue that his master is only complaining at the
absence of a final heroic couplet. He argues against a phrase of
Bradley, that Hal was trying "to buy the praise of the respectable
at the cost of honor and truth", that the word *respectability* had
not been invented (but the *thing* is visible enough here) and that
the change in Hal is "an instance of the phenomenon of 'con-
version'" (this does not join well onto his previous arguments
that Hal was never really a sinner). None of this, I think, is
adequate ground for doubting what seems obvious, that Shakespeare was deliberately aiming at a rather peculiar dramatic
effect, imposing considerable strain, as most critics have felt
whether they accepted it or not. The inherent tension between
the characters is given its fullest expression and then left
unresolved; as G. K. Chesterton remarked, this really is a "problem play", whereas the plays so called in the nineties were simply
propaganda plays – a man might fully recognise the merits and
importance of Henry V, and still doubt, without the dramatist
trying to decide for him, "whether he had not been a better man

when he was a thief". Of course, the play is not obtrusively a problem, because it simply tells a popular story, but to do that so strongly brings out what is inherent in it, and the apparently coarse treatment may involve profound or at least magical thinking. There seems room for the suggestion of J. I. M. Stewart, that Henry was felt to require before he arrived at Agincourt the *mana* which came from sacrificing the representative of a real divinity, or a tutor of heroes.

After imposing decent enough conditions on Falstaff, Henry sweeps out with the remark that the Lord Chief Justice must "perform the tenor of his word", and this is at once interpreted by the Chief Justice throwing Falstaff and all his company into the Fleet Prison; perhaps only till the mobs have dispersed, as Dover Wilson suggests. Neither he nor any other critic that I have seen discusses what would happen to Falstaff when he got there; a thing which would seem obvious to the audience but cannot to us. Surely it is likely that he would be smashed by the Fleet Prison. It assumed the prisoner to be a rich landowner who could toss money away before he got out, and it examined his sources of money and encouraged creditors to speak up. Lords at Elizabeth's court were commonly ruined if they were sent to the Fleet, living as they did on a speculator's market, and it is hard to see how Falstaff would do better. As for what are almost his last words, "Master Shallow, I owe you a thousand pound", which Dover Wilson calls "*the* last word", they are certainly a last boast, and I warmly agree that Shakespeare did not want to send the old boy off the stage whining and appearing broken, or even telling too much truth for that matter – nor did the King. But I think a contemporary spectator would reflect that, although ready money would be a great help to Falstaff "and his company" in the Fleet, it wouldn't take them at all far. And indeed, when the next play shows Falstaff dying as a free man in the tavern, I think this person might reflect that the King must have bought him out, paying off Shallow as well as the others. I would like to have a ruling from a historian on the point, but I suspect that the last boast of Falstaff was only just enough to get him off the stage.

I have next to argue that he was sure to die. Surely we have all met these strong old men, fixed in their habits, who seem unbreakable ("wonderful" as people say) till they get a shock, and then collapse very suddenly. He is over seventy, because he was breaking Scogan's head at the court gate fifty-five years ago; and his pox has been emphasised. The shock given to him is very severe all round; it does not matter whether ambition or love or his pleasures mattered most to him, he had lost them all, and had also lost his *mystique*; his private war against shame had been answered by public loathing of a kind which no tongue could get round; even his "company" would be reproaching him and jeering at him. As against this, which seems ordinary human experience, we have Dover Wilson arguing *both* that he was a study in increasing degeneration *and* that "the last thing Shakespeare had in mind" when he wrote the Epilogue of Part II "was a sad death for his fat knight", who was needed as a comic at Agincourt. Now, a certain amount of petty criminality can reasonably be shown among the troops at Agincourt, where it is punished fiercely, but does Dover Wilson mean that a searching picture of the third degree of degeneration would have fitted comfortably into the scene of national triumph? It seems rather hard on the Prince; who would also, I think, prefer not to be in danger of unbeatable comic criticisms from his old tutor at such a time. The idea that the text has gone wrong, I submit, comes from not seeing the story in the round; to have brought Falstaff to Agincourt would have thrown a serious jam into the gears of a rather delicate piece of machinery. But there again, it is rather too glib to talk in this technical way about the necessities of the playwright; what he manages to get out of them is an effect of truth. Given the two characters, that was the way it would have to end.

I want finally to consider what the plays meant to Shakespeare himself, as apart from the audience; there is no very definite conclusion to be expected, but one ought not to talk as if an achievement on this scale has no personal backing. It seems that Shakespeare, though of course he won his position in the Company much earlier, already perhaps from the *Henry VI* sequence, odd as it appears now, made his decisive position out of Falstaff. Not merely as a matter of money, which was very important, but also as a matter of trust from the audience, the triumph of Falstaff made possible the series of major tragedies; it was not merely an incident to him. I pursued the subject of the personal background to Falstaff in my *Pastoral* (pp. 102–9), and want to remark that I still believe what I said there, though this essay is concerned with something rather different. Indeed I think that to understand the many-sidedness of the legend he was using makes it more plausible to think he felt his own experience to be an illustration of it. I proved, I think, that the first soliloquy of the Prince, assuring the audience that he was going to abandon his low friends, is drawn almost line by line from the Sonnets trying to justify the person addressed. It seems inherently probable that the humiliation of Shakespeare's dealings with his young patron, which one can guess were recently finished, would get thrown into the crucible in which the Prince's friends had to be created. Falstaff looks to me like a secret come-back against aristocratic patrons, marking a recovery of nerve after a long attempt to be their hanger-on. But this was not done coarsely or with bad temper; the whole triumph of the thing, on its intimate side, was to turn his private humiliation into something very different and universally entertaining. I have been arguing that Falstaff is not meant to be socially low, even when he first appears, only to be a scandal to his rank; whereas Shakespeare of course had only a dubious profession and a suspect new gentility. There are warnings in the Sonnets that friendship with Shakespeare is bad for the patron's reputation, though we hardly ever get an actual admission of inferior social status (we do in the "dyer's hand"); he would rather talk obscurely about his "guilt". Snobbery, I think, had always seemed more real to him than self-righteousness, and even in the Sonnets we can see the beginning of the process that turned player Shakespeare into Falstaff, not a socially inferior friend but (what is much less painful) a scandalous one. Nobody would argue that the result is a life-like portrait of Shakespeare; though he must have known how to amuse, and talks in the Sonnets with a regret about his old age which was absurd even for an Elizabethan if he was then under thirty-five, and undoubtedly was what they called a "villainist" tutor, the type who could give broad experience to a young prince. The point is not that he was like Falstaff but that, once he could imagine he was, he could "identify" himself with a scandalous aristocrat, the sufferings of that character could be endured with positive glee. I am sure that is how he came to be liberated into putting such tremendous force into every corner of the picture.

APPENDIX

Since writing this in Peking, I have poked my nose into texts of the chroniclers, translator of Livius, Hall, and Holinshed, and the modern historian J. H. Wylie (*Reign of Henry V*). I find the subject is so confusing that one can hardly accuse the play of departing from history at all. It should be reported that the sources of Shakespeare do not strike one as devoted to patriotic whitewash. Perhaps their chief difference from the play is that they have more about money.

Thus critics often say that Shakespeare made Henry look more merciful by falsely denying that he sacked Harfleur; there is a bit of suppression of truth, but Henry did not sack it. He took care not to let his soldiers kill, rape, and burn; that is what Shakespeare makes him warn Harfleur against, and save it from. He did mulct the town very heavily, and he sent away "2000 of the poor and the women and children of every rank to save them from the soldiers" – so says Wylie, who argues that he meant in the end to replace the whole population by English settlers. Wylie does however report that the French at the time were surprised by his mercy (in the case of this particular town, where he may have had special plans). A John Falstaff was made lieutenant of captured Harfleur; so that is where Falstaff really went, of course he didn't go to Agincourt. To have to reject such entirely typical material must have given keen regret to the dramatist; but I am sure he never wrote it down; it would have been quite off the rails. The chronicler Hall says "the goods in the town were innumerable which were all prey to the English", but Wylie says you could keep your goods if you took an oath of allegiance to Henry. I am not clear what this involved in its turn.

In the same way, it is a possible point of view about the killing of the prisoners at Agincourt that Henry was chiefly interfering with his officers' ransom money. Holinshed says it was annoying for the French commanders to have French soldiers loot the English camp, because they were no longer trying to win the battle – "very many after were committed to prison, and had lost their lives, if the Dolphin had longer lived". He goes on to say how dolorous and terrible it was for Henry to order the killing of prisoners, but he seems to leave room for a suggestion that Henry meant "I can't afford profiteers here; you must destroy this property you have been collecting; the thing is getting out of hand." According to the modern Wylie, Henry when giving this order specifically excluded the killing of any Dukes or Earls, because they would be his own share of the ransom money. This detail does not appear in the chroniclers, and perhaps they did suppress that much as removing a possible source of credit for him.

Before nerving myself to approach the real confusions of history I looked up the great disintegrator J. M. Robertson on the killing of prisoners at Agincourt. As one would expect, he says that this bit of the play was written by three or four fools each of them quite indifferent to what was done by the others. In a case like this, where there really is something wrong, one can read him with much sympathy. But he also says a thing which I think shows an entirely wrong assumption. He denounces the speech of Henry to Harfleur, warning the citizens what a loot really means; the sickening cruelty of the threat, he says, is only made tolerable by an excuse disgraceful if true, that Henry had no control over his own army. Are these the heroes so soon to be exalted at Agincourt? and so forth. This highminded nineteenth-century point of view cannot survive a glance at the chroniclers, who did think it rather clever of Henry to manage not to let his troops behave appallingly. Shakespeare is keeping to the truth in expressing that ("Show mercy to them all"); but he might naturally become uncertain, as he read on, about how much truth he ought to put into this play.

J. M. Robertson, discussing the speech (IV.vii) which begins with that noble line

> I was not angry since I came to France

– it came over with great moral beauty in the film, because it means that no personal disaster could make him angry, only the suffering of children – points out that he says nothing whatever about these children. He says that the horsemen on yon hill offend his sight, therefore he orders a deceitful message to be sent to them, that if they attack he will kill his prisoners; whereas the audience knows that he has killed them already. That is, he hasn't been able to become gloriously angry before, because only now has he had enough blood to get drunk on it. This is really interesting criticism, because it shows what a knife-edge the great effects have to balance on. But it is none the less absurd; the intention is obviously the highminded one, that Henry was justly angered by an enemy atrocity, and was driven by it into a questionable reprisal. A critic does not have to be a whitewasher to think this, indeed he can say that the appeal to the gallery is coarse and false; but he must still recognise that Henry is repeatedly praised because he gave as much attention to a low-class Englishman (let alone a child) as to a Norman aristocrat, and also because he never boasted about the highminded motives which actually decided his behaviour. This, surely, is what makes us decide what we expect the passage to mean.

Robertson supposes three superimposed versions, none of them by Shakespeare. The first tried to alter the famous killing of prisoners into a mere threat (this desire for mercy is absurdly ascribed to Marlowe); the second gave the real story but did not bother to reconcile it with the threat; the third added the remarks of Fluellen and Gower, also presumably the two earlier soliloquies of the Boy, not bothering to remove any contradictions but meaning to suggest that the killing of the prisoners was a highminded reprisal. Passages are given to the different authors on grounds of style as well as logical coherence. Now Robertson's arguments from style are exposed to a fundamental objection, not unlike the objection to his argument from morality. The style of Shakespeare itself was very variable all along, even though, or perhaps because, he is the outstanding case of an author who kept on "developing" his style. It seems to me obvious that he could imitate the style of Marlowe whenever he thought that style would be suitable, because it is such a definite thing to imitate; and it is suitable here. As to the King of France, it is ludicrous to "prove" by a laborious count of double-endings that he can't be Shakespeare's; because Shakespeare wanted to make this character sound weak. J. H. Walter may be right in saying that the censor would have been annoyed if even a foreign royalty had been shamed, but Shakespeare could display the weakness of this man merely by giving him plenty of double-endings. Robertson really did have a good ear, and is very acute in other matters; one ought to read him for the incidental truths which he buried in his rather tragically irrelevant programme.

The strength of Robertson having driven me to the historians, I was impressed to find that they destroyed his case at once. The position is at once more puzzling and more natural than he had supposed. The entire layout of this rather subtle confusion about the prisoners is already present in Holinshed; that is, first the prisoners are killed, then Henry threatens to kill them, then we simply hear that the French have killed the boys in the camp. We need not invent three totally non-co-operative authors, who surely must have annoyed the actors bitterly, if we only want to know why the author of a History Play copied down what the chronicler said. We do, on the other hand, have to wonder why it was done so very tactlessly, in an age which expected tact about kings. *Henry V* as it stands gives such a bad impression of Henry that it is literally never acted, even nowadays, whereas the chroniclers give a reasonably good impression of him. A literary critic is not being fussy if he tries to explain why this occurred.

Holinshed says very little about anybody's motives, and I think he gives a better impression of Henry than Shakespeare does merely because, by telling more of the truth, he gives you the right timing. He says that, when the King heard the outcries from the lackeys and boys who had run away from the French spoiling of the English camp, he thought there was a danger of a second battle in which the mass of prisoners taken might be dangerous to his own army, so he ordered them to be killed at once, "contrary to his accustomed gentleness". When this lamentable slaughter was over (it was pity to see) the Englishmen disposed themselves in order of battle, ready to abide a new field; and at once they had a fresh onset to handle, from a separate group who had all that day kept together. After this had been won, the King saw that the French were again thinking of assembling for further battle, so he sent them his famous threat, and they parted out of the field and he made every man kneel down while they sang *Non Nobis Domine*. Holinshed introduces this part of his story with the doubtful phrase "Some write that . . . ", but he puts in the margin "a right wise and valiant challenge of the king". The opinion of a whitewasher would not be worth attention, but Holinshed has a sturdy enough morality; he has clearly decided that this action prevented further slaughter. His account does at least remove the combination of absurdity and meanness which made Dr Johnson say "he shows he is angry by threatening to kill his prisoners after he has killed them already"; in Holinshed there is enough lapse of time to let Henry get some fresh live prisoners. The stage always hurries things up, and here the most disgraceful part of the story is an accidental result of that.

In the same way, the idea that the killing of the prisoners was a just reprisal need not have been presented as an obvious delusion of the absurd Fluellen. According to Wylie, though later French historians rubbed in the barbarity of Henry at Agincourt, even his fiercest French critic at the time, though denouncing the carnage at Caen, did not blame him here. Two unexpected things were going on, as one need not be surprised to learn, which Henry could not have known to be independent of one another. I am rather doubtful how to interpret the learned Wylie when he says that the battle was as much arranged beforehand as a modern sports event; even there one can have large technical surprises, and I presume he does not mean to deny that Henry had planned one. What we were told at school, that the English long-bow-men won the battle by a trick, which was also what Shakespeare's audience had been told in *The Famous Vic-*

tories of Henry V, does not seem to get much attention from Wylie; but I presume he is only wincing away from the obvious. I am sure he is right about the general tone of the affair. The looting of the English camp, he says, was outside the rules, from the point of view of both sides; the looters seized Henry's crown and other holy objects, and raised a shout with *Te Deum* which meant that they had got hold of the King's magic again. Meanwhile the Duc de Brabant, who by bad timing had missed the earlier slaughter, was coming in with a fresh army for which the English hadn't been prepared, so the English couldn't again arrange the choice of ground for their new technical trick about archers. As I understand Wylie, the French not only blamed the looters as a matter of course but positively cursed the Duke for making his uninformed attack when the main event was over, thus causing death to a number of persons already captured whose status deserved attention. Hall says that the French blamed the looters for Henry's killing of the French prisoners, whereas Holinshed doesn't; but I have been impressed by the scholarly arguments that Shakespeare must have read all the sources, including some which were unpublished when he wrote, and if this is so the differences are unimportant. One can well believe that Government officials were willing to show him unpublished documents, at the price of a little briefing about how to take the right line on this tricky but important topic.

May I summarise my position: if you suppose that the single line "Then every soldier kill his prisoners" was marked by Shakespeare as cut when he altered his plan but somehow got into the printed texts, then you get a consistent treatment of the story. There is no way to tell whether Shakespeare decided to make these changes in the story about the prisoners while in solitude or because the censor ordered him to do it, because either case would leave just the same marks on his text. As to the pirated First Quarto, which gives a still more shocking treatment at this point, you must remember that the story was well known and that some audiences might prefer to have the treatment shocking. On the other hand, if you insist on making Shakespeare intend to retain this one line, you make Shakespeare thrust on the audience an epigrammatic and bursting hatred of Henry; the line if thrown back into the rather complicated treatment has the effect of giving Henry the comic fierce hard-to-beat wickedness of the Jew of Malta. I think a critic has to choose between two alternatives here.

I need also to explain the motives of the editors of the First Folio, who restored the line "Then every soldier kill his prisoners." I fancy they thought, rightly enough, that they had done their duty if they gave the printer, or had copied for him, their treasured original manuscript of the play. If they remembered a censorship of twenty years ago they would be rather pleased to beat it when it no longer mattered, and the line was universally known to be true to history; besides, it had sometimes been delivered, as we can presume from the first Quarto. The peculiar dramatic effect of it would not now bother them. I may now claim to have given intelligible and tolerable motives, though not specially good ones, to all the characters concerned in these queer bits of printing, as any theory about them needs to do.

3 *Hamlet*

One feels that the mysteries of Hamlet are likely to be more or less exhausted, and I have no great novelty to offer here, but it has struck me, in the course of trying to present him in lectures, that the enormous panorama of theory and explanation falls into a reasonable proportion if viewed, so to speak, from Pisgah, from the moment of discovery by Shakespeare. To do that should also have a relation with the impressions of a fresh mind, meeting the basic legend of the play at any date. I was led to it from trying to answer some remarks of Hugh Kingsmill, in *The Return of William Shakespeare*, who said that Hamlet is a ridiculously theatrical and therefore unreal figure, almost solely concerned with scoring off other people, which the dialogue lets him do much too easily, and attractive to actors only because "they have more humiliations than other men to avenge". A number of critics seem to have felt like this, though few have said it so plainly; the feeling tends to make one indifferent to the play, and over-rides any "solution of its problems", but when followed up it leads to more interesting country. I think it allows of a reconsideration of the origins, along which one might even take fresh troops into the jungle warfare over the text.

The experts mostly agree that Kyd wrote a play on Hamlet about 1587, very like his surviving *Spanish Tragedy* except that it was about a son avenging a father instead of a father avenging a son. In any case there was some early play on Hamlet. The only record of a performance of it is in 1594, under conditions which make it likely to have become the property of Shakespeare's Company; jokes about it survive from 1589, 1596, and 1601, the later two regarding it as a standard out-of-date object. A keen sense of changing fashion has to be envisaged; when Shakespeare's Company were seduced into performing *Richard II* for the Essex rebels they said they would have to be paid because it was too old to draw an audience, and it wasn't half as old as

Hamlet. A gradual evolution of *Hamlet*, which some critics have imagined, isn't likely under these conditions. We have to consider why Shakespeare rewrote a much-laughed-at old play, and was thus led on into his great Tragic Period, and the obvious answer is that he was told to; somebody in the Company thumbed over the texts in the ice-box and said "This used to be a tremendous draw, and it's coming round again; look at Marston. All you have to do is just go over the words so that it's *life-like* and they can't laugh at it." Kyd had a powerful but narrow, one might say miserly, theatrical talent, likely to repeat a success, so his *Hamlet* probably had a Play-within-the-Play like*The Spanish Tragedy*; we know from a joke it had a Ghost; and he would have almost all the rest of the story as we know it from the sources. For all we know, when Shakespeare created a new epoch and opened a new territory to the human mind, he did nothing but alter the dialogue for this structure, not even adding a scene. The trouble with this kind of critical approach, as the experienced reader will already be feeling with irritation, is that it can be used to say "That is why the play is so muddled and bad." On the contrary, I think, if taken firmly enough it shows how, at the time, such a wonderful thing as Shakespeare's *Hamlet* could be conceived and accepted.

The real "Hamlet problem", it seems clear, is a problem about his first audiences. This is not to deny (as E. E. Stoll has sometimes done) that Hamlet himself is a problem; he must be one, because he says he is; and he is a magnificent one, which has been exhaustively examined in the last 150 years. What is peculiar is that he does not seem to have become one until the end of the eighteenth century; even Dr Johnson, who had a strong grasp of natural human difficulties, writes about Hamlet as if there was no problem at all. We are to think, apparently, that Shakespeare wrote a play which was extremely successful at the time (none more so, to judge by the references), and continued to hold the stage, and yet that nearly two hundred years had to go by before anyone had even a glimmering of what it was about. This is a good story, but surely it is rather too magical. Indeed, as the Hamlet Problem has developed, yielding increasingly subtle and profound reasons for his delay, there has naturally developed in its wake a considerable backwash from critics who say "But how can such a drama as you describe conceivably have been written by an Elizabethan, for an Elizabethan audience?" Some kind of mediating process is required here; one needs to explain how the first audiences could take a more interesting view than Dr Johnson's, without taking an improbably profound one.

The political atmosphere may be dealt with first. Stoll has successfully argued that even the theme of delay need not be grasped by an audience, except as a convention; however, Dover Wilson has pointed out that the first audiences had a striking example before them in Essex, who was, or had just been, refusing to make up his mind in a public and alarming manner; his attempt at revolt might have caused civil war. One need not limit it to Essex; the Queen herself had long used vacillation as a major instrument of policy, but the habit was becoming unnerving because though presumably dying she still refused to name a successor, which in itself might cause civil war. Her various foreign wars were also dragging on indecisively. A play about a prince who brought disaster by failing to make up his mind was bound to ring straight on the nerves of the audience when Shakespeare rewrote *Hamlet*; it is not a question of intellectual subtlety but of what they were being forced to think about already. It seems to me that there are relics of this situation in the text, which critics have not considered in the light of their natural acting power. The audience is already in the grip of a convention by which Hamlet can chat directly to them about the current War of the Theatres in London, and then the King advances straight down the apron-stage and urges the audience to kill Hamlet:

> *Do it*, England,
> For like the hectic in my blood he rages,
> And *thou* must cure me.

None of them could hear that without feeling it was current politics, however obscure; and the idea is picked up again, for what seems nowadays only an opportunist joke, when the Gravedigger says that Hamlet's madness won't matter in England, where all the men are as mad as he. Once the idea has been planted so firmly, even the idea that England is paying Danegeld may take on some mysterious weight. Caroline Spurgeon and G. Wilson Knight have maintained that the reiterated images of disease somehow imply that Hamlet himself is a disease, and this gives a basis for it. Yet the audience might also reflect that the character does what the author is doing – altering an old play to fit an immediate political purpose. This had to be left obscure, but we can reasonably presume an idea that the faults of Hamlet (which are somehow part of his great virtues) are not only specific but topical – "so far from being an absurd old play, it is just what you want, if you can see what is at the bottom of it". The insistence on the dangers of civil war, on the mob that Laertes does raise, and that Hamlet could raise but won't, and that Fortinbras at the end takes immediate steps to quiet, is rather heavy in the full text though nowadays often cut. Shakespeare could at least feel, when the old laughingstock was dragged out and given to him as a new responsibility, that delay when properly treated need not be dull; considered politically, the urgent thing might be not to let it get too exciting.

Such may have been his first encouraging reflection, but the political angle was not the first problem of the assignment, the thing he had to solve before he could face an audience; it was more like an extra gift which the correct solution tosses into his hand. The current objection to the old play *Hamlet*, which must have seemed very hard to surmount, can be glimpsed in the surviving references to it. It was thought absurdly theatrical. Even in 1589 the phrase "whole Hamlets, I should say handfuls, of tragical speeches" treats Hamlet as incessantly wordy, and the phrase of 1596, "as pale as the vizard of the ghost which cried so miserably at the Theatre, like an oyster wife, Hamlet Revenge", gets its joke from the idea that her dismal bawling may start again at any moment, however sick of her you are (presumably she is crying her wares up and down the street). The objection is not against melodrama, which they liked well enough, but against delay. You had a hero howling out "Revenge" all through the play, and everybody knew the revenge wouldn't come till the end. This structure is at the mercy of anybody in the audience who cares to shout "Hurry Up", because then the others feel they must laugh, however sympathetic they are; or rather, they felt that by the time Shakespeare rewrote *Hamlet*, whereas ten years earlier they would only have wanted to say "Shush". This fact about the audience, I submit, is the basic fact about the rewriting of *Hamlet*.

The difficulty was particularly sharp for Shakespeare's Company, which set out to be less ham than its rivals, and the Globe Theatre itself, only just built, asked for something impressively new. And yet there was a revival of the taste for Revenge Plays in spite of a half-resentful feeling that they had become absurd. No doubt, the old ones had gone on to being occasionally revived; though Henslow records a performance of *The Spanish Tragedy* in 1597 as "new", with no record of previous performance since 1592; but also new ones were now being written with a rather different tone. Clifford Leech (*Shakespeare's Tragedies*, p. 51) has pointed out that the "induction" was revived in four plays around the turn of the century, and argues that it marks a new kind of self-consciousness about the situation of being in a theatre; one which led to greater realism but rather began by excusing the absence of it (*Antonio and Mellida*, *The Malcontent*, *Every Man Out of his Humour* and *Cynthia's Revels*). Indeed, J. M. Nosworthy has suggested, Hamlet's scenes with the Players are rather like an Induction put in the middle. Now, Kyd had been writing before the destruction of the Spanish Armada, therefore while facing a more immediate probability of conquest with rack and fire; the position had remained dangerous, but 1588 had made the Elizabethans feel sure that God was on their side. I think the wheel seemed to be coming round again, chiefly because of the succession problem (there was a considerable scare in 1599 that the Queen was dead and the Spaniards had landed), so that we ought not to regard this vague desire to recover the mood of ten years earlier as merely stupid. Perhaps the fashion for child actors, the main complaint of the Players in *Hamlet*, came back at this moment because children could use the old convention with an effect of charm, making it less absurd because more distanced. E. K. Chambers quotes a complaint by Jonson, when the Children of the Queen's Chapel started acting in 1600, that "the umbrae of ghosts of some three or four plays, departed a dozen years since, have been seen wailing on your stage here".

Shakespeare himself had hardly written a tragedy before. To have written or had a hand in *Titus Andronicus*, ten years before, only brings him closer to his current audience; his own earlier tastes, as well as theirs, were to be re-examined. Romeo does not suggest an Aristotelian "tragic flaw"; the source poem by Brooke blames the lovers for haste and greed, but Shakespeare though increasing their haste has a short prologue putting the blame on their families; the moral is against feuds. As a writer of comedies, his main improvement in technique had been to reduce the need for a villain so that the effect was wholly un-tragic, and meanwhile the series of History Plays had been on the practical or hopeful theme "How to Avoid Civil War"; even so he had manoeuvred himself into ending with the cheerful middle of the series, having written its gloomy end at the start when the public was grim and anxious. What Shakespeare was famous for, just before writing *Hamlet*, was Falstaff and patriotic stuff about Henry V. *Julius Caesar*, the play immediately previous to *Hamlet*, is the most plausible candidate for a previous tragedy or indeed Revenge Play, not surprisingly, but the style is dry and the interest mainly in the politics of the thing. One can easily imagine that the external cause, the question of what the audience would like, was prominent when the theme was chosen. If Essex came into the background of the next assignment, Shakespeare's undoubted patron Southampton was also involved. I am not trying to make him subservient to his public, only sensitive to changes of taste in which he had an important part; nor would I forget that the misfortunes of genius often have a wild luck in their timing. But he must have seemed an unlikely person just then to start on a great Tragic Period, and he never wrote a Revenge Play afterwards; we can reasonably suppose that he first thought of *Hamlet* as a pretty specialised assignment, a matter, indeed, of trying to satisfy audiences who demanded a Revenge Play and then laughed when it was provided. I think he did not see how to solve this problem at the committee meeting, when the agile Bard was voted to carry the weight, but already did see how when walking home. It was a bold decision, and probably decided his subsequent career, but it was a purely technical one. He thought: "The only way to shut this hole is to make it big. I shall make Hamlet walk up to the audience and tell them, again and again, 'I don't know why I'm delaying any more than you do; the motivation of this play is just as blank to me as it is to you; but I can't help it.' What is more, I shall make it impossible for them to blame him. And *then* they daren't laugh." It turned out, of course, that this method, instead of reducing the old play to farce, made it thrillingly life-like and profound. A great deal more was required; one had to get a character who could do it convincingly, and bring in large enough issues for the puzzle not to appear gratuitous. I do not want to commit the Fallacy of Reduction, only to remove the suspicion that the first audiences could not tell what was going on.

Looked at in this way, the plot at once gave questions of very wide interest, especially to actors and the regular patrons of a repertory company; the character says: "Why do you assume I am theatrical? I particularly hate such behaviour. I cannot help my situation. What do you *mean* by theatrical?" Whole areas of the old play suddenly became so significant that one could wonder whether Kyd had meant that or not; whether Hamlet really wants to kill Claudius, whether he was ever really in love with Ophelia, whether he can continue to grasp his own motives while "acting a part" before the Court, whether he is not really more of an actor than the Players, whether he is not (properly speaking) the only sincere person in view. In spite of its great variety of incident, the play sticks very closely to discussing theatricality. Surely this is what critics have long found so interesting about *Hamlet*, while an occasional voice like Kingsmill's says it is nasty, or Stoll tries to save the Master by arguing it was not intended or visible at the time. But, so far from being innocent here, what the first audiences came to see was whether the Globe could revamp the old favourite without being absurd. To be sure, we cannot suppose them really very "sophisticated", considering the plays by other authors they admired; to make *The Spanish Tragedy* up-to-date enough for the Admiral's Company (which was paid for in September 1601, and June 1602, in attempts to catch up with Shakespeare's *Hamlet* presumably – indeed I think with two successive *Hamlets*) only required some interesting "life-like" mad speeches. But that they *imagined* they were too sophisticated for the old *Hamlet* does seem to emerge from the surviving jokes about it, and that is all that was required. We need not suppose, therefore, that they missed the purpose of the changes; "he is cunning past man's thought" they are more likely to have muttered into their beards, as they abandoned the intention to jeer.

As was necessary for this purpose, the play uses the device of throwing away dramatic illusion much more boldly than Shakespeare does anywhere else. (S. L. Bethell, in *Shakespeare and the Popular Dramatic Tradition*, has written what I take to be the classical discussion of this technique.) A particularly startling case is planted early in the play, when the Ghost pursues Hamlet and his fellows underground and says "Swear" (to be secret) wherever they go, and Hamlet says

> Come on, you hear this fellow in the cellarage,
> Consent to swear.

It seems that the area under the stage was *technically* called the cellarage, but the point is clear enough without this extra sharpening; it is a recklessly comic throw-away of an illusion, especially for a repertory audience, who know who is crawling about among the trestles at this point (Shakespeare himself, we are told), and have their own views on his style of acting. But the effect is still meant to be frightening; it is like Zoo in *Back to Methuselah*, who says "This kind of thing is got up to impress you, not to impress me"; and it is very outfacing for persons in the audience who come expecting to make that kind of joke themselves.

Following this plan, there are of course satirical misquotations of the Revenge classics, as in "Pox! leave thy damnable faces and begin. Come – 'the croaking raven doth bellow for revenge'" (probably more of them than we realise, because we miss the contrast with the old *Hamlet*); but there also has to be a positive dramatisation of the idea, which is given in Hamlet's scenes with the Players. Critics have wondered how it could be endurable for Shakespeare to make the actor of Hamlet upbraid for their cravings for theatricality not merely his fellow actors but part of his audience (the term "groundlings" must have appeared an insult and comes nowhere else); but surely this carries on the central joke, and wouldn't make the author prominent. I agree that the Player's speech and so forth was a parody of the ranting style of the Admiral's Company (and when Hamlet praised it his actor had to slip in and out of real life, without turning the joke too much against the Prince); but even so the situation is that the Chamberlain's Company are shown discussing how to put on a modern-style Revenge Play, which the audience knows to be a problem for them. The "mirror" was being held close to the face. As to the talk about the War of the Theatres, people were curious to know what the Globe would say, and heard its leading actor speak for the Company; they were violently prevented from keeping their minds on "buried Denmark". What is technically so clever is to turn this calculated collapse of dramatic illusion into an illustration of the central theme. The first problem was how to get the audience to attend to the story again, solved completely by "O what a rogue" and so on, which moves from the shame of theatrical behaviour and the paradoxes of sincerity (Hamlet first blames himself for not feeling as much as the actors do and then for over-acting about it, feeling too much) into an immediate scheme to expose the king. Yet even here one might feel, as Dover Wilson said (with his odd power of making a deep remark without seeing its implications), that "the two speeches are for all the world like a theme given out by the First Violin and then repeated by the Soloist" – Hamlet has only proved he is a better actor, and indeed "rogue" might make him say this, by recalling that actors were legally rogues and vagabonds. We next see Hamlet in the "To be or not to be" soliloquy, and he has completely forgotten his passionate and apparently decisive self-criticism – but this time the collapse of interest in the story comes from the Prince, not merely from the audience; then when Ophelia enters he swings away from being completely disinterested into being more disgracefully theatrical than anywhere else (enjoying working up a fuss about a very excessive suspicion, and thus betraying himself to listeners he knows are present); next he lectures the Players with grotesque hauteur about the art of acting, saying that they must always keep cool (this is where the word "groundlings" comes); then, quite unexpectedly, he fawns upon Horatio as a man who is not "passion's slave", unlike himself, and we advance upon the Play-within-the-Play. The metaphor of the pipe which Fortune can blow upon as she pleases, which he used to Horatio, is made a symbol by bringing a recorder into bodily prominence during his moment of triumph after the Play scene, and he now boasts to the courtiers that he is a mystery, therefore they cannot play on him – we are meant to feel that there are real merits in the condition, but he has already told us he despises himself for it. Incidentally he has just told Horatio that he deserves a fellowship in a "cry" of players (another searching joke phrase not used elsewhere) but Horatio only thinks "half of one". The recovery from the point where the story seemed most completely thrown away has been turned into an exposition of the character of the hero and the central dramatic theme. No doubt this has been fully recognized, but I do not think it has been viewed as a frank treatment of the central task, that of making the old play seem real by making the hero life-like.

Dover Wilson rightly points out the obsessive excitability of Hamlet, as when in each of the scenes scolding one of the ladies he comes back twice onto the stage, each time more unreasonable, as if he can't make himself stop. "But it is no mere theatrical trick or device", he goes on, "it is meant to be part of the nature of the man"; and meanwhile psychologists have elaborated the view that he is a standard "manic-depressive" type, in whom long periods of sullen gloom, often with actual forgetfulness, are followed by short periods of exhausting excitement, usually with violence of language. By all means, but the nature of the man grows out of the original *donnée*; his nature had (first of all) to be such that it would make the old story "life-like". And the effect in the theatre, surely, is at least prior to any belief about his nature, though it may lead you on to one; what you start from is the *astonishment* of Hamlet's incessant changes of mood, which also let the one actor combine in himself elements which the Elizabethan theatre usually separates (e.g. simply tragedy and comedy). Every one of the soliloquies, it has been pointed out, contains a shock for the audience, apart from what it says, in what it doesn't say: the first in having no reference to usurpation; the second ("rogue and slave") no reference to Ophelia, though his feelings about her have been made a prominent question; the third ("To be or not to be") no reference to his plot or his self-criticism or even his own walk of life – he is considering entirely in general whether life is worth living, and it is startling for him to say no traveller returns from death, however complete the "explanation" that he is assuming the Ghost was a devil; the fourth ("Now might I do it pat") no reference to his obviously great personal danger now that the King knows the secret; the fifth ("How all occasions do inform") no reference to the fact that he can't kill the King now, or rather a baffling assumption that he still can; and one might add his complete forgetting of his previous self-criticisms when he comes to his last words. It is this power to astonish, I think, which keeps one in doubt whether he is particularly theatrical or particularly "life-like"; a basic part of the effect, which would be clear to the first audiences.

However, the theme of a major play by Shakespeare is usually repeated by several characters in different forms, and Hamlet is not the only theatrical one here. Everybody is "acting a part" except Horatio, as far as that goes; and Laertes is very theatrical, as Hamlet rightly insists over the body of Ophelia ("I'll rant as well as thou"). One might reflect that both of them trample on her, both literally and figuratively, just because of their common trait. And yet Laertes is presented as opposite to Hamlet in not being subject to delay about avenging his father or to scruples about his methods; the tragic flaw in Hamlet must be something deeper or more specific. We need therefore to consider what his "theatricality" may be, and indeed the reader may feel I am making too much play with a term that Elizabethans did not use; but I think it makes us start in the right place. The Elizabethans, though both more formal and more boisterous than most people nowadays, were well able to see the need for sincerity; and it is agreed that Shakespeare had been reading Montaigne about how quickly one's moods can change, so that to appear consistent requires "acting", a line of thought which is still current. But to understand how it was applied here one needs to keep one's mind on the immediate situation in the theatre. The *plot* of a Revenge Play seemed theatrical because it kept the audience waiting without obvious reason in the characters; then a theatrical *character* (in such a play) appears as one who gets undeserved effects, "cheap" because not justified by the plot as a whole. However, "theatrical behaviour" is never only "mean" in the sense of losing the ultimate aim for a petty advantage, because it must also "give itself away" – the idea "greedy to impress an audience" is required. Now the basic legend about Hamlet was that he did exactly this and yet was somehow right for it; he successfully kept a secret by displaying he had got one. The idea is already prominent in Saxo Grammaticus, where it is presented as wholly successful (the eventual bad end of Hamlet had a different cause). Many scholars recently have argued that Shakespeare looked up his sources more than we have supposed, and I imagine the text of Saxo could be borrowed for him when he was given the assignment, if he wanted a rapid check on the French version; "the Saxon who could write Latin" in 1200 would be an evidently impressive source of primitive legend. The differences from the French are not important, but if Shakespeare did look up Saxo he would get an even firmer reassurance that his natural bent was the right one; the brief pungent Latin sentences about Hamlet are almost a definition of Shakespeare's clown, and Dover Wilson is right in saying that Shakespeare presented Hamlet as a kind of generalisation of that idea ("they fool me to the top of my bent" he remarks with appalling truth). Here we reach the bedrock of Hamlet, unchanged by the local dramas of reinterpretation; even Dr Johnson remarks that his assumed madness, though entertaining, does not seem to help his plot.

Kyd would probably give him powerful single-line jokes when answering other characters; the extreme and sordid pretence of madness implied by Saxo would not be used. I think that Shakespeare's opening words for Hamlet, "A little more than kin and less than kind", are simply repeated from Kyd; a dramatic moment for the first-night audience, because they wanted to know whether the new Hamlet would be different. His next words are a passionate assertion that he is *not* the theatrical Hamlet – "I know not seems." Now this technique from Kyd, though trivial beside the final Hamlet, would present the inherent paradox of the legend very firmly: why are these jokes supposed to give a kind of magical success to a character who had obviously better keep his mouth shut? All Elizabethans, including Elizabeth, had met the need to keep one's mouth shut at times; the paradox might well seem sharper to them than it does to us. Shakespeare took care to laugh at this as early as possible in his version of the play. The idea that it is silly to drop hints as Hamlet does is expressed by Hamlet himself, not only with force but with winning intimacy, when he tells the other observers of the Ghost that they must keep silence completely, and not say "We could an if we would. There be an if they might" and so on, which is precisely what he does himself for the rest of the play. No doubt he needs a monopoly of this technique. But the first effect in the theatre was another case of "closing the hole by making it big"; if you can make the audience laugh *with* Hamlet about his method early, they aren't going to laugh *at* him for it afterwards. Instead they can wonder why he is or pretends to be mad, just as the other characters wonder; and wonder why he delays, just as he himself wonders. No other device could raise so sharply the question of "what *is* theatrical behaviour?" because here we cannot even be sure what Hamlet is aiming at. We can never decide flatly that his method is wrong, because the more it appears unwise the more it appears courageous; and at any rate we know that he sees all round it. There seem to be two main assumptions, that he is trying to frighten his enemies into exposing themselves, and that he is not so frightened himself as to hide his emotions though he hides their cause. I fancy Shakespeare could rely on some of his audience to add the apparently modern theory that the relief of self-expression saved Hamlet from going finally mad, because it fits well enough onto their beliefs about the disease "melancholy". But in any case the basic legend is a dream glorification of both having your cake and eating it, keeping your secret for years, till you kill, and yet perpetually enjoying boasts about it. Here we are among the roots of the race of man; rather a smelly bit perhaps, but a bit that appeals at once to any child. It would be absurd to *blame* Shakespeare for accentuating this traditional theme till it became enormous.

The view that Hamlet "is Shakespeare", or at least more like him than his other characters, I hope falls into shape now. It has a basic truth, because he was drawing on his experience as actor and playwright; these professions often do puzzle their practitioners about what is theatrical and what is not, as their friends and audiences can easily recognise; but he was only using what the theme required. To have to give posterity, let alone the immediate audiences, a picture of himself would have struck him as laying a farcical extra burden on an already difficult assignment. I think he did feel he was giving a good hand to actors in general, though with decent obscurity, when he worked up so much praise for Hamlet at the end, but you are meant to be dragged round to this final admiration for Hamlet, not to feel it all through. To suppose he "is Shakespeare" has excited in some critics a reasonable distaste for both parties, because a man who models himself on Hamlet in common life (as has been done) tends to appear a mean-minded neurotic; whereas if you take the *plot* seriously Hamlet is at least assumed to have special reasons for his behaviour.

We should now be able to reconsider the view which Stoll has done real service by following up: Hamlet's reasons are so good that he not only never delays at all but was never supposed to; the self-accusations of the revenger are always prominent in Revenge Plays, even classical Greek ones, being merely a necessary part of the machine – to make the audience continue waiting with attention. Any problem we may invent about Shakespeare's Hamlet, on this view, we could also have invented about Kyd's, but it wouldn't have occurred to us to want to. In making the old play "life-like" Shakespeare merely altered the style, not the story; except that it was probably he who (by way of adding "body") gave Hamlet very much better reasons for delay than any previous revenger, so that it is peculiarly absurd of us to pick him out and puzzle over his delay. I do not at all want to weaken this line of argument; I think Shakespeare did, intentionally, pile up all the excuses for delay he could imagine, while at the same time making Hamlet bewail and denounce his delay far more strongly than ever revenger had done before. It is the force and intimacy of the self-reproaches of Hamlet, of course, which ordinary opinion has rightly given first place; that is why these legal arguments that he didn't delay appear farcical. But the two lines of argument are only two halves of the same thing. Those members of the audience who simply wanted to see a Revenge Play again, without any hooting at it from smarter persons, deserved to be satisfied; and anyhow, for all parties, the suspicion that Hamlet was a coward or merely fatuous had to be avoided. The ambiguity was an essential part of the intention, because the more you tried to translate the balance of impulses in the old drama into a realistic story (especially if you make Hamlet older which you want to if he is to understand what he is doing) the more peculiar this story had to be made. The old structure was still kept firm, but its foundations had to be strengthened to carry so much extra weight. At the same time, a simpler view could be taken; whatever the stage characters may say, the real situation in the theatre is still that the audience knows the revenge won't come till the end. Their own foreknowledge is what they had laughed at, rather than any lack of motive in the puppets, and however much the motives of the Revenger for delay were increased he could still very properly blame himself for keeping the audience waiting. One could therefore sit through the new *Hamlet* (as for that matter the eighteenth century did) without feeling too startled by his self-reproaches. But of course the idea that "bringing the style up to date" did not involve any change of content seems to me absurd, whether held by Shakespeare's committee or by Stoll; for one thing, it made the old theatrical convention appear bafflingly indistinguishable from a current political danger. The whole story was brought into a new air, so that one felt there was much more "in it".

This effect, I think, requires a sudden feeling of novelty rather than a gradual evolution, but it is still possible that Shakespeare wrote an earlier draft than our present text. To discuss two lost plays at once, by Kyd and Shakespeare, is perhaps rather tiresome, but one cannot imagine the first audiences without forming some picture of the development of the play, of what struck them as new. Dover Wilson, to whom so much gratitude is due for his series of books on *Hamlet*, takes a rather absurd position here. He never edits a straightforward Shakespeare text without finding evidence for two or three layers of revision, and considering them important for a full understanding of the play; only in *Hamlet*, where there is positive evidence for them, and a long-recognised ground for curiosity about them, does he assume they can be ignored. He rightly insists that an editor needs to see the problems of a text as a whole before even choosing between two variant readings, and he sometimes actually asserts in passing that Shakespeare wrote earlier drafts of *Hamlet*; and yet his basis for preferring Q2 to F is a picture of Shakespeare handing in *one* manuscript (recorded by Q2) from which the Company at once wrote out *one* acting version (recorded by F), making drastic cuts and also verbal changes which they refused to reconsider. He says he is not concerned with "sixteenth century versions of Hamlet", a device of rhetoric that suggests a gradual evolution, too hard to trace. I am not clear which century 1600 is in (there was a surprising amount of quarrelling over the point in both 1900 and 1800), but even writing done in 1599 would not be remote from 1601. I postulate one main treatment of the play by Shakespeare, first acted in 1600, and then one quite minor revision of it by Shakespeare, first acted in 1601, written to feed and gratify the interest and discussion which his great surprise had excited the year before. To believe in this amount of revision does not make much difference, whereas a gradual evolution would, but it clears up some puzzling bits of evidence and I think makes the audiences more intelligible.

Dover Wilson's two volumes on *The Manuscripts of Shakespeare's Hamlet* are magnificently detailed and obviously right most of the time. I am only questioning this part of his conclusions: "we may venture to suspect that (always assuming Shakespeare to have been in London) *Hamlet* was not merely a turning-point in his career dramatically, but also marks some kind of crisis in his relations with his company". The idea that Shakespeare wasn't in London, I take it, is inserted to allow for the theory that he was in Scotland drafting his first version of *Macbeth*, which need not delay us. The cuts for time in the Folio seem to be his main argument, because he ends his leading volume (*Manuscripts*, p. 174) by saying that Shakespeare discovered his mistake if he imagined that the Company would act such a long play in full. "If" here is a delicacy only, because the purpose of the argument is to answer critics who had called our full-length *Hamlet* "a monstrosity, the creation of scholarly compromise" between rival shorter versions. I agree with Dover Wilson that Shakespeare did envisage a use for this whole text. But Dover Wilson had just been giving an impressive section (pp. 166–70) to prove that some of the Folio cuts are so skilful that Shakespeare must have done them himself – perhaps unwillingly, but at least he was not being ignored. Another part of the argument for a quarrel is that the producer "did not trouble to consult the author when he could not decipher a word or understand a passage", but this section argues that Shakespeare did make a few corrections in the Prompt Copy, when a mistake happened to lie near the bits he had looked up to make his cuts. Surely this makes the author look culpably careless over details rather than in a huff because he hadn't been consulted over details. Another argument uses errors which are unchanged in the Quartos and Folio to suggest that the Company repeated the same bits of petty nonsense blindly for twenty years. But Dover Wilson also argues that the Prompt Copy used for the Folio was "brought up to date" in later years, at least on such points as the weapons fashionable for duelling; the same might apply to some slang terms which were already out of date when the Folio was published, though he labours to restore them now from the Quarto. I think he presumes an excessive desire to save paper in this quite wealthy company; they are not likely to have kept the same manuscript Prompt Copy of their most popular play in constant use for twenty years. There would have to be a copying staff, in any case, to give the actors their parts to learn from. The baffling question is how the Folio *Hamlet* with its mass of different kinds of error could ever occur; and the theory of Dover Wilson is that it was badly printed from a copy of the Company's (irremovable) Prompt Copy made by a Company employee who was careless chiefly because he knew what was currently acted, so that his mind echoed phrases in the wrong place. Surely I may put one more storey onto this card castle. Hemming and Condell, I suggest, set this man to copy the *original* Prompt Copy, which so far from being in current use had become a kind of museum piece; they tried to get a basic text for the printer, and only failed to realise that it isn't enough in these matters to issue an order. The basic object to be copied had neither the later corrections nor the extra passages which had been reserved for special occasions, and the interest of the man who copied it is that he could scribble down both old and new errors or variants without feeling he was obviously wrong. It seems improbable that the Globe actors, though likely to introduce corruptions, would patiently repeat bits of unrewarding nonsense for twenty years; my little invention saves us from believing that, without forcing me to deny that Dover Wilson's theory has produced some good emendations.

We cannot expect to recover a correct text merely from an excess of error in the printed versions of it; and in no other Shakespeare play are they so confused. But surely this fact itself must have some meaning. I suggest that, while Shakespeare's *Hamlet* was the rage, that is, roughly till James became King without civil war, it was varied a good deal on the night according to the reactions of the immediate audience. This would be likely to make the surviving texts pretty hard to print from; also it relieves us from thinking of Shakespeare as frustrated by the Company's cuts in his first great tragedy. Surely any man, after a quarrel of this sort, would take some interest in "at least" getting the printed version right. No doubt there was a snobbery about print to which he was sensitive, and also the text belonged to the Company; but neither question would impinge here. The Company must have wanted a presentable text for the Second Quarto, designed to outface the First, and even the most anxious snob can correct proofs without attracting attention. Indeed there was at least one reprint of it during his lifetime, in which the printer can be observed trying to correct mistakes, obviously without help from the author (for example over the line which Dover Wilson well corrects into "Or of the most select, are generous chief in that", *chief* meaning "chiefly"). You might think he fell into despair over the incompetence of the printers, but they could do other jobs well enough, and were visibly trying to do better here. The only plausible view is that he refused to help them because he wouldn't be bothered, and I do not believe he could have felt this if he had been annoyed by the way *Hamlet* had been mangled at the Globe. I think he must have felt tolerably glutted by the performances.

Critics have long felt that the First Quarto probably contains evidence for a previous draft by Shakespeare which is hard to disentangle. This theory has been blown upon in recent years by E. K. Chambers and Dover Wilson, who regard Q1 as a perversion of the standard Globe performance; but I think the point of view I am recommending helps to strengthen it. One must admit, on Dover Wilson's side, that a text published in 1603 cannot be trusted to be unaffected by changes in the performance supposedly made in 1601; the idea that this was a travelling version, suited to audiences less experienced than the Globe ones, seems a needed hypothesis as well as one suggested by the title-page. Also, though often weirdly bad in detail, it is a very workmanlike object in broad planning; somebody made a drastically short version of the play which kept in all the action, and the effect is so full of action that it is almost as jerky as an early film, which no doubt some audiences would appreciate. There seems no way to decide whether or not this was done independently of the pirating reporters who forgot a lot of the poetry. The main change is that the soliloquy "To be or not to be" and its attendant scolding of Ophelia is put before the Player scene, not after it; but a producer wanting a short plain version is wise to make that change, so it is not evidence for an earlier draft by Shakespeare. The variations in names might only recall Kyd's names, perhaps more familiar in the provinces. What does seem decisive evidence, and was regularly considered so till Dover Wilson ignored rather than rebutted it, is that this text gives a sheer scene between Horatio and the Queen alone, planning what to do about Hamlet's return to Denmark; surely this would be the pirating hack. The text here seems particularly "cooked up" or misreported, and Duthie has argued convincingly that it is made out of bits vaguely remembered from Shakespeare or Kyd in other contexts. But this only shows what the pirates did when they forgot what Shakespeare wrote, here and elsewhere; it does not prove that Shakespeare never wrote such a scene. And the adapter would not invent it, because what he wanted was action; it is less like action to have Horatio report Hamlet's adventures than to let the hero boast in person, nor is it inherently any shorter. Besides, the change fits in with a consistently different picture of the Queen, who is not only made clearly innocent of the murder but made willing to help Hamlet. Dover Wilson does not seem to deal with this familiar position beyond saying "Shakespeare is subtler than his perverters or his predecessors", assuming that the Q1 compiler is his first perverter; and he argues that the Queen is meant to appear innocent even of vague complicity in the murder in our standard text of *Hamlet*. But surely it is fair to ask what this "subtlety" may be, and why it deserves such a fine name if it only muddles a point that was meant to be clear. Why, especially, must the Queen be given an unexplained half-confession, "To my sick soul, as sin's true nature is . . . ", a fear of betraying guilt by too much effort to hide it? Richard Flatter, I think, did well to emphasise how completely this passage has been ignored by critics such as A. C. Bradley and Dover Wilson, whose arguments from other passages to prove that she was meant to seem innocent are very convincing. Surely the only reasonable view is that Shakespeare in the final version wanted to leave doubt in the minds of the audience about the Queen. You may say that the adapter behind Q1 just got rid of this nuisance, but you are making him do an unlikely amount of bold intelligent work. It is simpler to believe that he preferred an earlier version, which made the Queen definitively on Hamlet's side after the bedroom scene.

One might also recall, I think, that on the usually accepted dating there is a pause just after *Hamlet* in the usual speed of production by Shakespeare; here if anywhere he had time to revise a play, and this play is the one which gets the most contemporary reference, therefore would be most worth revising. It seems natural to connect the pause with the general anxiety until James became King without civil war – I take it that the revision made the play even better fitted to this growing state of public sentiment.

Dover Wilson used to believe in two versions by Shakespeare and apparently does so still, or if not he must be praised for giving the evidence against his later view with his usual firmness. Harvey's note praising a *Hamlet* by Shakespeare, he recalls, needs to predate the execution of Essex in February 1601, whereas the remarks about the War of the Theatres, and a hint at the siege of Dunkirk in the soliloquy "How all occasions do inform against me", belong to the summer of that year. This note by Harvey, written on the flyleaf of a book, in a rather affected style which could refer to dead men as if alive, has given rise to extremely confusing arguments; some of them take the play back to 1598, which I don't believe. I am not arguing that it gives strong evidence, only trying to recall that the position I take here is the normal one. If we are to believe in a revision for the 1601 season it should include these items (presumably the whole of the soliloquy, because it all refers to Dunkirk if any of it does), also the new position for "To be or not to be" and for the scolding of Ophelia, and a number of changes about the Queen, interesting for her actor but not long in bulk. The idea that the main text was written before the death of Essex and the revisions after it should perhaps have more meaning than I can find; perhaps anyway it corresponds to a certain darkening of the whole air. But there is no need to make this revision large or elaborate, and I agree with the critics who have said that the actors would have found trivial revisions merely tiresome. The points just listed seem the only ones we have direct evidence for, and are easily understood as heightening the peculiar effect of *Hamlet* for a public which had already caught onto it. May I now put the matter the other way round; I do not believe that our present text of *Hamlet*, a weirdly baffling thing, could have been written at all except for a public which had already caught on to it.

The strongest argument is from the soliloquy "How all occasions". Dover Wilson says that the Company omitted this "from the very first" from the Fortinbras scene, "which was patently written to give occasion to the soliloquy". But no producer would leave in the nuisance of an army marching across the stage after removing the only point of it. Fortinbras had anyway to march his army across the stage, as he does in Q1 as well as F, and presumably did in Kyd's version. The beginning of the play is a mobilisation against this army and the end a triumph for it; the audience thought in more practical terms than we do about these dynastic quarrels. But that made it all the more dramatic, in the 1601 version, to throw in a speech for Hamlet hinting that the troops at Dunkirk were as fatuous for too much action as he himself was for too little. It is only a final example of the process of keeping the old scenes and packing into them extra meaning. What is reckless about the speech is that it makes Hamlet say, while (presumably) surrounded by guards leading him to death, "I have cause and will and strength and means / To do it", destroying a sheer school of Hamlet Theories with each noun; the effect is so exasperating that more than one critic, after solving all his Hamlet Problem neatly except for this bit, has simply demanded the right to throw it away. Nobody is as annoying as all that except on purpose, and the only reasonable view of why this speech was added is that these Hamlet Theories had already been propounded, in discussions among the spectators, during the previous year. But the bafflement thrown in here was not the tedious one of making a psychological problem or a detective story insoluble; there was a more immediate effect in making Hamlet magnificent. He finds his immediate position not even worth reflecting on; and he does get out of this jam, so you can't blame him for his presumption at this point. His complete impotence at the moment, one might say, seems to him "only a theatrical appearance", just as his previous reasons for delay seem to have vanished like a dream. Here as elsewhere he gives a curious effect, also not unknown among his critics, of losing all interest for what has happened in the story; but it is more impressive in him than in them. By the way, I would like to have one other passage added by Shakespeare in revision, the remarks by Hamlet at the end of the bedroom scene (in Q2 but not F) to the effect that it will only cheer him up to have to outwit his old pals trying to kill him; this seems liable to sound merely boastful unless afterwards proved genuine by his private thoughts, but if the soliloquy is being added some such remark is needed first, so as to prepare the audience not to find it merely unnatural.

One might suppose that this dream-like though fierce quality in Hamlet, which becomes perhaps his chief appeal two centuries later, was not invented till the 1601 revision. I think this idea can be disproved. The moral effect is much the same, and hardly less presumptuous, when he insists at the end of the play on treating

Laertes as a gentleman and a sportsman, though he has already told the audience (in high mystical terms) that he is not such a fool as to be unsuspicious; and the moral is at once drawn for us – this treatment unnerves Laertes so much that he almost drops the plot. The fencing-match no less than the Play scene is an imitation which turns out to be reality, but that is merely a thing which one should never be surprised by; Laertes ought still to be treated in the proper style. "Use them after your own honour and dignity; the less they deserve, the more merit is in your bounty"; this curious generosity of the intellect is always strong in Hamlet, and indeed his main source of charm. One reason, in fact, why he could be made so baffling without his character becoming confused was that it made him give a tremendous display of top-class behaviour, even in his secret mind as expressed in soliloquy. Now the paradoxical chivalry towards Laertes (which commentators tend to regard as a "problem" about how much Hamlet understood) is marked in Q1, whose author was clearly not bothering much about the revised version by Shakespeare, and wanted his Hamlet to be a knock-down hero. The idea was not too subtle for the audience of a simplified version of Shakespeare's *Hamlet*; on the other hand it seems clearly not due to Kyd. We feel this because of their styles, but probably a state of public feeling corresponds to it; the casual remark of Hamlet in the graveyard, that all the classes are getting mixed, has probably some bearing on his behaviour. An awareness of social change had been arising in that decade, especially of a thing which in itself had been happening for some time (encouraged though not caused by Elizabeth), the arrival of a new aristocracy which felt that grand behaviour has to be learned.

Thus another reason why there is a suggestion of theatricality about the royal behaviour of Hamlet may well be that he is presented as honestly trying to do it, like a man learning a new job. Commentators have felt it to be shifty of him to apologise to Laertes merely by saying he is mad; the audience has seen that he did not kill the man's father out of madness. No doubt, as Bradley remarked, he could hardly have said anything else; but he is still in part the Hamlet of the fairy-story, who cannot tell a lie though he can always delude by telling the truth. What he is really apologising for is the incident "I'll rant as well as thou"; there, as he has already remarked to Horatio, he is "very sorry he forgot himself". Oddly enough, neither he nor Laertes so much as mention that he has killed Laertes's father, either in the quarrel or the scene of apology for it. Hamlet of course realises that he and Laertes have the same "cause", and says so (rather obscurely) to Horatio, as a reason why he is sorry for the quarrel; and Laertes does at last mention it to him, when they are dying side by side like brothers, but even then Hamlet evades accepting forgiveness, because he recognises no guilt. The quarrel, on the surface merely about proper behaviour at a funeral, could only be recognised by the bystanders (who have not been officially told how Polonius died) as about whether Hamlet is to blame for driving Laertes's sister mad; here too he completely denies guilt, by claiming to have loved her greatly. But to have scuffled with Laertes while they both kicked her body in her grave was disgustingly theatrical; he feels it may really be described as a fit of madness, and apologises for it as such. According to Q2, he took the occasion to slip in a secret apology to his mother, for having acted theatrically on another occasion to her ("And hurt my mother" Q2, "And hurt my brother" F). I can hardly believe that this extra twist is more than a misprint, though it has been accepted by good critics; but it would be powerful if the actor could get it over, because the occasion when he was rude to *her* was when he happened to kill Polonius, for which you might suppose he was apologising to Laertes. To worry about one's style of behaviour rather than one's incidental murders now appears madly egotistical, but it would then appear as immensely princely behaviour. It seems clear that Shakespeare made Hamlet a model of princeliness as a primary element in his revivification of the play.

But one would not want Hamlet to be a complete hero all along (as in Stoll); and indeed to make obvious in the theatre that his behaviour is princely one needs sometimes to show him trying to correct it. We only know that he fought in the grave from a stage direction in the First Quarto, presumably because only a private company would need to be told it; but some critics have felt that only a vulgarised version could want anything so coarse. They are right to find it shocking, but not to assume that the shock could not be meant. There is no doubt that Laertes gets into the grave, because he demands to be buried with her, and Hamlet at once competes with his theatricality, so may naturally join him there (the graves were broader and shallower than ours). Indeed the whole suggestion of the Grave-digger scene is that Hamlet will soon get into a grave, so there is a symbolical point in having him do it at once. But to have them trampling on her corpse while they fight to prove which of them loves her most has a more powerful symbolism; the effect of their love has been to torment her and threaten her with contempt. The Hamlet of the sources descends to sordid behaviour in his pretence of madness; the great prince can only win by being more low-class than you or I dare be. We may be sure that Kyd did not want this, but Shakespeare restored about as much of it as the stage could bear. The revulsion of his Hamlet from doing it (already clear when he insists to the players that one should always be calm) was I think clear to the first audiences; they were ready for him to feel that he must have been mad to be so unprincely as to fight in the grave. There are other times, of course, when his behaviour is extravagantly princely without effort or thought.

I take it, then, that one way and another a good deal of mystery got into Shakespeare's first version of *Hamlet*, which had started with the intention of reviving the old play by making it life-like. Then, when the audiences became intrigued by this mystery, he made some quite small additions and changes which screwed up the mystery to the almost torturing point where we now have it – the sky was the limit now, not merely because the audiences wanted it, but because one need only act so much of this "shock-troops" material as a particular audience seemed ripe for. No wonder it made the play too long. The soliloquy "How all occasions" is a sort of encore planned in case an audience refuses to let the star go, and in the big days of *Hamlet* they would decide backstage how much, and which parts, of the full text to perform when they saw how a particular audience was shaping. This view gives no reason to doubt that the whole thing was sometimes acted, with the staff of the Globe extremely cross at not being allowed to go home earlier. I am not clear how much this picture alters the arguments of Dover Wilson from the surviving texts, but it clearly does to a considerable extent. Everyone says that the peculiar merit of the Elizabethan theatre was to satisfy a broad and varied clientele, with something of the variability of the Music Hall in its handling of the audience; but the experts do not seem to imagine a theatre which actually carried out this plan, instead of sticking to a text laid down rigidly beforehand. It is unlikely to have happened on any scale, to be sure, except in the very special case of *Hamlet*. But if you suppose it happened there you need no longer suppose a quarrel over some extras written in for occasional use. And there is the less reason to suppose a quarrel, on my argument, because the Company must have accepted Shakespeare's 1601 revision as regards both

Ophelia and the Queen, for example treating the new position for "To be or not to be" as part of the standard Prompt Copy, eventually recorded in the Folio. (One would never swap back the order of scenes "on the night".) I imagine that this excitement about the play, which made it worth while keeping bits for special audiences, had already died down by 1605, when the Company sent plenty of Shakespeare's manuscript to the printer (as Dover Wilson says) just to outface the pirate of Q1; one no longer needed to keep extras up one's sleeve. But I should fancy that the claim on the title-page, "enlarged to almost as much again as it was", does not refer to the extreme shortness of the pirate's version; advertisements even when lying often have sources of plausibility, and it would be known that a few of the Globe performances had been remarkably long.

If, then, the First Quarto gives evidence about the first draft, the main changes for 1601 concerned Ophelia and the Queen; whom I will consider in turn. The scolding of Ophelia by Hamlet, and the soliloquy "To be or not to be" before it, were put later in the play. The main purpose in this, I think, was to screw up the paradoxes in the character of Hamlet rather than to affect Ophelia herself. I have already tried to describe a sort of Pirandello sequence in his behaviour from meeting the Players to the Recorder scene, which raises problems about whether he is very theatrical or very sincere, and this is much heightened by putting his hysterical attack on Ophelia in the middle of it; especially beside the utter detachment of "To be or not to be", which J. M. Robertson found so incredible in its new position as to demand grotesque collaboration theories. The first version by Shakespeare must have carried the main point of this sequence, because even the First Quarto makes him take an actual "pipe" after the Play scene and use it to claim he is a mystery ("though you can fret me, yet you cannot play upon me"); but this was a crucial part to "heighten" if you wanted to heighten the mystery as a whole.

One might also feel that the change had another purpose; combined with the new doubts about the Queen it gives the play a concentrated anti-woman central area. The worst behaviour of Hamlet is towards Ophelia, whether you call it theatrical or not; the critics who have turned against him usually seem to do so on her behalf, and his relations with the two women raise more obvious questions about whether he is neurotic than his delay. The first question here is how Shakespeare *expected* the audience to take the scolding of Ophelia, admitting that an audience has different parts. We can all see Hamlet has excuses for treating her badly, but if we are to think him a hero for yielding to them the thing becomes barbaric; he punishes her savagely for a plot against him when he has practically forced her to behave like a hospital nurse, beginning with his melodramatic silent visit. I feel sure that Dover Wilson is getting at something important, though as so often from a wrong angle, when he makes a fuss about adding a stage direction in II.ii, and insists that Hamlet must visibly overhear the King and Polonius plotting to use Ophelia against him. No doubt this is better for a modern audience, but we need to consider the sequence of changes in the traditional play. In our present text, even granting Dover Wilson his tiny stage direction, what Hamlet overhears is very harmless and indeed what he himself has planned for; it was he who started using Ophelia as a pawn, however much excused by passion or despair. Kyd, one would expect, gave solid ground for Hamlet's view that Ophelia is working against him; she would do it high-mindedly, in ringing lines, with distress, regarding it as her duty since her lover has become mad, and never realising what deep enmity against him she is assisting; but still she would do something plain and worth making a fuss about. Hamlet's scolding of her for it would follow at once. The agile bard, with gleaming eye, merely removed the adequate motivation for the scolding of Ophelia, a habit to which he was becoming attached. Then for his revision he took the scolding far away even from the trivial bit of plotting, no more than was essential to explain the sequence, that he had left in for his Hamlet to overhear; thus making Dover Wilson's view harder for a spectator to invent. One can respect the struggle of Dover Wilson to recover one rag of the drapery so much needed by Hamlet, but if this was the development the Globe Theatre is not likely to have given any.

We should recall here, I think, the rising fashion in the theatres for the villain-hero, who staggers one by being so *outré*, and the love-poems of Donne, already famous in private circulation, which were designed to outrage the conventions about chivalrous treatment of women. Also the random indecency of lunatics, a thing the Elizabethans were more accustomed to than we are, since they seldom locked them up, is insisted on in the behaviour of Hamlet to Ophelia whether he is pretending or not. The surprising instruction of the Ghost – "Taint not thy mind" – was bound to get attention, so that one was prepared to think his mind tainted. I think the Shakespeare Hamlet was meant to be regarded by most of the audience as behaving shockingly towards Ophelia, almost too much so to remain a tragic hero; to swing round the whole audience into reverence for Hamlet before he died was something of a lion-taming act. This was part of the rule that all his behaviour must be startling, and was only slightly heightened in revision. But to see it in its right proportion we must remember another factor; the theatre, as various critics have pointed out, clung to an apparently muddled but no doubt tactical position of both grumbling against Puritans and accepting their main claims. The Victorians still felt that Hamlet was simply highminded here. D. H. Lawrence has a poem describing him with hatred as always blowing and snoring about other folks' whoring, rightly perhaps, but in Hamlet's time this would feel like the voice of lower-class complaint against upper-class luxury, as when he rebukes the Court for too much drink. All Malcontents rebuked luxury; this aspect of him would not need to be "brought out".

Here I think we have the right approach to another Victorian view of Hamlet, of which Bernard Shaw is perhaps the only representative still commonly read: that he was morally too advanced to accept feudal ideas about revenge, and felt, but could not say, that his father had given him an out-of-date duty; that was why he gave such an absurd excuse for not killing the King at prayer. (Dr Johnson thought it not absurd but too horrible to read.) Without this obscure element of "discussion drama", Shaw maintained, the nineteenth century would never have found Hamlet interesting; and of course Shaw would also feel it highminded of him to be a bit rough with the women in a Puritan manner. This Hamlet Theory has been swept away by ridicule too easily, and I was glad to see Alfred Harbage defend it with the true remark that no moral idea was "remote from the Elizabethan mind". Indeed it is not so much feudal as royal persons who cannot escape the duty of revenge by an appeal to public justice; this is one of the reasons why they have long been felt to make interesting subjects for plays. But I think Shakespeare's audiences did regard his Hamlet as taking a "modern" attitude to his situation, just as Bernard Shaw did. This indeed was one of the major dramatic effects of the new treatment. He walks out to the audience and says "You think this an absurd old play, and so it is, *but I'm in it*, and what can I do?" The theatrical device in itself expresses no theory about the duty of revenge, but it does ask the crowd to share in the question. No wonder that one of the seventeenth-century references, dropped while describing some- one else, says "He is like Prince Hamlet, he pleases all."

This trait of his character has rightly irritated many critics, most recently perhaps Salvador de Madariaga, whose lively book on Hamlet has at least the merit of needing some effort to refute it. He finds him a familiar Renaissance type of the extreme "egotist", as well as a cad who had been to bed with Ophelia already. The curious indifference of Hamlet to the facts does make him what we call egotistical, but this would be viewed as part of his lordliness; "egotism", I think, is only a modern bit of popular psychology, quite as remote from medical science as the Elizabethan bit about "melancholy" and much less likely to occur to the first audiences. The argument that Hamlet has been to bed with Ophelia gives an impression of clearing the air, and I think greatly needs refuting; I am glad to have a coarse enough argu- ment to do it without being suspected of undue chivalry. We need a little background first. Madariaga points out that the corre- sponding lady in the sources did enjoy Hamlet's person on a brief occasion, and argues that the audience would take the story for granted unless it was firmly changed; he then easily proves that the actress of Ophelia can make all references to her virginity seem comic, but this doesn't prove she was meant to. The only "source" which most of the audience would know is the play by Kyd which we have lost, and there is a great simplicity about the drama of Kyd which is unlikely to have allowed any questionable aspect to his hero. The legend itself, I agree, gives Hamlet a strong "Br'er Fox" smell, and Shakespeare had a nose for this, but the tradition of the theatre would let him assume that Ophelia represented pure pathos and was somehow betrayed. Kyd would be likely to introduce the idea that this lady, who needs a bit more dignity in the sources (though she loves Hamlet and was his foster-sister) was regarded as Hamlet's prospective Queen. Shakespeare gave this a further twist; he implies at her first appearance that her father and her brother are angling to make her Queen. To be sure, they don't say that to the girl, and still less to Hamlet's parents, but we need not believe their over- eager protestations about the matter; the fuss made by Polonius about never having thought of such a thing seems to me just the way he would behave if he was manoeuvring for it, and I think this would be likely to occur to some members of the first audi- ences. The placid lament of the Queen over the grave of Ophelia, that she had expected her to marry Hamlet, sounds as if she had long known it was in the wind. (Not that this detail can have much effect on the stage, but it is a faint piece of evidence about how Shakespeare regarded the situation, and meant his actors to interpret it.) I do not know that any critic has taken it like that, but presumably the first audiences were more accustomed to such situations than we are. What her brother and her father do tell her, very firmly, is that the urgent thing is not to go to bed with him too quickly; her whole position depends on it; and she agrees to hold off in a pointed manner. Surely the audience will assume that this important family plan is being carried through; unless, of course, she leers and winks as Madariaga recommends, but that would only make her seem a fool. The impact of the poetry that introduces the character has a natural right to interpret her; it is hauntingly beautiful and rather unsuited to the brother who speaks it:

> The chariest maid is prodigal enough
> If she unmask her beauty to the moon

and so forth; the whole suggestion is that she must hold off from Hamlet, as part of her bid for grandeur, and yet that tragedy may come of it. However, I agree that these vast prophetic gestures towards all human experience could easily suggest just the opposite, that she is sure to have done what she is advised against; a more definite argument is required. In the Play scene, when Hamlet is offensively jeering at her for her supposed lust, and she is trying to laugh it off (pathetically and courageously; it is unfair of Madariaga to say this proves she is used to such talk), she says "you are keen, my lord, you are keen", meaning to praise his jokes as highminded general satire against the world, though they are flat enough bits of nastiness, and he answers:

> It would cost you a groaning to take off my edge.

Now the conviction that it is fun to make a virgin scream and bleed, especially at her wedding, was far too obvious to the Elizabethans for this to mean anything else; I can imagine alternatives, but do not believe in them and will wait for them to be advanced by some opponent. The point is not that Hamlet's remark has any importance on the stage, but that the first audiences took for granted one view of her or the other, from the production if not from the tradition (an ambiguity here, I think, would only confuse the production), whereas we have to learn what they took for granted by using details which at the time merely seemed to fit in. This detail, I submit, is enough to prove they assumed her to be a virgin.

I am not trying to whitewash Hamlet; he is jeering at the desires of the virgin which he is keen to excite and not satisfy, and this is part of what sends her mad. But to jeer at a prospective Queen for having yielded to him already would be outside the code; the more loose the actual Court habits were (a point Madariaga uses) the more ungentlemanly it would seem, and Hamlet never loses class, however mad. He also keeps a curious appeal for the lower classes in the audience as a satirist on the upper class, as I have tried to describe; even here, some of the audience would probably enjoy having jeers against an aggressively pure young lady whose family are angling for a grand marriage; but for this purpose too he needs to be unworldly rather than to have been to bed with her already. What seems more important to us is his "psychology", and that gives the same answer; the whole point of his bad temper against her, which he builds up into feverish suspicions, is that it arises because she has shut him out, not because she has yielded to him. In the Nunnery scene, when he runs back for the second time onto the stage because he has just thought of a still nastier thing which he can't bear not to say, he says "I have heard of your paintings too", heard that women in general paint their faces. It is almost a Peter Arno drawing. He calls her obscene because all women are (like his mother) and a prostitute because she is plotting against him (like a nurse). To allow any truth to his accusations against her seems to me throwing away the dramatic effect.

But of course there is a grave solemn truth, never denied, which is simply that Ophelia did want to marry him and ought not to have been accused of lust for it. Madariaga regards her behaviour when mad as proof of incontinence when sane, an idea which strikes me as about equally remote from an Elizabethan audience and a modern doctor. She sings a song in which the man says to the woman "I would have married you, as I promised, if you had not come to my bed", which seems to ask for application to her own case; but many of the parallels in her mad talk work by opposites; indeed the agony of it (as in the mad speeches added to *The Spanish Tragedy*, for instance) is that we see her approaching recognition of the truth and then wincing far away again. "They say a made a good end" is her comment on the father who died unshriven, and "Bonny sweet Robin is all my joy" deals with her appalling lover before she walks out to death. Well might she reflect that the girls in the ballads, who came to a simpler kind of disaster by giving too earlier, met a less absolute frustration than the girl who held off because she was being groomed for queenhood; and surely this idea is the point of her vast farewell: "Come, my coach; . . . Sweet ladies, good night." The German *Der Berstrafte Brundermorde* interprets this by making her say she wants her coach because she has to dine with the King. But we can argue more directly from the poetry of the thing. When she brings out this ballad the wicked King, who never falls below a certain breadth of sentiment, says "Pretty Ophelia", a quaintly smoking-room comment which directly tells the audience what to feel. Soon after, her brother echoes the word in a rage, saying that even in the madness forced upon her by Hamlet she turns Hell itself to favour and to prettiness, but the King saw that "pretty" is right at once. Recently I was being asked by a student in Peking what to make of the

> long purples
> Which liberal shepherds give a grosser name
> But our cold maids do Dead Men's Fingers call them.

Why are the obscene thoughts of these peasants necessary in the impossible but splendid description of her death? At the time, I could only say that the lines seemed to me very beautiful, and in the usual tone about Ophelia, so I felt sure they didn't carry any hint that would go outside it. Also, no doubt, the maids give the flower this unmentioned name "when they laugh alone", and here the Love of a maid did become Death and fumble at her, but there is a broader, and one might well say a prettier, suggestion behind all these hints at her desire; that nobody wants her to be frigid. A certain amount of teasing about the modesty required from her would be ordinary custom, but the social purpose behind both halves of this little contradiction is to make her a good wife. Indeed to struggle against these absurd theories about her is to feel as baffled as she did by the confusions of puritanism; it makes one angry with Hamlet, not only with his commentators, as I think we are meant to be. Being disagreeable in this way was part of his "mystery".

Turning now to the Queen: Dover Wilson argued that the First Quarto was merely a perversion of the single play by Shakespeare, with a less "subtle" treatment of the Queen. I do not think we need at once call it subtle of Shakespeare to make her into an extra mystery by simply cutting out all her explanations of her behaviour. The idea of a great lady who speaks nobly but is treacherous to an uncertain degree was familiar on the stage, as in Marlowe's *Edward II*, not a new idea deserving praise. No doubt the treatment is subtle; several of her replies seem unconscious proofs of complete innocence, whereas when she says her guilt "spills itself in fearing to be spilt" she must imply a guilty secret. But we must ask why the subtlety is wanted. An important factor here is the instruction of the Ghost to Hamlet, in the first Act, that he must contrive nothing against his mother. I think this was supplied by Kyd; he would see its usefulness as an excuse for the necessary delay, and would want his characters to be high-minded. (It would be a natural extension of Belleforest who treats the Queen with great respect.) Also he had to give his Ghost a reason for returning later, because the audience would not want this interesting character to be dropped. In Kyd's first Act, therefore, the Ghost said Claudius must be killed and the Queen protected; then in the third Act, when Hamlet was questioning her suspiciously, the Ghost came back and said she hadn't known about his murder, supporting her own statement to that effect; meanwhile he told Hamlet that it would be dangerous to wait any longer about killing Claudius, because the Play scene has warned him. Hamlet had felt he still ought to wait till he knew how much his mother was involved. The Ghost had already forgiven her for what she had done – perhaps adultery, probably only the hasty remarriage to his brother – but had not cared to discuss it much; the tragic effect in the third Act is that he clears up too late an unfortunate bit of vagueness in his first instructions. This makes him a bit absurd, but the motives of Ghosts seldom do bear much scrutiny, and he is better than most of them. (On this account, Hamlet is still liable to have different motives in different scenes for sparing the King at prayer, but that seems a normal bit of Elizabethan confusion.) Thus there is no reason why Kyd's Queen should not have satisfied the curiosity of the audience fully; she would admit to Hamlet that her second marriage was wrong, clear herself of anything else, offer to help him, and be shown doing it. Shakespeare, in his first treatment of the play, had no reason not to keep all this, as the First Quarto implies; his problem was to make the audience accept the delay as life-like, and once Hamlet is surrounded by guards that problem is solved. But if we next suppose him making a minor revision, for audiences who have become interested in the mystery of Hamlet, then it is clearly better to surround him with mystery and make him drive into a situation which the audience too feels to be unplumbable.

Richard Flatter, in his interesting book *Hamlet's Father*, has done useful work by taking this reinterpretation of the Ghost as far as it will go. He points out that the Ghost must be supposed to return in the bedroom scene to say something important, and yet all he does is to prevent Hamlet from learning whether the Queen helped in his murder; such then was his intention, though he had to deny it. After this Hamlet does up his buttons (stops pretending to be mad) and has nothing left but a highminded despair about his duties to his parents; that is why he talks about Fate and refuses to defend himself. In effect, he can now only kill Claudius after his mother is dead, and he has only an instant to do it in before he himself dies, but he is heroic in seizing this moment to carry out an apparently impossible duty with pedantic exactitude. To accuse him of delay, says Flatter with considerable point, is like accusing Prometheus of delay while chained to the Caucasus. This result, I think, is enough to prove that the Flatter view was never a very prominent element in a play which hides it so successfully. He produces interesting evidence from stage history that her complicity in the murder was assumed as part of the tradition; but I can't see that the German version has any claim to echo a pre-Shakespearean play, whereas the First Quarto gives evidence that it was Shakespeare who first started this hare, in his revision of 1601. He goes on to claim that the theme of a Ghost who, so far from wanting revenge, wants to save his unfaithful wife from being punished for murdering himself, wants even to save her from the pain of confessing it to their son, is an extraordinary moral invention, especially for an Elizabethan poet; and so it is, for a playwright in any period, if he keeps it so very well hidden. Here, surely, we are among the vaguely farcical "Solutions of the Hamlet Problem" which have been cropping up for generations. But we need also to consider why they crop up, why the play was so constructed as to excite them. I think the Flatter theory did cross the keen minds of some of the 1601 audiences, and was intended to; but only as a background possibility in a situation which encouraged a variety of such ideas.

Indeed, an opposite position to the Flatter one is also left open, and I have heard from people who still hold it; that the Ghost is a devil, and only comes back in the third Act to prevent

the Queen from being converted by Hamlet. One might suppose
that if she had been fully converted the tragedy would have been
avoided, though it is not clear how. Dover Wilson has written
well about the variety of views on ghosts expressed by the characters in the first Act, and therefore expected in the audience; but
then he seems to assume that the whole audience, after the first
Act, is swung over to one view, that the Ghost is genuine. It was
not their habit to be converted so easily. The official Protestant
position was that all apparent Ghosts are devils trying to instigate
sin; also that Purgatory does not exist, so that this Ghost in saying
it has come from Purgatory must be lying. Few of the audience
would be inclined to worry about such points, but the technique
of Shakespeare aims at breaking up any merely aesthetic "sus-
pension of disbelief" – you are made to consider how people
would *really* react to a Ghost. To think it a devil had both the
safety of being official and the charm of being cynical; after
admitting the idea at the start, the playwright could expect it to
remain alive in the audience somewhere. Certainly the whole
audience is meant to believe in the murder, otherwise the thing
would be too confusing (this may be why the King's confession
"aside" had to be added in III.i); but even a devil, for bad purposes, could "speak true". From the point of view of James I, as
I understand, any usurper once legally crowned had the Divine
Right, and only a devil could supernaturally encourage murder
of him. That Hamlet is stirring up misery among a lot of otherwise contented people is a prominent suggestion of the play, as
several critics have pointed out – he is a disease, and presumably
the Ghost made him virulent. Thus you could not only think the
Ghost in the bedroom scene startlingly good, but also startlingly
bad; though most of the audience was not likely to think either.

   We need to step back here, and consider why it is possible for
such radically opposed theories to be held by careful readers; it
would be trivial merely to jeer at the long history of theories
about *Hamlet*, because they bear witness to its peculiar appeal.
The only simple view is that the play was constructed so as to
leave them open. This may seem to make it a mere trick, but the
popular feeling about ghosts had always this curious ambivalence; the novelty was in getting an author who could put it
directly on the stage. As for raising doubts about the Queen, I
think that the fundamental reason why the change was "subtle",
to recall the term of Dover Wilson, was something very close to
the Freudian one which he is so quick at jumping away from; to

make both parents a mystery at least pushes the audience towards fundamental childhood situations. But it would have a sufficient immediate effect from thickening the atmosphere and broadening the field.

We should now be prepared to consider the Freudian view of *Hamlet*, the most extraordinary of the claims that it means something very profound which the first audiences could not know about. I think that literary critics, when this theory first appeared, were thrown into excessive anxiety. A. C. Bradley had made the essential points before; that Hamlet's first soliloquy drives home (rather as a surprise to the first audiences, who expected something about losing the throne) that some kind of sex nausea about his mother is what is really poisoning him; also that in the sequence around the Prayer scene his failure to kill Claudius is firmly and intentionally tied up with a preference for scolding his mother instead. I have been trying to argue that his relations with the two women were made increasingly oppressive as the play was altered, but in any case the Freudian atmosphere of the final version is obvious even if distasteful. Surely the first point here is that the original legend is a kind of gift for the Freudian approach (even if Freud is wrong); it need not be painful to suppose that Shakespeare expressed this legend with a unique power. There is a fairy-story or childish fascination because Hamlet can boast of his secret and yet keep it, and because this crazy magical behaviour kills plenty of grown-ups; to base it on a conflict about killing Mother's husband is more specifically Freudian but still not secret. The Freudian theory makes a literary problem when its conclusions oppose what the author thought he intended; but it seems clear that Shakespeare wouldn't have wanted to alter the play if he had been told about Freud, whether he laughed at the theory or not. Then again, what is tiresome for the reader about the Freudian approach is that it seems to tell us we are merely deluded in the reasons we give for our preferences, because the real grounds for them are deep in the Unconscious; but here the passage to the underground is fairly open. A feeling that this hero is allowed to act in a peculiar way which is yet somehow familiar, because one has been tempted to do it oneself, is surely part of the essence of the story. There is a clear contrast with Oedipus, who had no Oedipus Complex. He had not wanted to kill his father and marry his mother, even "unconsciously"; if he came to recognise that he had wanted it, that would weaken his bleak surprise at

learning he has done it. The claim is that his audiences wanted to
do it unconsciously – that is why they were so deeply stirred by
the play, and why Aristotle could treat it as the supreme tragedy
though in logic it doesn't fit his case at all, being only a bad-luck
story. This position is an uneasy one, I think; one feels there
ought to be some mediation between the surface and the depths,
and probably the play did mean more to its first audiences than
we realise. But Hamlet is himself suffering from the Complex, in
the grand treatment by Ernest Jones, though the reactions of the
audience are also considered when he makes the other characters
"fit in". And this is not unreasonable, because Hamlet is at least
peculiar in Saxo, and Shakespeare overtly treats him as a "case"
of melancholy, a specific though baffling mental disease which
medical textbooks were being written about.

What does seem doubtful is whether they would think his
mental disease was what made him spare the King at prayer, as
is essential to the Freudian position; or, if you don't think that
matters, whether they could at least suspect that the real reason
was not the one he gave, as is believed by almost all modern
critics. Here I want to propose a conjecture, which would put the
first audiences in a much more intelligible position. In the first
place, the incident is likely to have been in Kyd's version. What
so many critics have felt is, not so much that the motive of Hamlet
is too wicked, but that it sticks out; it is unprepared-for; and one
thinks of other cases in Shakespeare where this is due to a certain
strain between the story he has taken over and the characters he
has invented for it. If then Kyd introduced the incident, we may
presume he gave Hamlet the plain motive of wanting to send
Claudius to Hell, and intended it to be believed. We have next to
ask why; and we must remember that, when Kyd wrote Hamlet,
the fashion for condoning revenge in the theatre had not yet
arisen; besides, a revenger who killed a king was a particularly
shocking one – to treat him as a hero might be positively dangerous. The immediate problem before Kyd, inventing the
Elizabethan drama, is how to turn the story in Belleforest into a
stage tragedy. A good deal has to be changed, because the
incidents convenient for treatment don't end in tragedy; besides,
to use the later formula, he needs a crisis in the third Act
sufficient to give him his catastrophe in the fifth. In the structure
of the play as we have it, the crisis is the refusal of Hamlet to kill
the King at prayer; in no other case does he evidently refuse an
opportunity, and the effect of his refusal here is the death not

only of the hero but of almost the entire cast. Surely there had to be some "point" in the incident, some reason why it mattered; and for an Elizabethan moralist there would be a very obvious point, so obvious as to be hard for the dramatist to evade, even if he had wanted to. Hamlet goes too far here; he wants too much revenge. If he killed Claudius he would be impeccable (except on the theory of James I, but that was rather wild), because he is the real King, with the Divine Right, and Claudius is a murderer as well as a traitor; Hamlet would only act like an established King signing an order for execution. But even then it would be wrong not to allow the criminal the consolations of religion in the condemned cell; ordinary opinion would allow frightful cruelties against a regicide, but a plan to send him to Hell it would think outrageous. When Hamlet wants that, he goes outside his legal position; he becomes simply a wicked revenger, though he could still get sympathy for his reckless courage. He commits a tragic error of statecraft which is also a sin, forgiveable in his circumstances perhaps but his own fault, and such a fault is enough to spoil an otherwise righteous plan of revenge. Perhaps the moral was expressed by the Ghost, which gives him something to say when he reappears; but the structure of the plot made it very plain anyhow. If it is asked why we have no record of this moral, the answer is that it came to be thought unfashionably heavy; maybe that was a reason why the play was laughed at, though nobody would dare say so outright.

A number of Victorian critics, including Bernard Shaw, as I was recalling earlier, thought that Shakespeare had to write a Revenge Play for his coarse audience but that, because he was morally so "advanced", he added hints that revenge was wrong or at least out of date. One or two recent critics, sternly recalling us to the high sense of duty of a purer time, have argued that it was the unquestioned duty of Hamlet to send his father's murderer to Hell. This idea that the Elizabethans were all heathens seems to be comical; the first audiences had heard any number of sermons denouncing revenge under any circumstances. The Victorians were right in feeling there was some twist about the matter, but they got it the wrong way round; the old play was the one which would naturally have the moral, not the new one; and so far as Shakespeare seems against revenge he is "backward". But I think that, while fully realising the horror of the thing, he made positive efforts to turn Hamlet into an up-to-date revenger. G. B. Harrison has well pointed out that Hamlet

happens to succeed, to an appalling degree, in his desire to kill
Claudius during some act of deadly sin. Claudius knows it is the
poisoned cup the Queen wants to drink from (as an intimacy with
her son) and orders her not to; but she insists, and he only says
(aside) "It is the poisoned cup. It is too late." When the poison
takes effect he says "She swounds to see them bleed." In real life
he might not have time to save her, but surely Harrison is right
about the best way to act it. "Claudius could save the Queen, but
that would betray himself. He has now killed the woman for
whom he contrived two murders . . . and can only wait for the
end" – actually he is more set on life than that when he says "Oh,
yet defend me, friends; I am but hurt." The actress of Gertrude,
says Harrison, should make her realise what Claudius has done
as she dies; she does, of course, contradict him and try to save
Hamlet. I should think Shakespeare added this detail deliberately, to give Hamlet what he wanted. Also he makes Hamlet
report with glee that he sent Rosencrantz and Guildenstern to
their deaths positively ordering "no shriving time allowed",
which might prevent discovery of his plot but would be bound to
appear strikingly wicked. They are old friends against whom
even he alleges nothing but meddling, not any knowledge of the
order to kill him when he gets to England. I should imagine that
Shakespeare both added the detail about no shriving and cut out
all evidence that these characters know of the King's intention. I
imagine indeed he felt a certain ironical willingness to make his
revenger very bad; he could fit that in easily enough, if it would
help to make Hamlet popular. At the same time, I readily agree,
he was not absorbed into the fashion he was making use of; the
inherent humanity of his treatment makes an eerie contrast to
it. Indeed there are repeated suggestions that Hamlet is exasperated by being put into a situation so unwelcome to him, so that
when he does act he plunges into his role with wilful violence. At
the words "no shriving time allowed" Horatio coolly interrupts
and asks "how was this sealed?", and Hamlet can boast that
Heaven had provided the right seal to carry out this order, and so
forth, ending after eight lines with a mention of the fight with the
pirates. Horatio returns rather broodingly to the earlier detail:

> So, Guildenstern and Rosencrantz go to it.

On this mild hint Hamlet becomes boisterously self-justifying.
They are not near his conscience; it was at their own risk that they
came near a great man like himself. Horatio says only:

Why, what a King is this!

and Hamlet with importunate eagerness asks him whether he
doesn't now think it is "perfect conscience" to kill Claudius, who
has tried to kill Hamlet as well as all his other crimes, and with
such cozenage too. The repetition of "conscience", I think,
shows the gleaming eye of Shakespeare. Critics, so far as I have
noticed, take Horatio's remark to mean that Claudius is wicked
to try to kill Hamlet, and this is perhaps what Hamlet thinks he
meant; but I had always assumed, and still do, that he meant
"what a King you have become"; it is Hamlet who is now acting
like a king, almost too like a king, after a long period when he
didn't.

I am putting in an appendix some remarks about the background of the play, which I hope support this theory about
sparing the King at prayer; I want now to consider the effects on
members of the first audiences, most of whom may be presumed
to know the old play well enough. An idea that Hamlet doesn't
realise what he is doing here in all its implications, one may say,
had always been present, as part of the moral. In the new play
Hamlet is no longer blamed for the motive he gives; indeed,
when the Ghost says he has been neglecting to kill the King
because "lapsed in time and passion" it is rather pointedly
ignored. The audience is set free, I think, among other possible
reactions, to regard the motive as an excuse. Also Hamlet's
failure even to think of his personal danger, now that the King
knows his secret, would be more glaring for Elizabethans than
for ourselves (as Dover Wilson pointed out); it suits the habitual
lordliness of his mind, but is evidently not justified on this
decisive occasion. There is a suggestion "You thought you were
going to be bored by this old moral anecdote, but you had not
really considered the whole situation it describes." That there is
some puzzle about it could easily occur to them, and the puzzle
joins on very naturally to his mental disease.

The idea of a man grown-up in everything else who still acts
like a child towards his elder relations could occur to a reflective
mind, not only be sensed by the Unconscious, as soon as
behaviour like Hamlet's was presented as a puzzle. The trouble
with it if made prominent would be from making the hero con-
temptible, but Hamlet has many escapes from that besides his
claim to mental disease. That his mother's marriage was considered incest made his initial disturbance seem more rational

then than it does now; but his horror and jealousy are made to feel, as T. S. Eliot pointed out for purposes of complaint, a spreading miasma and in excess of this cause. I do not think Dover Wilson need have suspected that Eliot hadn't heard about incest, even for a rival effort at dodging Freud; there was admittedly an excess, because the old play was admittedly theatrical. Unconscious resistance to killing a *King* is what the audience would be likely to invent, if any; for Claudius to talk about the divinity that doth hedge a king is irony, because he has killed one, but we are still meant to feel its truth; there may be some echo of the current view of Hamlet, as one critic has suggested, in the grand scene of Chapman with the repeated line "Do anything but killing of a King." It would fit well onto the highminded aspect of Hamlet, as having an unmentioned doubt about the value of his revenge. But none of this is a rebuttal of the Freudian view; the feeling about a King is derived very directly from childhood feelings about Father.

We have to consider, not merely how a play came to be written which allows of being searched so deeply so long after, but why it has steadily continued to hold audiences who on any view do not see all round it. The Freudian view is that it satisfies the universal Unconscious, but one feels more practical in saying, as Hugh Kingsmill did, that they enjoy the imaginative release of indulging in very "theatrical" behaviour, which in this case is hard to distinguish from "neurotic" behaviour. The business of the plot is to prevent them from feeling it as an indulgence, because the assumption that Hamlet has plenty of reasons for it is always kept up. If we leave the matter there, I think, the play appears a rather offensive trick and even likely to be harmful. Indeed common sense has decided that people who feel encouraged to imitate Hamlet, or to follow what appear to be the instructions of Freud, actually are liable to behave badly. But the first audiences were being asked to consider this hero of legend as admittedly theatrical (already laughed at for it) and yet unbreakably true about life; in one way because he illustrated a recognised neurosis, in another because he extracted from it virtues which could not but be called great however much the story proved them to be fatal. So far as the spectator was tempted forward to examine the "reasons" behind Hamlet he was no longer indulging a delusion but considering a frequent and important, even if delusory, mental state, and trying to handle it. If one conceives the play as finally rewritten with that kind of purpose and that kind of audience, there is no need to be astonished that it happened to illustrate the Freudian theory. The eventual question is whether you can put up with the final Hamlet, a person who frequently appears in the modern world under various disguises, whether by Shakespeare's fault or no. I would always sympathise with anyone who says, like Hugh Kingsmill, that he can't put up with Hamlet at all. But I am afraid it is within hail of the more painful question whether you can put up with yourself and the race of man.

HAMLET APPENDICES

I would much prefer to make this essay on *Hamlet* one consecutive piece, but as everyone has found about *Hamlet* the subject begins budding off you, and it had better be allowed to take its natural course. However, these extra little essays are intended to be subordinate; they are meant to give a tolerable amount of support to assertions which were made in the main essay. I wish that the subject was less obscure, but the fact that people at the time wanted it to be obscure does seem to me enough to make a competent historian feel less baffled; all he really needs to feel is that not he but some earlier people were baffled, and I should think they were. My remarks are therefore very comforting for him, and he need not attack me for them. It seems a fussy introduction, but I am asking to be allowed a brief glance at various learned fields. Consider the enormous fact that the books about *Hamlet* would alone completely fill a sheer house. I am rather interested in the reflection that this already defeats what is called "scholarship", because nobody has read them all. If he did, he would only be a monster. The historian of *Hamlet* is therefore already in the situation envisaged by the great Toynbee, when he said that a historian a thousand years hence, with thousands of millions of documents to choose from, could only try to write a good novel.

I
REVENGE PLAYS

There is perhaps an initial obstacle here, because a critic living in a fairly placid society needs to bring his mind round before he can find the subject of Revenge very real or interesting. But in the modern world it has become painfully familiar to have some

social group or nation take into its head that it has been unbearably wronged, so much wronged that it positively *ought* to cut off
its nose to spite its face; and this is the fundamental situation of
the Revenge Play, which is practically always concerned with the
painful and distorting effects of revenge regarded as a duty.
Indeed, anyone who has to do administrative work is likely to
come to feel that the basic purpose is not so much to do justice as
to prevent anyone from coming to feel too much wronged; there
is always a suggestion of handling the waters which might otherwise flood the plain. No doubt the classical themes for drama,
especially as rehashed by Seneca for recitation to his peculiarly
high, bloody, and tottering society, were much concerned with
revenge; but the Elizabethans can't be accused of merely copying
this, and perhaps the best straightforward Revenge Play is the
almost literal History of *III Henry VI*. The first spectators, as is
often said, must have felt accustomed in real life to meeting persons who felt unbearably wronged; such indeed is what Marston
says, with obvious conviction because with a splendour
unfamiliar to him, in the Prologue to *Antonia and Mellida*; we
need not perhaps puzzle our heads to know why, the question is
rather why other periods and peoples have not expressed the
sentiment in similar plays. At any rate we should recognise a certain connection between reality and these apparently unreal
objects; we had better not remain content with saying they are
"derived from Seneca".

Thus the first thing to be said about the Revenge Play is that,
though it became a rather tiresome and brutal fashion, the basic
idea of it is not at all inhumane and has a natural permanence in
the relations of the individual to society. A wrong has been done
which is not recognised as such by the existing social system, and
it is so great that the person wronged *ought* to act independently
of society, or at least you must expect him to. In one way he
becomes an outlaw, but in another he becomes a judge; the
theatricality of the Revenger can be justified because such a man
ought to appeal to the judgement of other men, though he cannot
do so by the accepted rules. As a test of his sincerity, he should
be ready to welcome death for himself as well as for his enemies,
so long as he can thereby impress enough other people with the
idea that this was a wrong. He is thus inherently trying to get the
rules improved, not merely to break them. But he is not expected
to be conscious of this, because it is assumed that he cannot do it
by normal means, from within his society, using the ideas which

he accepts from it. He can only affect other people by an extremity of feeling and behaviour which seems to them mad; and seems mad to him too, because the only ideas he has ready are those of his society. Indeed there seems to the audience to be nothing else in the world except these ideas, and yet the revenger is coming from outside them; therefore he is mixed up with the supernatural.

One needs to get clear, I think, both that a great theatre is rare in human history, and that, although when it happens it always uses this theme, no other great theatre has used it so fully and directly as the Elizabethan. Thinking of the ancient Greeks, the Renaissance French and Spanish, and the Japanese Noh plays, which are about all you *can* think of, the amount of madness in the Elizabethan play is bound to stand out. The Japanese are I think our chief rivals there, and this rather drives home the oddity of it; where did the Elizabethans get this idea? They must at least have made a selection if they "derived" it from the *Hercules Furens*, and after that they must have invented the significance of it. I suspect that they derived it literally from Hamlet himself, recently made conveniently accessible in the French of Belleforest, which is full of the significance of this peculiar theme; and, from what one can gather, the *Hamlet* of Kyd must have been the first good Elizabethan play. The reader would naturally be irritated if asked to believe this guesswork, but I had best write it down at once as giving him the purport of the rest of the essay. The Hamlet story looks to me historically as well as dramatically important, and I hope at least that the revenge theme does not appear dull.

It would be natural to ask why I have to argue here, why revenge ever came to seem dull; and the answer of course is that no splendid formula can be turned on like a tap. The playwright needs an important enough story, and deep enough understanding of how the characters react in it. When Marston makes Piero, at the beginning of *Antonio's Revenge*, say

> I have no reason to be reasonable

he is hitting the centre of the formula and making it ring like a gong, but this is not enough. Nor would a critic do enough who pointed out that Piero hasn't enough reason to reject reason; the author agrees that Piero is the villain, and he gets an appalling revenge back on himself. The critic must fall back on an over-all judgement, a thing which could be expressed in a lengthy argument but would then be unfitted to convince a receptive mind already able to react either way; it is very important to be able to give reasons, but not always useful. I agree with current opinion that Marston's plays are intolerable; the effect is somehow *voulu*; like so many things which were once the height of fashion, they have become stuffy. But when the formula really works it is, one may say, the essential reason for having a theatre; because it treats the audience as a jury.

My account of the formula may seem too theoretical and too conscious of the idea of revolutionary progress; I think it is the fundamental one, but the Elizabethans had local reasons for their fashion, and would have given a rather different account. Here the basic assumption of the Revenge Play is that Honour has duties which Christianity refuses to recognise. They can be spoken of as entirely separate moral systems; thus Claudius has a tone of cosy piety, even if with the voice of the Devil, when he says to Laertes

> No place, indeed, should murder sanctuarize;
> Revenge should have no bounds.

To take Honour quite seriously, one would think, necessarily erected it into a rival religion (rather like the medieval Love), but this was seldom done; however, it was taken pretty seriously by respectable persons, and not only as an imaginative indulgence. Even the idea that it is smart to invent a new and extra horrible revenge, a theatrical one so as to catch public attention, joins on to the cult of Honour; because that in itself is deeply confused with the idea of being well thought of by the world. The Elizabethans, I suspect, felt a little ashamed of being provincials compared to southern Europe, and especially in not having so much of the Code of Honour; in practice they tended to revolt against it, very rightly as most of us would think, but they hadn't the nerve to boast of doing that. They found it convenient to insist that the Italians were very wicked, as one could see from Machiavelli; because the other side of this quality was something they weren't sure they had enough of. The reason why the first big Revenge Play is *The Spanish Tragedy* is that the Spaniards had an appalling amount of Honour; as indeed the play reminds us at the beginning (I.ii):

> Yet shalt thou know that Spain is honourable.

To this extent, even if no more, the artificial form provided an experience they wanted to examine.

The desire to display Honour, even at the risk of the soul, was thus mixed up with a desire to be high-class; but there was another way of looking at the plays which let them join on more directly to the morality of real life. The plays were about foreigners, of the Romance language-group, for whose wild actions one could feel a certain romantic sympathy because the whole set-up was pretty wild over there. Here at home, it was felt, we aim at a civilised community; a private individual ought to appeal to public justice and renounce revenge, and he ought to stick to this even in cases where the law is not just to him, because there is a public policy about it which ought to be supported. This was the settled principle, but even at home, and without giving oneself airs about Honour, there were cases where one could seriously doubt whether holding to it would be reasonable. In any case, of course, Christ had enjoined forgiveness; but one did not have to be anti-Christian to realise that his doctrines need to be applied with moderation; somewhere in the background of the judgement there would be an estimate of how the consequences in a given society worked out. Royal persons when dispossessed made a separate case, because they inherently could not appeal to public law, and yet they themselves in some sense embodied public law, as the rightful final court of appeal on earth; so that revenge might be their duty even as Christians. When the succession is in doubt, various nobles may plausibly make this claim; and indeed *III Henry VI* is extremely like one of the later Revenge Plays, except that it is more sensible.

This state of public feeling, I think, made the legal status of characters in Shakespeare more prominent than it is now. Orlando in *As You Like It* is only a private individual, therefore not entitled to revenge himself on his brother. But he has no hope of redress by public law as the present government stands, therefore it is noble of him not to let the lion eat his brother. Othello is the governor of an island under martial law, so he has powers of life and death; it is very wrong of him to kill his wife and try to kill Cassio, but he is not legally a criminal; except that he possibly becomes one, by bad luck, because Cassio is made governor over his head before the plan is completed. One must think of the more sober part of the audience as habitually making this kind of legal estimate, so that the super-heated atmosphere of an all-out

Revenge Play would seem to them morally shocking, as it was meant to do, and does to us.

I realise that these remarks are rather prosy, but I think we tend to imagine the Elizabethan ideas on revenge as more remote from us than they really are. To collect "parallels" from other plays of plans to send your enemy to Hell, for instance, does not in itself show what the audience thought about them. Such a play was meant to concentrate on a rather peculiar mood of tragic exasperation; the mood was admired in a way, as a kind of fashion, but the ordinary moral judgements went on firmly underneath it. Thus I do not think it unreasonable to suppose that the Ur-Hamlet, which was quite possibly the earliest Elizabethan Revenge Play, carried a moral (if only as an excuse) which the audience could think normal and respectable.

II

TITUS ANDRONICUS

It would be foolish to deny that *Titus Andronicus* is a bad and nasty play but the essential technical skill of Shakespeare is already strong in it; his power, that is, to stop churning out a play and think instead "Why is anybody interested in this plot?" and then throw the answer naked on the stage. To a spectator who had been all agog about the play so far, Act V, Scene ii must have been astounding poetry; because it rises into a larger air, and tells him what he is feeling about. Titus is not as mad as his enemies think, that is why he defeats them, but he is quite mad enough at this point to speak with an oracular penetrating power: indeed, unless he had obviously meant what he said, he could not have deceived them. The practical objection to revenge, I should have remarked before but these things are so well known, is that it doesn't stop; it tends to produce an endless bloodfeud, unlike the process of law even when bad. Titus has been dragged into revenge by the wickedness of his enemies, and realises that he is joining wickedness, as the audience is expected to agree, because it is essential to the play that he must be killed after succeeding in his revenge. What forced him to join was not any intensity of wickedness but the process of jeering, when they return to him in mockery his own hand and the heads of his two sons, breaking the promise which exacted them; that called out Honour, because he would be less than a man if he didn't revenge it, though nothing less would make him revengeful. What is impressive about Titus is the way he drives home this peculiar octopus-like truth as he embraces his three victims (Tamora and her two sons), who imagine he is their victim. He pretends to mistake each person precisely in the manner considered original when used ten years later in love-poems by Donne, for the incarnate Universal or envisaged Platonic Ideal of his or her special crime, and the point of doing this is that it enables him to say safely (just as Hamlet could tell the truth safely) that they are inherently self-destructive; by appointing himself as their avenger he is merely letting himself collapse into one of the forces of Nature. This ingenuity is not his own, though he expands it with glee; it is introduced by the wicked Queen Tamora, who imagines like many later politicians that she can make madness convenient to her. She claims to be Revenge in person:

> *Tam.* Show me a thousand that have done thee wrong,
> And I will be revenged on them all.
> *Tit.* Look round about the wicked streets of Rome,
> And when thou findst a man that 's like thyself,
> Good Murder, stab him, he's a murderer.
> Go thou with him, and when it is thy hap
> To find another that is like to thee,
> Good Rapine, stab him; he's a ravisher.
> Go thou with them; and in the emperor's court
> There is a queen attended by a Moor;
> Well mayst thou know her by her own proportion
> For up and down she doth resemble thee.
> I pray thee, do on them some violent death;
> They have been violent to me and mine.
> *Tam.* Well hast thou lessoned us; this shall we do.
> But would it please thee, good Andronicus,
> To send for Lucius, thy thrice-valiant son,
> Who leads towards Rome a band of war-like Goths,
> And bid him come and banquet at thy house . . .

and so forth. Obviously this conference reaches full agreement.

This bit of the play, I submit, must be by Shakespeare and proves that he had once been seriously present among these roots of Elizabethan drama, which he can throw up into the air and yet catch again when he comes to rewrite *Hamlet*. I do not think it gives the slightest reason to suppose that he wrote the original *Hamlet*, as some critics have suggested; what we have is a power-

ful young mind, trying at an accepted form, choosing as hell-up
a story as his grammar school could suggest to him and then at the
climax taking his theatrical stand on the bare interest of an
analysis of its inherent meaning. You can see how that scene
went over big, and he felt he could trust himself after that had
gone over big. My business here is merely to point out that he
includes all the intelligent ideas that can be extracted from *The
Spanish Tragedy*; the revenger acts only on the combination of
insult with unbearable wrong, and then he pretends to be half-
mad, and really is half-mad, otherwise he could not deceive his
enemies, but he has strength of character enough to use this
queer condition to their destruction – of course at the cost of his
own life, but both he and his audience have long regarded that as
forfeit. Apart from the shortage of jokes, which one can understand Shakespeare finding hard to let in, it is a firm statement of
the ideology of early or untarnished Revenge Play, and throws in
at the end some tearing metaphysical poetry. The roots of the
Elizabethan drama, I think, only seem to us dull because they are
familiar; Shakespeare does give us one bit of information about
his mind, he laughs at what he thinks funny, and he expresses
very little contempt for Kyd.

Perhaps I may remark on a note in the new Arden edition of
Titus Andronicus, introducing this splendid passage; the note is
attached to the second line of those quoted.

Tam.	These are my ministers, and come with me.
Tit.	Are they thy ministers? What are they called?
Tam.	Rape and Murder; therefore called so
	'Cause they take vengeance of such kind of men.
Tit.	Good Lord, how like the empress' sons they are,
	And you the empress; but we worldly men
	Have miserable, mad, mistaking eyes.
	O sweet Revenge, now do I come to thee . . .

Note: Wilson calls this question "an inconsistency surely too glaring to
        be explained as Titus's lunacy". Possibly ll. 44–59 were an after-
        thought, not fully integrated with the context at the "foul
        papers" stage. It is clear, though the editors do not comment on
        it, that Titus knows at l. 45 who Tamora's attendants are.

If these critics have really never encountered a difficult old man
they had better read James Thurber, who does not exaggerate
the experience they have been deprived of. However, the
modern lunatic revival of pedantry is making a real point here,

but of course a dramatic point and not as it supposes any evidence for "revision". Tamora comes in (as she has told the audience) planning to tell the old man she is not herself but Revenge, but she is frightened of him enough to bring her two sons to help her. The old man accepts this story with glee, and immediately adds that her two sons are Rape and Murder (as in his life of course they are). He makes a thrilling speech of fifteen lines to this goddess of Revenge, saying from its first words that he will do anything as her servant so long as she kills Rape and Murder. It is merely at the end of this one speech that he sharply asks her back "What are these men?" and she has to go on playing the game she started, but now accepting the lead he has called, so she says

> Rape and Murder; therefore called so
> 'Cause they take vengeance of such kind of men

so Titus makes the fine speech I have already quoted, saying they must all three kill themselves as soon as they meet themselves. Now this is genuine old-man behaviour; and the spectacle of the firm Tamora getting knocked down when she thinks she can win him over, merely because she shouts his own lines back at him, had been familiar to Shakespeare before he left Stratford. Just for once in this bad play you get a strong dramatic effect, and instead of thanking God for it all these critics leap on it and say it is hopelessly bad because it is the accidental consequence of a revision. But the world is wide, and the point they draw attention to is really worth looking at.

III

DER BESTRAFTE BRUDERMORD

A rival reason why Hamlet spared the King at prayer has been brought forward; I am not sure whether only by A. A. Jack (*Young Hamlet*, 1950) from whom I take it. He argues from the late German version *Der Bestrafte Brudermord* (or *B.B.*) that the Ur-Hamlet spared the King at prayer because he was in chapel, and to kill him there would be sacrilege, whatever he happened to be doing. A. A. Jack uses rather lyrical language about the simple power of this brilliant dramatic invention, and maintains that Shakespeare assumed that his audience would assume it; the old play was known, and the staging would prove the scene to be a chapel. Nothing else is required, he says contentedly, to destroy the Romantics and prove that Hamlet never delayed, not even once. But the brilliant dramatic invention seems to me too trivial for Kyd, let alone for Shakespeare; it makes the crisis of the play just one more stage in an obstacle race, a technical question of etiquette, producing an "Oh Brother" effect. It does seem possible, I confess, that Shakespeare had heard of this idea, because he makes Laertes, as the opposite of Hamlet, say he would do anything at once to revenge himself on the murderer of his father, such as "cut his throat in a church". But the fact that this was an obvious extreme of revenge does not force us to tie it onto Kyd's Hamlet.

I am therefore glad to point out that it is not clearly expressed even in the German *B.B.* The stage direction, on which all is supposed to depend, calls for a "temple", which need not be Christian. The King prays to "the gods", and I should think the German audience would get to know, because they would like it, that the story was an ancient North-European one, therefore pre-Christian. There is also a vaguely comic reference to the Pope: the remorseful Queen says "if the Pope had not allowed the marriage it would never have taken place", but we need not expect these ideas to be very definite. There is no dramatic build-up to the idea of sacrilege, and the text does not even refer to being in a "temple". Surely "temple" in the stage direction might be written in by an editor who merely thought it a natural place for a King to pray. The staging available to these troupers in Germany was not so elaborate that it could force the audience, without any words at all, to realise that the whole point of the scene was that it took place on consecrated ground. I would be foolish to deny that the human reality which lies behind the idea of consecrated ground also lies behind the scene as written by Shakespeare, but this is general; it gives you no evidence that *B.B.* must have been derived from Kyd.

We are less in danger of making false deductions from the speech of Hamlet in *B.B.* if we admit its merits. I quote the Variorum translation:

Thus long have I followed the damned dog, till I have found him. Now is the time, when he is alone. I will slay him in the midst of his devotions. (*Is about to slay him.*) But no, I will first let him finish his prayer. But ah, when I think of it, he did not first give my father time for a prayer, but sent him to Hell in his sleep and perhaps in his sins. Therefore will I send him after to the same place. (*Is again about to run him through from behind.*) But hold, Hamlet, why shouldst thou take his sins upon thyself? I will let him finish his prayer, and let him go this time, and give him life; but another time I will fulfil my revenge.

Now it may have been a well-known superstition among seventeenth-century Germans that if you killed a man in sanctuary you took over by magic the guilt for all his sins. It is a possible belief; but A. A. Jack needs to offer some evidence for it, and he offers none. Also we need not presume it, because the audiences would still find the speech interesting without any such belief. What is really shown here, I think, is the inherent strength of the Hamlet story, even when handled summarily. Two ideas are present in this brief text: that it is unsporting or something to stab a man in the back while he is praying (one at least pauses before it), and that young Hamlet wants to treat Claudius as badly as Claudius treated old Hamlet. We can easily feel the first in the Shakespeare version, even though the second claims to oust it. The *B.B.* author, so far as one can follow him, makes Hamlet think Claudius will go to Hell if he is killed *before he has finished* his prayer, and still makes Hamlet refuse to do it; this might be claimed as a noble variant, but it is not presented clearly enough to be so intended; the author simply gives him confused decent feelings. What is curious, I think, is that this accidental turning upside-down of the official stage situation does not alter the real one; the motives seem inherently more complicated than the expression of them. In the same way, the audience of *B.B.* could be trusted to feel that the revenger is afraid of becoming a sinner like his victim, merely because revenge was an "unlucky" form of duty. We need not invent an invisible theatrical tradition about sacrilege. Indeed, the idea is made rather prominent in the prologue to *B.B.*, where Night says:

Kindle a fire of revenge, and let the sparks fly over the whole realm; entangle kinsmen in the net of crime; and give joy to Hell, so that those who swim in the sea of murder may soon drown.

A reasonable spectator need not be surprised after this to find Hamlet at least for a moment afraid of getting entangled in the net of crime. In fact, the adaptation seems to me remarkably good at this point; if you had to do it so shortly and colloquially, and keep your Hamlet homely and natural, you could not convey the confusion of his mind more strongly.

It has been argued that the prologue comes from Kyd, whereas the rest comes from a shortened version of Shakespeare such as

Q1; because the prologue foretells things that don't happen in the play. Also the play has a few extra references to Fortinbras and the throne of Norway, a branch of the subject which Shakespeare left obscure; thus, it is said, Kyd had two plays on Hamlet, using the extra space for a Danish civil war in which Fortinbras became involved. We must suppose that Shakespeare worked mainly from the second. There is nothing painful about this theory, but the evidence seems very slight. If the prologue doesn't fit *B.B.* anyhow, the adapters may just as well have taken it from any Revenge Prologue; they can only have regarded it as a suitable bit of noise. Contrariwise, anybody might want to make the Fortinbras situation rather more definite. It is perhaps tantalising, but I don't think anything can be deduced from *B.B.*

IV

SAXO AND BELLEFOREST

Plunging forever deeper into the heart of the question, I shall now offer my opinion on Saxo and Belleforest, at whom I have peeped in the very convenient edition of Israel Gollancz (*The Sources of Hamlet*). I shall quote Belleforest from the English translation given by Gollancz, first known as of 1608, but possibly older (so that it might in an earlier form have been used by Shakespeare), unless a difference in the French seems worth notice. The Victorian translation of Saxo tends to be romantic; both versions need checking against the text on the opposite page whenever a detail is important. I ought to admit that without this machine I would have felt the French and Latin too hard to approach.

It struck me that the impression of them usually left by critics of *Hamlet* is rather out of proportion. Belleforest gives a full and straightforward translation of Saxo, merely omitting some riddles which had become tedious or obscure and adding a good deal of moral reflection; if Kyd, for example, ever tried checking it against the Latin he would be likely to stop almost at once, feeling there was no need; and "the Saxon who knew Latin" is so far from being primitive that he copies from Livy instead of keeping to the wilder legends that we would like to know. What I have not seen remarked is that they both load Hamlet with magical and symbolical splendour; we tend to think of the Elizabethan stage as making him more of a mystery, but it seems rather to have reduced his claims. Belleforest compares him both to

Brutus and to King David, and the chief *mystique* of the Tudors lay in boasting their descent from these two (at least, I am not sure which Brutus it was, but the name had a magic for the "British" reader). Also, it would appear from Belleforest that he had acted exactly like Prince Hal, the first genuinely English king, the forerunner of the Tudors – he made himself despised in youth as a means to become the greatest king of his time. This was a formidable political combination. (And, come to think of it, is anything known about why Shakespeare's son was christened Hamnet in 1585? I have read somewhere that it was then quite a common Christian name, and considered a pet form of Hamlet; but when did this practice begin and end? It sounds as if they attached some importance to the remote barbarian.) What is more, he was a practising sorcerer, though in a part of the story that did not reach the stage (even if the Ur-Hamlet did have two parts, it seems clear that their extra time was used on Fortinbras and civil war, not on Hamlet's career in England and Scotland). At the Court of England he made startling accusations against his hosts and their banquet, which turned out to be true though he could only have known them by magic. Or rather, Saxo leaves a doubt whether this was done by magic or merely by a fairy-story exquisiteness of apprehension, like the princess who was black and blue from the one pea under the nineteen mattresses. Belleforest however, after repeating the details, adds a rather lengthy argument that it is not heretical to believe he could tell the past, as apart from the future; no doubt there was plenty of sorcery among pagan Danes, "and Hamlet, while his father lived, had been instructed in that devilish art, whereby the wicked spirit abuseth mankind, and advertiseth him (as he can) of things past". It is like what Plato says, he goes on, about the inspiration of poets (a surprising addition to Hamlet's claims). When Hamlet comes home the courtiers fear him at sight, and Belleforest adds to Saxo that some of them saved their lives by running away, because they foresaw he had prepared some "tour de maistre" (English version "legerdemain"). This is not surprising if he was known to be a sorcerer before he started pretending to be mad.

On the other hand, Belleforest whittles down the view of Hamlet as a demi-god, which is strong in Saxo. The King of England said Hamlet must have "more than mortal wisdom" (*supra mortalem*) "or more than mortal folly"; Belleforest makes it either a complete fool "ou des plus sages de son temps" (or one of the wisest princes of his time – the English is often vaguely more royalist). When the King found the remarks true he "venerated" his wisdom "perinde ac divinum", "tanquam coeleste"; Belleforest has "beholding in him some matter of greater respect than in the common sort of men" ("le commun des hommes"). When he kills Feng, Saxo addresses him as worthy of immortal fame, because he had hidden under folly a wisdom more august than that of man ("augustiorem mortali ingenio"); Belleforest reduces this to "trompa . . . les plus sages". Going back to the first test of Hamlet, when they showed him to the lady, a friend of Feng said a stronger plot was needed to break the unfathomable cunning of such a mind ("inextricabile calliditatis ingenium"); Belleforest rather pleasingly makes this "un galant si rusé". One must agree that it is a bit Freudian or childlike to feel such deep wonder at his contriving to make love in private while in "a distant and impenetrable fen". In these details of style Belleforest removes the primitive or simply pagan idea of a demi-god, but he takes care to recognise it in his final praise of Hamlet, saying he "sought to gather a multitude of virtues, that might make him equal to those that by them were esteemed as gods". In any case, he puts much the same feeling back by his scandalised argufying over Hamlet as sorcerer. The chief relic of this in Shakespeare seems to be the two hints by Hamlet that he is a contrast to Hercules.

I was saying earlier that the mystery of Hamlet in Shakespeare is only a full development of what is inherent in the legend; this needs defending, because several critics have rightly made an opposite point. In the old story, they say, everybody knew that Claudius had killed his brother, so Hamlet might be expected to revenge him; Hamlet could therefore only save his life by pretending to be mad, either till he had prepared a trick or simply till he had grown up. This practical story is clear in Belleforest. The reason why a mystery came into Hamlet was merely that Kyd, when preparing the first play about him, was determined to have the usual Ghost of theatrical revenge; it must tell a secret, so the murder must be a secret, so Hamlet had much better not let Claudius know that he knows the secret; in fact, he is mad to pretend to be mad. Shakespeare then picked on this confusion and erected it into a mystery.

This is fair enough, but one can still call the reasonableness of the sources a "rationalisation" of the forces at work. The glee of the child in showing his cleverness safely, boasting about his secret and still keeping it, and the consequent sense of magical power – that seems to be the basis. Now the Hamlet of Saxo and Belleforest conveys a great deal of this pleasure. Hamlet in Belleforest

counterfeiting the madman, many times did divers actions of great and deep consideration, and often made such fit answers, that a wise man would soon have judged from what spirits so fine an invention might proceed; for that standing by the fire and sharpening sticks like poinards and pricks, one in smiling manner asked him wherefore he made those little staves so sharp at the points? I prepare (saith he) piercing darts and sharp arrows to revenge my father's death. Fools, as I said before, esteemed these his words as nothing; but men of quick spirits, and such as had a deeper reach, began to suspect somewhat, esteeming that under that kind of folly there lay hidden a great and rare subtlety, such as might one day be prejudicial to their prince,

so then they test him with the lady. One feels the suspicion did not require very great ingenuity. Saxo has the same incident but does not allow the boast to cause the leakage. Both the occupation and the answer, he says, were laughed at, but the thing ("res") helped his purpose afterwards. In the story this "thing" must be the occupation, because he used the sticks to net down the courtiers before he burned them alive; but perhaps in magic it was the answer that helped him. In any case, it was his "solertia" here that first made the deeper observers suspect his cunning; the work was trivial, but he could not be imbecile if he was such a good craftsman; besides, he went on taking care of his sticks ("which madness would gambol from"). This seems less his own fault than the more common-sense Belleforest version, but it is not clear why the sticks had to be prepared so early; an almost magical foreknowledge is assumed. The reason why he had to make the rash threat seems to be that he always told the truth when directly asked, though in a style which would only be laughed at; both Saxo and Belleforest emphasise this, in different places. When nobody believes he has enjoyed the lady, and he says he has, though it would be fatal if they believed him (so we are told, though it can only be for some magical or Freudian reason, since they must have known that not all lunatics are impotent) Saxo says with triumph that none could open the secret lock of the young man's wisdom. Here is enough basis for the Recorder speech, if Shakespeare had read it; Belleforest has the incident but not the phrase. He welcomes the truthfulness as a high moral virtue (perhaps with a certain jesuitry of sentiment, as the forgery was hardly truthful); but Saxo merely enjoys it as an extra boast, or as part of the technique of the magic; that is why he will never allow it to cause suspicion. The insults of Hamlet at the English Court, though not intended to deceive, carry the same gleeful feeling that if you are clever enough you can be as rude as you like with positive advantage; both Saxo and Belleforest say that the King admired his behaviour so much as to give Hamlet his daughter in marriage. The idea that this habit is likely to bring trouble on a man in the end does not occur to either of them, though it would seem a natural reflection even among primitives. Saxo finds no tragic flaw in him, and Belleforest only the lustfulness of marrying a second wife; which we need not laugh at, because the moral reaction seems to chime with a more ancient one. The idea that he died because he accepted the advances of a Queen who had always killed her suitors, though the death is only a later effect of her character, does seem to give a further Freudian or White-Goddess twist to his story. In any case, the mechanics of adding the Ghost did not radically alter the character of Hamlet.

I have been assuming that Belleforest does let Hamlet enjoy the lady in the woods, which has been denied, and certainly he is very furtive about it; but the English is a mistranslation. A friend warns Hamlet that it would be dangerous to accept, which disturbs him because he loves her, but she too warns him of the treason, because she loves him,

and would have been exceedingly sorrowful for his misfortune, and much more to leave his company without enjoying the pleasure of his body, whom she loved more than herself. The prince in this sort having both deceived the courtiers, and the lady's expectation, that affirmed and swore that he never once offered to have his pleasure of the woman, although in subtlety he affirmed the contrary, every man thereupon assured themselves that without all doubt he was distraught of his senses . . .

ayant le jeune seigneur trompe les courtesans, et la fille, soustenans qu'il ne s'estoit avance en sorte aucune a la violer, quoy qu'il dict du contraire, chacun s'asseura veritablement il estoit insense . . .

The translator has taken the grammar as "trompa la fille", but that makes "la fille soustenans" very clumsy – it needs to be another participle clause following "ayant"; or for that matter the girl, like Hamlet, might deceive the courtiers, which would give a reasonable time-order and explain the otherwise baffling pair of commas before and after *et la fille*. Belleforest does not tell us what happened, only what they both said afterwards. The clause *in subtlety* is added by the translator to make certain that Hamlet was lying, but Belleforest did not use it, because he knew quite well that Hamlet could not lie – he says it at the end of Chapter III:

> the prince that never used lying, and who in all the answers that ever he made (during his counterfeit madness) never strayed from the truth (as a generous mind is a mortal enemy to untruth) answered and said, that the counsellor he sought for was gone down through the privy . . .

Besides, the phrase "un galant si rusé" lets his knowledge peep out. I agree that he is rather hoping to deceive the reader by his tortured bit of grammar, because he is an extremely moral author labouring to make this part of the story more decent; but he does not literally tell the story wrong, and I should think a knowing reader at the time would get his meaning. Indeed, that the only spot on Hamlet was his concupiscence was the final moral, and the language need not apply only to his accepting the Queen of Scotland who killed her suitors.

The idea that Saxo found Hamlet in Livy and merely adapted the story of Brutus has a certain appeal for the debunker, as if a jungle expedition were to find itself on Hampstead Heath, but the later parts of the story, such as the fiend-like Queen, were not taken from Livy. The only detail so specific that it must have been borrowed is the symbolical hollow stick with gold inside, which Saxo might merely regard as an elegant way to draw the parallel. There must have been *some* northern legend about a hero who cunningly appeared foolish, in a revenge situation, because Saxo would have to appear plausible; and the fact that he could dignify it with this learned parallel might argue for it an extreme antiquity, or a tendency to recur everywhere.

The two authors take rather different views of the rights of revenge. Saxo takes the matter for granted except in the set speech of Hamlet after killing Feng; Hamlet says he has killed not a King but a fratricide, also a tyrant who broke the laws, and "your hands were equally bound to the task which mine fulfilled", but I chose to do it alone without risk for you. The two arguments rather suggest a double standard, but the idea is not positively excluded that it is anybody's duty to kill a King who behaves badly enough. Belleforest has heard of Divine Right, not surprisingly, and says it is always wrong to kill a King; also he makes Hamlet say (to his mother) that, as everyone knows, promises to traitors, perjured persons, and murderers need not be kept anyhow, *but*

if I lay hands upon Fengen, it will be neither felony nor treason, he being neither my king nor my lord, but I shall justly punish him as my subject [French "vassal"], that hath disloyally behaved himself against his lord and sovereign prince.

The force of "but" is a double standard again; some people might doubt the general argument, though he won't admit that the common-sense view in favour of it is wrong, but in his particular case he is morally impregnable. This would be firmly accepted by Elizabethans, and likely to occur to them in the theatre; but it would not cover, as I have already said, the refusal of Hamlet to kill Claudius till he can be sure of sending him to Hell. This presumed the separate morality of the Revenge Play.

Belleforest is well able to feel that, even the idea that it adds to your honour to get your revenge in a theatrical manner, so as to catch public attention. Where Saxo praises Hamlet because he "not only found in his subtlety means to protect his own safety, but also by its guidance found opportunity to revenge his father", Belleforest praises "un nouveau genre de punition et non excogite supplice" ("a new and unexpected kind of punishment" accepts this sentiment with worldly coolness). When the pages and courtiers mocked at his pretended madness

he noted them well enough, minding one day to be revenged in such a manner, that the memory thereof should remain perpetually to the world.

The main point of this addition seems to be not the malice but the desire for fame; there is also the delight in Machiavellian behaviour as such, which is crucial to the Revenge Play:

. . . and he that will follow this course must speak and do all things whatsoever that are pleasing and acceptable to him whom he meaneth to deceive . . . for that is rightly to play and counterfeit the fool, when a man is constrained to dissemble and kiss his hand, whom in heart he could wish a hundred foot depth under the earth, so he might never see him more, if it were not a thing wholly to be disliked in a Christian, who ought by no means to have a bitter gall, or desires infected with revenge.

The English version heightens the surprise at the end of this long sentence, when we are jerked out of fantasy into sober morals, because the French has a full stop before "if"; but I should think it means by that a snort of disgust. The mixed feelings of Belle-forest allow him to express all sides of the question; "if vengeance ever seemeth to have any show of justice" it is when our fathers are unjustly murdered; and besides, God himself avenges wrong, though slowly; and the Athenians put up statues to those who had killed tyrants. King David comes in twice; he "counterfeited the madman among the petty Kings of Palestine to preserve his life from the subtle practices of those Kings", thus setting the pattern for Hamlet, and also when on his deathbed told Solomon to revenge him. The holy King cannot have wanted revenge, says Belleforest, so he must have done this as an example to us, to show that the desire for revenge deserves praise "ou le public est interesse" ("prince or country" says the more royalist trans-lator). David on his deathbed (I Kings 2:8) says he promised Shimei "*I* will not put thee to death with the sword", so now he can tell Solomon to do it; yet at the time, we are told (II Sam. 19:23), what he swore was "Thou shalt not die." The Old Testa-ment seems a particularly bad guide to conduct here, but what Belleforest means is an appeal to public spirit. Of course we can-not know that Shakespeare either had an English version avail-able or would read the French, still less what he thought about the question in general; but he would have found here a broad and thorough look-round of it.

Finally a rather baffling detail may be pointed out. In Belle-forest, not Saxo, Hamlet says while killing Fengon:

When thou comest to Hell, forget not to tell thy brother (whom thou traitorously slewest) that it was his son that sent thee thither with the message, to the end that being comforted thereby his soul may rest among the blessed spirits, and quit me of the obligation that bound me to pursue his vengeance.

This implies very strongly though it need not assert, that the father had to stay in Hell till he was avenged. Belleforest cannot seriously have believed that, but he might be using rhetoric as a cover for a bit of folklore. The Ghost seems to be already walk-ing. No wonder it told Hamlet to hurry up.

4 *Macbeth*

J. Dover Wilson's arguments, in his edition of the play (1947), for an early revision by Shakespeare himself, designed to shorten it for a Court performance, seem to me valuable but untrue. Valuable, that is, because they draw attention to points you do not easily notice otherwise, and untrue because these points add to the dramatic effect when noticed: it is therefore unnecessary to suppose they are confusions due to revision.

All this is separate from the generally accepted opinion, not questioned either by Dover Wilson or myself, that the scenes and passages involving Hecate were added by Shakespeare especially to please James I. Admittedly, if that is so, it makes an unusually short play even shorter; and many critics have used that as an argument for believing in substantial cuts. I don't mean to deny the possibility, but don't feel that much can be built on it. In any case, the play gives great opportunities for trick staging with the witches (they always had a resinous white smoke, says Dover Wilson, but didn't start flying on wires till after Ariel had done it in *The Tempest*; a year or two later, on his dating, than Middleton's first vulgarisation of *Macbeth* in 1610); it was probably altered a little whenever it was done with new machinery. It doesn't seem likely that the audience would complain of being given short measure, and surely that would be the only practical objection to a short text.

However, if I may chatter about my prejudices at once, so as to help the reader's work of judging my whole position, I do feel sympathetic to a theory which would put the first draft of the play earlier. *Macbeth* is now generally put later than *Lear*, but it seems much more satisfactory to have *Lear* at the end of the main tragic series; as a matter, that is, of the development of Shakespeare's thought and feeling, and this seems to me a stronger argument than the one from style which has also been plausibly advanced. You then have some kind of breakdown after *Lear*,

137

rather accidentally recorded in *Timon*, and then a recovery which always remained in some important way partial, so that after this recovery he always felt somehow above his characters, even in *Antony and Cleopatra* never again really part of them. He could have fallen back on an old style, presumably, merely because it suited the case in hand; but what you are really trying to envisage is an entire development under heavy pressure. However, this kind of thing only makes me want to put *Macbeth* before *Lear* and after *Othello*; I don't see that there is a strong argument, either from style or development, to help Dover Wilson in trying to put the first draft of the play considerably earlier.

On his general thesis, that many Shakespeare plays bear marks of repeated revision, I feel less inclined to prattle about the psychology of the Bard; it is a delightful occupation, but the guesses are so liable to cancel one another out. One would think he had neither the time nor the inclination for revising, but the more you make him careless about his old work the more possible it seems that he threw away the perfect first version of *Macbeth* just to get through one Court performance quick enough. What does seem to me incredible is that the Company would allow him to do it; the decision rested with them, and it was not at all in their interest. They made their money out of the public performances, and only needed the Court for protection; at least this is commonly accepted, though perhaps one could argue that James was paying much more than Elizabeth had done (the evidence given by Harbage, for instance, seems to deal mainly with Elizabeth): but anyway the public performances were still important to them. The Globe audience was going to demand to see a play all the more after it had been honoured by performance at Court, and that audience would demand the full text – they wouldn't even know what the Court cuts had been. Dover Wilson describes many other details of procedure, but he never I think explains exactly how a full Shakespeare text so often got lost after a performance at Court; and for that matter why, if the surviving bits of *Measure for Measure* had to be dragged up to full length by a hack for the public stages after this process, the same did not have to be done for *Macbeth* too. One can hardly suppose it was left for Middleton four years later; these fighting little theatres were on a repertory basis. I presume he means they all got too drunk to carry the text home (though not their individual parts in some cases); a plausible theory, because James does seem to have gone in for tossing the drink around; but surely somebody could have been sent home with the full text, even if they had risked bringing it with them. There were plenty of servants about; one wouldn't think the actors were mingling with the throng very much anyway; surely they could manage to get drunk without losing the most important bit of property they had brought. They were rather property-minded characters. You can imagine it happening once, but there would be a good deal of fuss about not letting it happen again.

The only standard argument for putting *Macbeth* later than *Lear* seems to be the Porter's joke about equivocation, which is held to be a direct reference, beyond doubt, to the trial of the leading Jesuit Garnet from the end of March 1606 onwards (that is, none of the other arguments seem to me decisive). One cannot simply reply that the joke was added when it was topical, because it fits in with so major a cry as Macbeth saying "I now begin / To doubt the equivocation of the fiend", let alone minor phrases which merely echo the story; they cannot all have been added later, because that assumes a dramatist who didn't know what he was writing about to start with. However, I think it is dangerous in this process of dating to neglect the element of luck; in fact it seems fair to be rather superstitious about the luck of a man of genius, in such matters, because he can feel somehow what is going to become "topical". Obviously the idea that equivocation is important and harmful and above all protean did not simply become discovered at the trial of Garnet; it would be as plausible to say that the trial went off as it did because that was felt (these state trials of course were as elaborately prepared beforehand as any in recent history). The echoes of the Shakespeare play in other people's plays, usually called in evidence, come very soon after the trial – while it was topical; provokingly soon if you want to argue that Shakespeare had rushed out his masterpiece in between. Indeed the current theory, as I understand,makes him not merely write it but prepare it for a Court performance (with elaborate business presumably) between May and early August of 1606; surely that amount of pace is too hot. And on the other hand none of these echoes come early enough to support the pre-equivocation draft of 1602 posited by Dover Wilson. I think Shakespeare simply got in first with this topic, in 1605, and did not have to add anything to make it look startlingly topical in its second year. It was already about what was really happening; for that matter, I should think it just comfortably predated the actual Gunpowder Plot affair.

By the way, Dover Wilson's argument that the prattle of the child Macduff must be a later insertion intended as a reference to the Garnet trial (because he says a traitor means one who "swears and lies") does seem to me absurd. The argument is that the child uses the word in a different sense from that of Ross, who has just said it, so the effect is artificial and can't have been in the first draft; but obviously children often do do that. This seemed to need fitting in here, but I wish to avoid fussing about trivialities; probably no one would deny that there may have been cuts and insertions by Shakespeare. The very specific proposals of Dover Wilson about what was cut are what I want to examine here.

In the first place, he feels that the murder of Duncan comes too quickly, or anyway abnormally quickly; the hesitation of Macbeth is a key dramatic effect which in most plays would be given space. This is true, but the whole point about Macbeth is that he is hurried into an ill-considered action, or that he refuses to consider it himself: "let not light see" – "the eye wink at the hand" – "which must be acted ere they may be scanned"; the play is crowded with such phrases, and its prevailing darkness is a symbol of his refusal to see the consequences of his actions. These consequences are to be long drawn out, but the choice of killing Duncan is to be shown as the effect of two or three shocks close together. Dover Wilson proposes whole scenes to be added before the murder of Duncan, and I think this would not merely be less "exciting" but off the point of the play. A. C. Bradley, to be sure, has said this already, but I don't think he recognised enough the "psychology" as the contemporary audience would see it, which was rather what we now call "existentialist". Problems about free will, which are raised particularly sharply by prophetic witches, were much in the air, and also the idea of the speed with which the self-blinded soul could be damned. One might perhaps imagine that Shakespeare cut down his first version to get the right effect, but that he really intended the effect, and wasn't merely pushed into it by a Court performance, seems hard to doubt.

Some remarks by Dover Wilson on the state of mind of Macbeth, which only bear indirectly on the question of cuts, had better be looked at next. Murderous thoughts, we are told, first come to him, not before the play nor yet on hearing the prophecy, but on hearing that he has become Thane of Cawdor so that half of the prophecy has been fulfilled. The temptation fills him with horror: "the symptoms would be meaningless" unless he were "an innocent spirit reeling under an utterly unforeseen attack". This first assault of the Tempter is viewed in moral terms, and Macbeth repels it as such, but the idea continues to "mine unseen". When Duncan appoints Malcolm his heir, though the deed seems as terrible as ever, Macbeth "has moved appreciably nearer to it". I should have thought he clearly plans to do it: the words are:

> Stars, hide your fires;
> Let not light see my black and deep desires:
> The eye wink at the hand: yet let that be
> Which the eye fears, when it is done, to see.

The chief thought here, surely, as in all these habitual metaphors of darkness, is that Macbeth wants somehow to get away from or hoodwink his consciousness and self-knowledge and do the deed without knowing it. His first meeting with his wife helps forward this process, as Dover Wilson agrees. But by the stage of the I.vii soliloquy ("if it were done . . . ") he has reached "a new stage of his disease"; he is thinking not morally but purely from self-interest, says Dover Wilson. Yet "the voice of the good angel can still be heard by us, though not by Macbeth, speaking through the poetry which reveals his sub-conscious mind". (A. C. Bradley ought to be given credit here, I think.) The proof that his objections are now only prudential is that those are the only ones he makes to his wife (but they are the only ones he *dares* make) and this is why he is won over by her plan to hide the murder – though obviously open to suspicion, it gives him "the talisman his soul craves", an *appearance* of safety (so far from that, it seems to me, what wins him over is her reckless courage). After the murder he has no morality but only bad dreams of being assassinated, which drive him on from crime to crime (but it is the suppressed feeling of guilt, surely, which emerges as neurotic fear – that is *how* he is "possessed", if you regard him as possessed).

All this discussion about when he is thinking "morally" seems to me to ignore the central fact that there are two moral systems in view, even though one of them is firmly called a bad system. When the witches lead off with "fair is foul and foul is fair" they are wicked; but when Macbeth says their soliciting "cannot be good, cannot be ill" he is in real doubt; and the first soliloquy of Lady Macbeth is presented as a quite laborious and earnest inversion of moral values. The Machiavellian or the Ambitious Man has his moral struggles no less than the Christian or the loyal feudalist, and what prevents Macbeth from confessing his scruples to his wife is a genuine moral shame.

> Thou wouldst be great,
> Art not without ambition, but without
> The illness should attend it; what thou wouldst highly
> That thou wouldst holily,

and so on, is not meant merely as obvious moral paradox from the author but as real moral blame from the deluded speaker; a man *should* be ambitious and *should* have the "illness" required for success in that line of effort; it is good to will highly, and slavish to will "holily". The inversion of moral values is sketched as an actual system of belief, and given strength by being tied to the supreme virtue of courage. Of course it is presented as both wicked and fallacious, but also as a thing that some people feel. (Dover Wilson indeed makes this point himself, by saying that she regards the private murder as a glorious act, just as Macbeth does killing in battle. But Macbeth is involved in this puzzle too, as is rubbed in by the irony of "nothing affeared of what thyself didst make, strange images of death".) There is a good deal of truth, in fact, in the Victorian joke that the Macbeths commit the murder as a painful duty. Indeed they never seem to regard royalty as a source of pleasure at all. Lady Macbeth regards the crown as an "ornament", a satisfaction to pride; and Macbeth says in so many words, "I have no spur / To prick the sides of my intent, but only / Vaulting ambition, which o'er-leaps itself." Unless you regard this moral paradox as already obvious, given from the start, it is natural to feel that the characters are practically unmotivated and must have been explained in early passages which are now cut.

The great question "How many children had Lady Macbeth?" had better be fitted in here. The question cannot be regarded as merely farcical, as one might say, "Who wants children anyhow?" Macbeth is far more concerned to found a royal line than to be King himself; he howls on and on against the threat that his descendants will be supplanted by Banquo's. When Lady Macbeth says she would kill her child she is felt to be ridiculous as well as devilish, because without a child the main purpose would be defeated. But the murdered or the helpless child comes echoing back into the play all through (as Cleanth Brooks pointed out); it is the one thing strong enough to defeat Macbeth and the whole philosophy he has adopted. In the story, however, we are left in doubt whether the Macbeths have any children; it would be symbolically appropriate if they hadn't, but Macbeth's talk would be absurd unless they have, as perhaps it is; and there the matter is left. It is the only crux in the play, I think, which need be regarded as a radical dramatic ambiguity.

The first of Dover Wilson's arguments for a cut scene is what he calls the "ambiguity" of Banquo. A. C. Bradley remarked that only Banquo knew what the witches had told Macbeth, and by keeping silent after the murder, though suspicious in soliloquy, he "yielded to evil". Dover Wilson says that this "shows Bradley at his weakest", because Shakespeare could not possibly have intended to show to James I the supposed founder of his line as a criminal. Besides, James believed in the Divine Right of Kings, even of usurpers once legally crowned, and would have thought Banquo's behaviour merely correct. Exactly; the King would find nothing to complain about, and other persons in the audience could look at the character in other ways – surely this second point of Dover Wilson destroys his previous argument that a scene has been cut. Besides, if James was the person to whom Banquo needed justifying, it is absurd to suppose that the scene justifying him was cut out precisely to suit performance before James.

It seems to me, in any case, that all the lords are meant to be "ambiguous", in the quite flat vague sense that we feel any of them may be playing his own game during this period of confusion, though we never get it clear. "Cruel are the times, when we are traitors, and do not know ourselves" – the point could hardly be rubbed in more firmly, with even the child Macduff prattling about whether his father is a traitor too. It is not merely a literary effect; it is what people really do feel in times of civil war, and Shakespeare had a practical and lasting fear of civil war. The witches say it is "fog" in the first scene, and fog it remains not only in Macbeth's mind but in all the nobles'; we are given two sheer scenes (II.iv and III.vi) of suspicious gossip between persons hardly worth naming, to intensify the thing merely. Ross in the first of these scenes is clearly telling lies to Old Man. Old Man tells a prodigious story about what the birds did on the night

Duncan was murdered, so Ross says on that night Duncan's horses turned wild in nature and began kicking their stalls down. "Tis said they ate each other" says eager Old Man, and Ross says "They did so, to the amazement of my eyes / That looked upon it. Here comes the good Macduff." Surely even a very superstitious audience would realise that he has waited to see how much Old Man will swallow; he is "spreading alarm and despondency". But this isn't meant to reduce the magic of the play to farce; the idea is that a fog of evil really has got abroad, and as likely as not did produce prodigies; the fact that Ross is telling lies about them only makes it all worse. In short, I believe that the various muddles which have occupied the minds of critics (the kind of thing which allowed the Victorian Libby to produce a rather impressive argument that Ross was the villain all through) were deliberately planned to keep the audience guessing but fogged.

On this basis, I think, we can advance with tolerable firmness upon the baffling confusions about the previous Thane of Cawdor. At the beginning of the play messengers arrive from two battlefields; they speak obscurely, but we learn that Cawdor was assisting the King of Norway, who was at the southern battlefield. We then see Macbeth returning from the northern battlefield; he is met by Ross and Angus, who are sent to tell him he has been given the thaneship of Cawdor, and he has never heard of the treachery of Cawdor; Angus says he doesn't know whether Cawdor "was combined / With those of Norway, or did line the rebel / With hidden help and vantage"; and Ross says nothing about it, though he was the messenger from the south in the previous scene. Dover Wilson points out that the prophecy of the witches, that Macbeth will become Thane of Cawdor, "loses half its virtue" if Macbeth has just been fighting Cawdor and knows he is a traitor; but anyhow the audience must be meant to gather that he doesn't know it. "The real explanation", says Dover Wilson (thus I think giving an example of what he calls "Bradley at his weakest", the treatment of a play as a historical document) is that Cawdor had *secretly* helped both the Norwegian invader and the Scotch rebel lord; so this must have been said plainly in one of the cut lines. This rule that secrets have to be said plainly, one is tempted to observe, would lighten the work of the historian if properly carried out. But the historian has still got to worry about how Macbeth managed to fight two decisive battles, practically on the same day, in both Fife and Inverness, north and south of east Scotland and more than a hundred miles apart. The messengers came in almost simultaneously; of course he could conceivably have done it by moving as fast as the messengers – a horse relay system has to be envisaged, though we see him returning from the battle on foot. But there is nothing in the deliberately confused scene I.ii to convince a practical listener that Macbeth went to a new battlefield; so far from that, as soon as he had finished with the rebels (we are told, I.ii.30, by the messenger from the northern battlefield) he and Banquo began to fight the invaders; then Ross comes in from the southern battlefield and never mentions Macbeth, though he uses the peculiar term "Bellona's bridegroom" which practically all commentators assume to mean Macbeth in person. Duncan, to whom these things are told, expresses no interest whatever in the conduct of the campaigns but only attends to the passing phrase about the traitorship of Cawdor, adding that Macbeth shall succeed him. This need not make Duncan look weak; he is dealing with the only immediate essential point. It is only reasonable to suppose that the Norwegians, holding the sea and fully informed by the traitor, would attack at two points at once. I hope I do not appear subtle here; I am trying to follow what the first audiences would make of it. They were very much better-trained than I am on picking up the spoken word; they also thought very keenly, after succeeding in hearing words, along their own lines of military and political strategy. They would certainly notice that Duncan never examines the case of Cawdor, and is only told of Cawdor's confession by his child Malcolm, who may easily have been lied to. I do not mean that there is a *story* about Cawdor to be dug out of the Shakespeare text, only that the fate of the previous Thane of Cawdor (from the point of view of the first listeners) was already made a baffling and fateful thing before Macbeth began to howl out "And therefore Cawdor shall sleep no more, Macbeth shall sleep no more." In fact, everybody feels this; it is the poetry of the thing. All Macbeth's inheritance is appalling; here he inherits from a man who, in spite of a circle of contradictory gossip, remains baffling and is assumed to need no trial. The smashing irony of "There's no art / To find the mind's construction in the face . . . O worthiest cousin" is transferred obviously by Duncan from Cawdor to Macbeth as soon as Macbeth enters. We do not have to worry about Cawdor; he is presumed to be in the usual fog. But his name does sound like Fate in the play, merely because Macbeth has got to be the same kind of thing all over again. Perhaps it is

tedious to say something so obvious; but editors who try to tidy
the play really do need to be told the obvious. So far from being
a cut version of a tidy historical play now unfortunately lost, it is
a rather massive effort, very consistently carried out, to convey
the immense confusion in which these historical events actually
occur.

Various minor arguments are often produced for believing in
cuts, for example the large number of incomplete lines. It seems
to me that they merely give a more dramatic and vigorous
rhythm. The most extreme case of this uneasiness in the editorial
ear is "Toad, that under cold stone," which practically every
editor since Pope has wanted to tinker with because it "doesn't
scan", whereas of course it is a wonderfully powerful sound
effect. However, Dover Wilson is not particularly guilty here;
and one cannot blame his ear for feeling that there is something
peculiar about the beginning of the play – the whole second scene
is pretty close to turgid rant. I think it was needed, however hard
it may be to stomach, just to get enough pace at the beginning;
the audience has to be thrown into a wild and whirling situation
right away. Has to be, that is, if you are going to get to the murder
of Duncan very quickly; certainly, if you are going to put in a lot
of extra scenes before it, you will want a different beginning, but
to argue from one to the other is only to argue in a circle. The
same applies to the complaints of editors about the "abruptness"
of scene iv, the way Duncan weeps for joy over the loyalty of
Macbeth, dooms himself by making Malcolm his heir, and
arranges an immediate death by inviting himself to Macbeth's
castle, actually in three consecutive sentences. Surely it is absurd
to say that this masterly piece of compression cannot have been
intended, merely *because* it is so compressed. You might as well
say that Wagner must have composed the first draft of his music
for a single flute, because he cannot have intended to be so noisy.
As to the arguments that the audience needs to be told where
Macbeth's castle is before Duncan says "from hence to
Inverness", so that an earlier passage must have been cut – the
audience are told it in the next sentence; as soon as their interest
in the subject has been aroused. As to the arguments that the
appearance of a third murderer for Banquo, and Macduff's
desertion of his wife and family, are puzzling and therefore must
have been prepared for in earlier passages now cut – of course,
they are *meant* to seem puzzling; they are part of the general
atmosphere of fog and suspicion.

Dover Wilson speaks with great confidence about a passage in Malcolm's curious scene of self-accusation:

> Nay, had I power, I should
> Pour the sweet milk of concord into hell,

and so on. "That here we have an instance of re-writing after the completion of the original dialogue cannot, I think, be denied", he says, and the reason is that the passage is aimed at pleasing James; instead of following Holinshed and accusing himself of falsehood, he accuses himself of contentiousness, "a strange vice and expressed in strangely modern terms", says Dover Wilson (oddly), but this would please James who was a pacifist. The change was made "because Shakespeare had come to know more of his royal master's mind in the interval". This seems to me a really remarkable case of arguing in a circle. Dover Wilson himself suggests that Shakespeare went to Edinburgh in 1602 or so and wrote the first draft of the play there specifically to curry favour with a possible future King of England; if this is true, it seems quite unnecessary to suppose he had to learn a rather prominent fact about the mind of James four years later. In any case, the mind of Shakespeare himself can reasonably be considered when we wonder why he wrote something down. He thought civil war a real and horrible danger, and he was right in fearing it would come; we need not suppose he was lying to flatter the King when he says it here. And he hardly alters the Holinshed moral anecdote at all, from this point of view; he merely illustrates it. The objection to lying in kings is that by lying they make people quarrel; you don't want a child's copybook rule against lying here, you want to relate the harmfulness of lying to the appalling scene before you; and that is all he does. Surely it is absurd for Dover Wilson to call this a case where revision "cannot be denied".

However, his major thesis does not turn on these dubious minor points; it raises two important questions, and many people will feel it to give them probable and reasonable answers. He maintains that the full play of *Macbeth* gave a much more prolonged struggle between Macbeth and his wife, in which things that now seem baffling to a careful reader, if not to an audience, were given intelligible preparation. I do not want to treat this as absurd; in fact it seems rather wilful to argue, as I am now doing, that the first part of the play was intended to be as thin and confused as so many critics have found the existing text. On the other hand, since we cannot recover these lost scenes if there were any, it does seem at least tolerably useful to show that we can get along without them; and I think that to answer the two questions on that basis (chiefly, of course, by collecting previous opinions) improves or restores the play a good deal.

The first main argument is that Lady Macbeth, in her second soliloquy and her first two conversations with her husband, repeatedly says or appears to say that she is going to kill Duncan herself; but then without further explanation it turns out that both she and Macbeth assume Macbeth is going to do it. It does seem likely that this change of plan would at least have been mentioned. By the way, what seems to me a more immediate argument for some cut in I.vii is that she makes Macbeth change his mind so ridiculously quickly; he says with apparently settled conviction "We will proceed no further in this business", and within thirty lines he is merely asking for a good plan. The answer here, surely, is that all poetic drama uses poetry as a substitute for repetition of arguments and "sleeping on" a problem and such like; the convention feels natural because it is clearly what the stage requires – the characters talk so powerfully that the story can move forward. In real life the Macbeths would argue for half the night, but the audience is actually presented with the morning after a few minutes of action. Here you might possibly invent some arrangement about the time, but the same device is used later in the play with no break at all; the banquet at which Banquo's ghost appears leads us on to dawn in a few minutes, and this seems a natural consequence of the brief exhausted worrying of the Macbeth couple after dismissing their guests. These conventions of course have been much discussed, and they are not questioned here by Dover Wilson. I wanted to remark that we should only accept Elizabethan conventions if they are in a sense natural, that is, such as modern actors and producers can make an audience accept. It is off the point to list "the Elizabethan conventions", as some critics have done; because the Elizabethans did not formulate such things and rather imagined they were free from them. In the case of Lady Macbeth, we can say that the mere force of her two speeches is enough to prevent Macbeth from looking too ridiculous; but also that, even if it isn't, the main point of the story is that he let himself be hurried into a wrong decision.

The second main argument, from the same scene, is that she scolds him because, though unwilling to do the murder now that "time" and "place . . . adhere", he had been willing to promise he would do it when he needn't act, and she finds this a typical mark of cowardice. It seems obvious to deduce that the promise was made before the battle, therefore of course before the meeting with the witches; but Dover Wilson maintains that this would spoil the whole shock of their prophecy. He therefore argues that Macbeth must have visited his wife after seeing the witches and before reporting to the King on his conduct in the battle; a scene has therefore been cut. But a definite geography can be fitted together; Macbeth has been fighting near the east coast, because the Norwegian invader could throw in fresh troops when the rebel was defeated; he walks westwards to the King's head-quarters to report; and his wife is in his castle at Inverness, a day's ride to the west again. He has a positive duty to report to the King before going to her. Surely this kind of point was firm in the Elizabethan mind, however foggy everything else was made. (Even if you are determined to have him gallop between the two battlefields instead of staying at one of them, he still has an obli-gation to report before he goes home.) In this scene with his wife, now lost, says Dover Wilson, he must have sworn he would kill Duncan when occasion arose, and she in her turn must have insisted, probably using her now misplaced invocation to the "spirits that / tend on mortal thoughts", that she would do it her-self. In our text "I.v", jammed together from bits of the lost scenes, she is still assuming she will do it herself; and the change of plan by which Macbeth does it, says Dover Wilson,

ought by all dramatic rights to be explained to the audience. This was originally done, I suggest, by means of a further dialogue between hus-band and wife, preceded perhaps by a scene in which, going into the bed-room knife in hand, she cannot bring herself to do it.

So three whole scenes are to be added before we finish with Duncan. The first objection, I think, must be that this pains-taking treatment would throw away the whole impression of "fog" which has been established at the start; the impression, that is, of a fatal decision made hurriedly in confusion. The play that Dover Wilson is imagining, or rather not imagining, would be like a "debate" by Racine. Also I do not see why, in the first of these lost scenes, Lady Macbeth insisted that *she* would kill Duncan, if the whole point of the scene was to make *him* swear he would do it. Also the arguments keep on being drawn from our existing text as though it were the original text, though that is what is being denied; if Lady Macbeth *didn't* say she would kill Duncan as late as our "I.v" (because her remarks to that effect have been dragged in from an earlier scene) then you can't require further scenes which presume that she *did* say it. However, this amount of confusion might be justified. What does seem clear is that the play supposed by Dover Wilson would not do what *Macbeth* does. I suspect he would have two jealous hell-hounds, each of them greedy to be first at the kill. In any case, he would not have an atmosphere of wincing and horrified determination, in which a crucial decision is scrambled through hurriedly and confusedly.

Before reaching this bold theory, Dover Wilson recalls various older suggestions about why Lady Macbeth says Macbeth had broached the enterprise before:

(1) on psychological grounds as a bold lie or as an exaggeration, based on his letter to her, and (2) on technical grounds, as an "episodic intensification" like the allusion to Lady Macbeth's children, or as a piece of dramatic legerdemain resorted to in order to stress at this juncture the less admirable side of Macbeth's character. The trouble with this last explanation, in some ways the most plausible of the four, is that as no spectator or reader apparently observed the point until 1865, it can hardly have been intended to stress anything.

But surely it can add to the atmosphere without the critics arguing about it first; both the actors and the audience are always doing a great deal of "interpretation" which doesn't get written down. I am anxious not to ignore these partial ways of swallowing the effect, without which it would no doubt have long been felt as obtrusively confused. Instead of that it feels like a fierce strain on your attention, intelligible somehow but intensely far from common life – new factors keep being thrown in. To that extent it should I think be called a "dramatic ambiguity"; but all the same I think the text here is meant to yield one straightforward story about what happened.

If we take "I.vii" as it stands, surely we have to believe that Macbeth *did* broach the enterprise to his wife before the battle and before meeting the witches, and before the play; what is more, we have to feel that this belated piece of news about Macbeth is credible on the spot, though it comes as a dramatic surprise. Lady Macbeth goes on to hint that he was half drunk at the time. At least, I am not sure that her metaphor in itself need carry much weight, but an actor could easily emphasise the lines so as to make it prominent:

> Was the hope drunk
> Wherein you dressed yourself? Hath it slept since
> And wakes it now, to look so green and pale . . .

It is not hard to believe that she could drink with him till he talked rashly; she boasts very soon after that she drank the grooms under the table and was only made bold by it. The argument against believing in this previous conversation, according to Dover Wilson, is that the first witch scene, "depicts the terror of Macbeth's soul when the idea of murder *first* comes to him", and the first speech of his wife "makes it clear that so far he has refused to entertain any but honourable thoughts". As to the second point, she only makes clear that he has been deciding *against* the murder; how can she know all this, about how much he wants to do it, and fears to do it, if they have never mentioned the subject to each other? No doubt in real life she could, but surely the dramatic impression is that this kind of topic is practically the small talk of the Macbeth household. As to the first point, which I agree is stronger and must be answered by imposing a greater dramatic strain, it is a commonplace that Macbeth and Banquo react quite differently to the witches. Banquo is needed in the scene as the innocent mind, which accepts the prophecy about himself as merely a statement about the future; Macbeth, because he already has murder in view, immediately accepts *his* part of the prophecy as a kind of order that he must bring it about. What horrifies him so much is that the witches appear as an externalisation of his secret, guilty daydreams; partly he feels exposed, but even worse he feels that the imaginary world has become real and must now be acted upon. The reaction is immediate; the sequence is:

3. Witch All hail, Macbeth! that shalt be king hereafter.
Banquo Good sir, why do you start, and seem to fear
       Things that do sound so fair?

and almost his first words alone call it "this supernatural *soliciting*"; whereas so far from tempting him to act, they have if anything told him that there is no need for action; he is sure to become King. This actually occurs to him a few lines later ("If chance will have me king, why chance may crown me, / Without my stir"), and he seems to throw the idea aside till Duncan appoints Malcolm his next heir. Then it comes back to him

strongly, but he has already begun to waver away from it again by
the time he meets his wife. Incidentally, the phrase "my thought,
whose murder yet is but fantastical" does not sound to me as if
the thought first came into his mind a few moments ago; the point
is rather "in spite of hearing the witches just now, my thought is
still only imaginary; the fatal decision has still not been taken".
Surely none of it sounds like a man who has never thought of such
a thing before. Bradley makes most of the points along this line,
and I feel Dover Wilson ought to have done more to recognise
them. But he might still say that they are the "weak side" of
Bradley, deductions in the study which are ineffective on the
stage. I do not agree, though no doubt the effect depends largely
on the actor and the production. We are not meant, probably, to
decide in the first witch scene that Macbeth has already discussed
the murder; but we are meant to be in a position to reflect, when
his wife brings out her accusation, "after all, he didn't act like a
man to whom the idea was new, such as Banquo, and he has gone
on wavering ever since; she is probably exaggerating, but they
probably have talked about it before".

This seems to me an important point, because if accepted it
would clear up a lot of muddling about the idea of Fate, which has
become almost habitual in critical writing on *Macbeth*. Shakespeare I think always uses the word with a fairly clear suggestion
that it stands for an excuse, and for his audience it was at best a
learned classical idea, not one that they couldn't avoid taking
seriously. The dramatic trick, in the structure of the first Act of
Macbeth, is that the audience is put through what appears to be
an experience of Fate but is then expected to think more sensibly.
The audience is anyway expected to be frightened by the witches,
and during the first meeting of Macbeth with the witches the
audience might as it were be stampeded into the immediately
plausible theory of Dover Wilson, that Macbeth had an innocent
mind before now but has at once been forced into a damnable
intention by a supernatural power. But afterwards, listening to
Lady Macbeth, and no longer frightened by the witches, they are
to recover their theology; they should think "Yes, after all, a
witch *couldn't* have made him do it, unless he had weakened his
own will before." "Compare the case of Banquo", they could go
on; and this line of thought was not difficult for them, because
they had assumed Macbeth to be wicked before they came; their
chief engagement in the witch scenes would be from puzzles
about the limitations of the powers of devils and the free will of

man. That the self-blinded soul would fall fast when pushed by witches would still be a natural expectation, fulfilled by the dramatic structure. I don't say that a modern producer could easily recover this movement of thought, but it does prevent what I have just called "a dramatic trick" from being a mere cheat.

The strongest modern attack on *Macbeth* was made by Robert Bridges, whose central charge was this:

It would not be untrue to the facts as Shakespeare presents them to precede the drama with a scene in which Macbeth and Lady Macbeth should in Machiavellian composure deliberate together upon the murder of Duncan, but plainly such a scene would destroy the drama.

A simple distinction is needed here; to act such a scene would destroy the sequence of feelings which the audience is meant to go through, but to believe that it happened doesn't destroy the drama, in fact the audience are meant to have come round to that (apart from the "composure") by the end of the first Act. A certain amount of surprise is quite usual in plays; what Bridges seems to have felt is the old Puritanical objection to all plays, that they don't tell all the truth all the time.

Macbeth's first meeting with his wife in the play (end of I.v) requires good acting. He is gravely shaken by the thought of guilt but has still not decided to incur it. He leaves it to her to raise the topic at all. She can see just what he is feeling, and begins at once to twist him into action. She pretends that the indecision and conscience in his face are merely the outward marks of a savage determination; let him hide them, and there will be no more trouble. It is too much effort for him to start to unwind this misunderstanding; he merely says it will have to be discussed later. But meanwhile his wife, who knows he is going to say this, has cut the ground from under him by implying that *she* is going to do the murder, so he needn't worry about it again. She does not however say this in so many words, and no doubt assumes that he will not be able to leave her carrying all the burden. The words are framed with a grim and triumphant ambiguity, as is obvious at once, but one does not easily notice that the ambiguity carries this twist of personal argument as well:

> He that's coming
> Must be provided for; and you shall put
> This night's great business into my dispatch,

> Which shall to all our nights and days to come
> Give solely sovereign sway and masterdom.

The whole thrill of the first phrase is that it means "I have to do my housework next; I have to get ready a grand dinner-party; don't you worry, you have only to keep your face straight" as well as "somebody has to *plan* how to kill the guest"; but neither idea says quite positively that she will do the killing. It is true, of course, that her soliloquy just before has prayed for cruelty enough to use a knife, which she rightly fears she may not have; but this is a matter of preparing enough determination for her share in the murder, not of saying she is determined to reject the help of her husband. The balance of the thing seems to me to be kept just right.[1]

The next great scene between them is in I.vii, after Macbeth has said "We will proceed no further in this business." She has to rally all her powers, makes a variety of accusations against him for *not* being ready to do it, and says she would have killed her baby *if* she had sworn to kill it as Macbeth has sworn to kill Duncan; she never says that *she* has sworn to kill Duncan. But there is again the obscure threat against him, very hard for him to stand up against, that perhaps if he refuses he will only be thrusting the work upon *her*. Macbeth's first words when he yields are "If *we* should fail" and from then on they both assume they will work together. Finally in II.ii, after making the chamberlains drunk and leaving the daggers beside them, she remarks that she thought of doing it herself before Macbeth came, but found she couldn't; she had already planned for him to come, and has only to ring a bell to bring him.

This seems to me a consistent story, not leaving any need for three extra scenes that would destroy the pace; hard to get across in the acting, no doubt, but that need not astonish us. The curious thing, rather typical of the combination of grasp of mind with wilfulness in Dover Wilson, is that he admits nearly all of it himself. It is agreed that Macbeth's mind has been "rendered temptable by previous dalliance of that fancy with ambitious thoughts"; it is agreed that, by offering to do the murder, his wife "leads him unconsciously forward by removing from his path the terror that

---

[1] As to the much discussed problem about whether Lady Macbeth "really" faints, it seems to me quite invisible; she probably wouldn't know herself. She is only keeping going by an effort of will, and she can see that this is a good time to stop the effort.

immediately confronts him". Perhaps it is unnecessary to answer at such length a theory to which its propounder, very fairly, has already given the essential answers.

II

It struck me that this essay seemed rather too confident, so I turned to a work of attractive confidence and vigour by J. M. Robertson, *Literary Detection* (1931), concerned to prove that a great variety of hands mangled the play of *Macbeth* incessantly from its first drafting by Kyd; very depressing to read, naturally. The great days of Disintegration are over, but the subject cannot be ignored; I noticed G. B. Harrison recently (*Shakespeare's Tragedies*, 1951) saying that the collaborator must have written such things as

> Thoughts speculative their unsure hopes relate,
> But certain issue strokes must arbitrate.

We need not pretend it is good, but I think that Shakespeare, a peaceable man, was usually embarrassed when he had to write something particularly soldierly; it is rather the same even with Fortinbras. Also one cannot call the theatrical effect bad; these laboured confusing patches somehow add to the wild foggy background. We cannot say they are certainly not Shakespeare's because they aren't in "his style".

The main argument for disintegration is from "tags" or repeated phrases, and the results seem valuable in showing what a large common stock the Elizabethans could draw upon. Robertson assumes that a "tag" could not be repeated unless deliberately, and uses such phrases as "Shakespeare does not go about picking from Kyd in general". I think he often echoed Kyd, but without noticing it, and would only have been mildly interested if you had told him so. The fact that what amounts to "Give me the daggers" is said by a woman in both *Soliman and Perseda* and *Arden of Faversham* seems worth knowing as part of the mental background of the audience (for instance, it shows they would not find Lady Macbeth incredible); but we need not think Shakespeare would avoid repeating it. Indeed a dramatist who worked under such a taboo would have to become very eccentric. We might go so far as to deduce that Shakespeare did not despise the Kyd part of his background.

Many of the objections of Robertson seem to me worth

answering but in no need of so startling an answer; for example, "the man who can see nothing absurd in the blood-boltered Sergeant ploughing his gory way from Fife up to Forres, ahead of the mounted nobles, is capable of any bluff" (since it is about 150 miles). But it is enough to assume there were two battles, with Macbeth and the Sergeant at the near one; a natural presumption from the two messengers – I don't deny that a line or two making it clearer may have got cut. The "aside" of Macbeth at the end of "I.iv", announcing his treachery to the King in Council, is absurd in itself and "the couplets are utterly out of place in an aside" – a good point, but it isn't meant to be an "aside"; it is a soliloquy on the apron-stage after the Council scene is over. "Shakespeare never brought the primary exposition of Macbeth's growth of purpose to clearness because he was hampered by a composite recast of an old play." But there is a positive merit in having his growth of purpose a mystery which only gradually clears. "The juggling cauldron stuff is extraneous to the very idea of Fate", therefore can't be Shakespeare's; "what the play needed, for him, in that kind, was just the really thrilling sense of 'Fate and metaphysical aid'". The devil, in short, ought to be presented as a gentleman; I think Shakespeare hadn't got all this respect for Fate, and would regard the sordidness of the witches as a traditional and proper thing to show about them.

The undue refinement in this last case is perhaps a natural result of no longer believing in the witches; I agree that they can't be seen in their original proportions by a modern audience. But I think a certain wincing away from the play causes many of Robertson's other objections, as in the sustained argument that the Porter's scene cannot be Shakespeare's. Middleton's *Blurt Master-Constable* makes the servant of a prostitute say "I am porter in Hell", so Middleton wrote it. But the familiarity of the idea was no objection to it; the audience would only see the point more readily. And the idea is not merely to provide "comic relief", which Robertson easily shows wasn't always required. The idea is that the servants regarded the victory and the visit of the King as an occasion for a gaudy night; only their masters regarded it as an occasion to enter Hell.

The repeated use of theatrical couplets at the ends of the scenes appeared particularly vulgar to Robertson, and he throws out a number of them which seem to me to sum up the thought of the play particularly vividly, such as

> The eye wink at the hand; yet let that be
> Which the eye fears, when it is done, to see.

and even "Hover through the fog and filthy air" is called a "vacuous tag-line", though it establishes from the start the theme of fog that Robertson always ignores. Even the central lines

> But cruel are the times, when we are traitors
> And do not know ourselves, when we hold rumour
> From what we fear, yet know not what we fear,
> But float upon a wild and violent sea,
> Each way, and move

are said to be certainly not Shakespeare's because they have "no sense". Here one must lose patience, I think; no one who had experienced civil war could say it had no sense. I find I take *know ourselves* to mean chiefly "ourselves know", as with a comma between the words, but "know the right name for our actions, and therefore in some degree our own natures" is also prominent; *hold rumour* could be like "hold parley with", be ready to entertain such a rumour, or simply "hold onto it" by believing it; the compactness is rather strained but surely not unlike Shakespeare. I still feel strongly what I said about *move* here in my *Ambiguity* (end of Chap. II) but the passage is still very good even if you regard it as incomplete or are determined to emend "move" to "none".

Robertson takes "Before my body / I throw my warlike shield" as admittedly intolerable, known even by its defenders to be very bad; he jeers at E. K. Chambers for saying one could not deny it to Shakespeare merely on grounds of style, and says "Chambers does not distinguish between the sense of style and the sense of sense". This case seems worth attention, because I suspect the trouble is merely that the critics don't see the point. "I will not yield" and so on, says Macbeth,

> Though Birnam Wood *be* come to Dunsinane,
> And thou opposed, *being* of no woman born,
> Yet I will try the last; before my body
> I throw my warlike *shield*. Lay on, Macduff,
> And damned be he that first cries "hold, enough".

The argument is "*although* the protections promised by the witches have failed me, *yet* I will try the bodily protection which is all I have left"; once you notice this idea, surely, you have nothing to grumble about.

5   The Globe Theatre

Many good things have been destroyed in our time; the procedure ought not to feel surprising; and yet it seems gratuitous to
have the standard techniques of propaganda used against the
equipment of Shakespeare's theatre. The busy work has been
going on for twenty or thirty years now, especially against the use
of an upper and inner stage; and this offers a good occasion for
the looney quality which seems essential to propaganda, because
nobody could read the plays with the original stage directions
without finding that they treat the "above" and the "within" as a
matter of course. This indeed is how our standard views of the
Elizabethan stage have been built up – they had to be, because
we are extremely short of information otherwise; but the
opponents, as I understand, maintain that such work (using
insight and intuition and what not) does not count as evidence at
all. What the authors *say*, and even what they can be felt to
intend, is probably only medieval symbolism or something; the
Devil alone knoweth the heart of man. But the impressions of a
foreigner during a brief visit to London, as sketched by a friend
who had never been there, and could not draw – that's real hard
evidence; "we have no *right*" to belittle it, they say (but any stage
with a back to it has a central aperture, the place for a grand
entry). I suspect that the Wimsatt Law, which says a reader must
never understand the intention of an author, has been at its fell
work here too. A strange collapse of the sense of reality, another
failure of nerve, has been going on. There is no agreement on any
alternative plan among the attackers; they operate on various
fronts, though nearly always with the same virulence and
unreason. Thus some would allow the occasional use of an upper
stage, only maintaining that it was tiny, ineffective, impossible to
see into. One of the reasons offered for this arrangement (which

158

no designer could have preferred) was that Elizabethan carpenters could only build small cells, like bees, so that their "above" could only be 3 or 4 feet long. And meanwhile all around this sad little object extended the tall galleries ("vast" was what Dekker called them) built for the spectators. This is my favourite example, and I am sorry to have lost the reference; it has the genuine reek of high-pressure wartime propaganda.

I can believe that there was a good motive behind all this, though in many cases it must have been working unconsciously. The J. C. Adams version of the Globe Theatre had come to be felt, by a wide variety of people, as failing to satisfy the high expectations that had been formed. This version (*The Globe Playhouse*, 1942, revised second edition, 1961) is so far ahead of the others that it is automatically what people attack if they attack the traditional Globe, and it really is a magnificent reconstruction, meant of course to include all previous good ideas. But it needs to be altered at two or three crucial points, most of them familiar, though I think I have one new idea. We need not really be surprised that this debate takes upon itself some of the confusions of an election. Many people feel that the theatre of Shakespeare should be a kind of model. Though holding a mass audience, it was intimate, human, fast-moving, passionately real though without any fuss about stage illusion, and all this made it very democratic. Of course some critics want to refute the picture and prove that he wrote for the palace or for stately homes, but they still regard it in political terms. The disillusion with Adams began, apparently not long after his first publication, among theatrical producers, and was not in political terms; a few of them made attempts at trying it out, and practically all who tried turned against it. I have no documentation here, and the only phrase that sticks in my mind is: "The actors walk off into a private room, and the audience overhears the play through a keyhole." This is absurd, but Adams did make excessive demands upon his inner and upper stages. I propose to bring historical evidence to show that the actual Globe was more what is needed, and I want to hurry to that constructive part of the programme, but for the rest of this first section I must try to give an adequate reply to the opponents.

Leslie Hotson's book (*Shakespeare's Wooden O*, 1959) is extremely different from the sour works produced later; it flows with hope and satisfaction. He feels confident that his plan provides what everyone has always wanted from the Globe, and he is immensely well-informed, continually arguing from details of the plays. Indeed, when the modern wreckers quote from the plays they are nearly always taking an example from Hotson, and using his ingenious misinterpretation of it too, although not one of them believes in his theory. The trouble with Hotson is not merely that some of the details are incredible; he is caught up in a peculiarly intense conflict between democracy and the leader-principle. Sometimes he writes as a total theatre-in-the-round man, speaking as if Elizabethan actors had always to twist and turn, as if "on ice", presenting themselves in every direction. Every angle of the round stage must receive its due share of the benefits of equality. His most striking example of this, oddly enough, is not an actor but a fencer, who was to receive his prize in a probably octagonal theatre, and he first bowed seven times, all round (Hotson, p. 277). A solemn comment reminds us of the seven gates of London. But surely this man was bowing to all the sides of the octagon except the one behind him, the back of the stage, where there were no spectators; we may expect that his first and his last bows were the most profound ones, since they were to the twelvepenny men. The example does not mean what Hotson thought at all. May I add that I respect the idealism of people devoted to theatre-in-the-round and once cut *Hamlet* to half its length for a production by Peter Cheeseman, being allowed to meet the cast after seeing one of the performances. The play became an adventure story, very like the First Quarto; the actor of Hamlet would have preferred a more psychological treatment, but the healthiness of the technique sternly forbade it. These actors tramped down four lanes of entry to their stage, but if you take the theory to its logical extreme an actor cannot enter the stage from any direction; he can only emerge from a trap-door. It thus becomes a basic principle of Hotson that the actors must dress in the cellar (which they would certainly have refused to do). A great many stage hands need to be ready, wearing black so that they count as invisible; they put up "houses", skeleton boxes with curtains on all sides and sometimes an upper storey; each house stands over a trap-door. Usually an actor walks up in seclusion and is "discovered" when his curtains are opened all round. But very often half the audience will be on the wrong side of some obstacle; thus they can see Polonius behind the arras till Hamlet stabs him, but can only hear Hamlet and his mother. To be sure Polonius need only be behind a narrow token curtain, but all these artificial techniques (as in the Far East) impose an extra effort of imagination. Brecht might approve of it, as preventing you from identifying your self with the hero; but he did not let that theory short-circuit all his drama. The audience at the Hotson Globe cannot even identify themselves with a *place*; for example, we are supposed to have simultaneous presentation of events inside and outside a beleaguered city (the examples given to prove it seem to me easy to explain otherwise). An audience very soon stops imagining anything at all, when so much strain is put on its imagination; and surely this Noh-play technique is very unlike the Elizabethans, who though capable of staying in two minds about a character wanted to feel *completely* in a throne-room or a torture-chamber, and then in a flash completely out of it. The Hotson technique has no immediacy. But there is a more practical objection to it; it requires an enormous amount of rehearsal time, for many stage hands as well as the actors. An Elizabethan company during the season put on a different play every day, with only occasional days off; perhaps they had only a dozen ready, but they had new ones coming in. They were appallingly short of rehearsal time. More than any other known actors, they needed a sturdy permanent all-purpose set.

These complaints are against the egalitarian side of the theory, which asks the actor to face all sides at once; it has also an insolently aristocratic side, making him face backwards. Hotson maintains very strongly that grandees in expensive seats sat at the back of the stage, above it, while literary critics had stools below them; thus blocking all possibility of an inner and upper stage. It is to take their place, of course, that we need all the trap-doors with houses over them. An actor had to face these grandees, showing his contempt for the great majority of the audience, who were directly behind him. Surely one needs to consider here the history and tradition of the public theatres. They were not originally built to satisfy grandees, not even as much as the "private" theatres were. It was a scandal against Southampton, shortly before he took part in the Essex rebellion, that he was haunting the theatres instead of going to Court to face the Queen. The Induction to Marston's *Malcontent*, when it was transferred from the child actors at the Blackfriars to the Globe, in 1604, remarked that sitting on the stage was (still) forbidden at the public theatres though usual at the private ones. Of course, the public theatres wholly depended upon the legal protection of the Queen, which was given because they supplied the Court with occasional performances; but she paid only £5 a time, less than a full house would be. It was one of her methods for maintaining a splendid Court with little expense for herself. The theatres must make their living out of the people; naturally, they must obey the moderate demands of her appointed censor, but only a small selection from their plays was even expected to be worthy of her Court. The Hotson layout could only occur if the theatres had originally been built to suit grandees; but the designers gave a great deal of space to standing for a penny, and made a special effort to provide a third storey for twopence. Richer visitors did begin to come, very sensibly, around 1590, when the plays became good enough to print, and small galleries near the stage were allotted to them; at least, Henslowe's *Diary* seems to describe such a change at the Rose in 1592; but Burbage's Theatre had been built in 1576. I don't deny that these twelvepenny men were liable to obtrude themselves on the upper stage, a situation which would have been hard for the management to handle without the ready barracking from the main audience; but the upper stage, and the apron-stage too, had not been built for them – quite a lot of comment survives, all burning with this sentiment, and absurdly misinterpreted by my opponents.

While looking for arguments in favour of a tiring-house under the stage, Hotson found a possible quibble in the wording of the Hope and Fortune contracts; and it has been much used by his successors. He is splendidly ruthless when he extends his doctrine to the Hope, because it was to be used not only for a theatre but for the maltreatment of bulls and bears. The contract demands:

a fit and convenient tire-house and a stage to be carried or taken away, and to stand upon trestles good substantial and sufficient for the carrying and bearing of such a stage.

There ought to have been a comma after *tire-house*, to make plain that only the stage will be carried away; but this is already implied by the next clause, which would otherwise demand trestles good enough to support a tire-house; unless, indeed, the actors are to dress among the trestles. But what can possibly be done to make this place fit and convenient for them? When the trestles are removed, nothing must be left but bare sand, level with the rest of the arena; there must be nothing for an outraged bull to tumble into or bump against. The stage could not be more than 5 feet high, or many groundlings could not see over; so the actors must have dressed crouched down, by the light of chinks between the sackcloth hangings, knowing that anything that they failed to pick up would be thrown away by the bear-men. Ben Jonson is the only known author who had a play produced in this theatre (with his habit of quarrelling, he had to cast round), and he said it stank worse than Smithfield; but he reported no complaints from the actors. Hotson might well have lightened his appalling picture, because when he describes a visit to the Globe (*Shakespeare's Wooden O*, p. 24) the guide takes the rich visitor through the stage door at the back to a seat in a lords' room at the side of the stage, won by bribery as the house is packed; they pass the stairs for the actors to go down to the cellarage, and they see the actor of Gondomar carried in on his litter through one of the great slanted doors. On any theory, some actors did have to go down to the cellarage, though we may presume they dressed in some more convenient place first; and Hotson's actors are at least not excluded from the back of the stage.

He gives a splendid display of nerve when handling an apparently decisive reference (long known, of course) from Middleton's *Family of Love* (I.iii.100). The three gallants have been to the theatre, and say they saw "Samson excel the whole world in gate-carrying."

> *Dryfat* Was it performed by the youths?
> *Lipsalve* By youths? Why I tell thee we saw Samson, and I hope tis not
> for youths to play Samson. Believe it, we saw Samson bear the
> town-gates on his neck from the lower to the upper stage, with that
> life and admirable accord, that it shall never be equalled, unless the
> whole new livery of porters set their shoulders.

The Fortune Theatre did have a play about Samson in 1602, and Middleton's play, acted by the youths at Blackfriars, was printed in 1608 with a preface complaining that the book had been delayed too long; so there is no reason to doubt that the words are literal. One is tempted to assume that Samson carried an imitation of the gates up the hidden stairs at the back, reappearing triumphantly on the balcony stage; but Lipsalve insists that they saw the feat done. It would have much popular appeal, and the Fortune was still new; Henslowe might well have a ladder brought on, concealed in an imitation of a rocky bit of hillside. For that matter, Samson might well carry the city gates which had just been shown on the stage. The pair of them are first seen when he is admitted to the city; then they appear again, and someone unlocks them from behind, and lifts them off their hinges, and pushes them out separately; and now we see it was the hero Samson, who proceeds to carry them up the hillside. For this purpose, the gates appear in the aperture of one of the big side doors, leaving the centre for the mountain. I don't deny that they were probably a lighter pair of gates than the ones used for battle-pieces, but they had better be shown to be practicable. It is this comic realism, more like making the shadow of a rabbit with one's fingers than anything else, that Lipsalve has found charming.

Nobody could be charmed by the scene that Hotson describes:

The muscular actor bore the gates – property ones, like the "canvas stone" of Hercules Furens – from the city walls of Hell at Stage Left (the lower) up the "hill of Hebron" or Heaven above the Stage Right (the upper stage).

That is, the actor merely walked from one side to the other. What would happen when he *needed* merely to walk from one side to the other, on some other occasion unsuited to all this weight of symbolism? The plays must have been very hard to arrange. Hotson, of course, does not deny that a token mountain may also have been carried in for Samson to mount, but this extra pleasure is not what is meant by what Lipsalve says. Nor did Lipsalve mean, as you might suppose, that the actor walked from the left of the audience to its right. Lipsalve had at once translated what he saw into the symbolic experience of the aristocrats on the other side of the stage, although he and the vast majority of spectators saw the actor walk from right to left. (At least, Lipsalve had somehow got into trouble at Court, and no longer goes there; and there is no suggestion that he met former acquaintances in the lords' rooms – he and his friends are on a very informal footing, and quite at home with the tradesmen, so they presumably go to the threepenny seats.) In any case, he is not the man to say "Believe it, we saw Samson" do these things, if he only saw an extremely remote symbolical representation of it.

It amounts to another point about historical evidence: that the literary experience itself can give some. I do not know much about these long-ago audiences, but I have been allowed to meet Lipsalve. He is not a bad man, or even low-minded; he can be sententious or enthusiastic. But he is extremely down-to-earth; in fact, very close to the corresponding men in Restoration comedy. He has taken up the seduction of traders' wives very much as, in a later age, he might have taken up golf. He is the last man in an Elizabethan audience whose eye could be completely annulled by medieval symbolism.

I must now turn to a gloomier duty. The most learned, thorough and wide-ranging of the recent attacks upon the Elizabethan theatre emerges from a treatise by Glynne Wickham, *Early English Stages* (Vol. I. *1300–1576*; Vol. II. *1576– 1660*; Part I, 1963; Part II, 1972). His position needs to be faced, and besides, I will be needing to claim him as my authority at various points. His basic position is that the stage and tiring-house were independent structures, "with their own independent life" he eerily says, planted down inside the "frame" of the Elizabethan round or quasi-round theatre, like those for baiting bears and bulls. An immense accumulation of detail is supposed to prove this, but I cannot understand what argument can be implicit in it. There might be a false argument from evolution, supposing Darwin to have proved that men still have tails, but then, what corresponds to the monkey? Where does any tiring-house conduct an independent life inside a bull-ring? A presumption that ignorant carpenters such as Old Burbage could not have known how to relate a tiring-house to a frame is about all the historical argument we are given; it is eked out by devotion to the "De Witt sketch" and an energetic use of Hotson's quibble over the contracts. The Fortune contract says:

The frame of the said house to be set square and to contain fourscore foot of lawful assize every way square without and fortyfive feet of like assize every way within . . . And the said frame to contain three storeys in height . . . With a stage and tiring-house to be made, erected and set up within the said frame, with a shadow or cover over the said stage . . . With convenient windows and lights glazed to the said tiring-house . . .

This is hailed as fully justifying the "De Witt sketch", in which a wall marked "mimorum aedes" does appear to jut out from the round frame; how far one cannot guess, because Van Buchell drew so badly. If the actors had no escape to the back from this narrow cell (and the cast of *Hamlet* is at least thirty) it would have to be fairly deep; and then the spectators below at the sides, marked in the sketch "orchestra" meaning the expensive seats, would only see the blank sides of the tiring-house, with perhaps glimpses of actors dressing if the required windows are provided there. Wickham however suggests that the windows in the turret for the crane, shown by "De Witt", may have satisfied the contract; and I thought this was a joke till I found it copied on a theatre hand-out about the Globe. So the actors had to dress in the dark and then run up higher than the top gallery in order to tidy their hair before going on stage.

Where then is the evidence in the contract upon which so much depends? Wickham repeatedly says that it calls for a tiring-house "within the frame", and that that means in the yard. But the frame has just been said to "contain" the three storeys of the public galleries, and even Wickham would not toss all the spectators out into the yard. I grant that there is some looseness about the meaning of the term *frame*, but clearly it is sometimes used for the outside wall of the whole building, within which it is essential for the architect to work, and that is the relevant meaning here. It has been argued that erecting a house, even a special kind of house, would not be done inside another house; but the legal habit of using three words, as in "made, erected, and set up", is specifically intended to guard against this kind of objection. The word *tiring-house* had been extending its meaning to include all backstage equipment; at least, my party think so, and there is nothing here to prove us wrong. The *NED* shows that the word *erect* has now become slightly narrower; when Queen Elizabeth "erected" the East India Company she presumably did it indoors. And it does not alter the case if you take the word *frame* to mean "the main structure". Consider a *house* built round a yard, Buckingham Palace for instance. I think one can say definitely that the momentous sentence "the corpse is still within the palace" does not mean "it has been tossed out into the yard". Surely this particular quibble had better be given a rest.

The strangest invention by Wickham to maintain the separate life of the tiring-house (Part I, p. 306) was the erection upon it of the turret holding the crane. A logical necessity, he might well think, because the god must be let down from heaven in front of the tiring-house; and he gives drawings of this tall narrow building, "a free-standing erection", rising up higher than the top gallery of the main building and there offering like a flower the necessarily heavy crane. Please remember it is built on a swamp. Wickham is rather prone to wonder what such an ignorant carpenter as Old Burbage could possibly have known, and I can tell you one thing; he would know that this eerie contraption would blow down in the first high wind. Come to think of it, the mere presence of this crane, which had to be supported by the whole building, is enough to prove that the tiring-house was inside the frame. Even Wickham, after his fancy has carried him so far, allows a connection between the frame and the tiring-house, though not for bodily support; threepenny spectators are allowed to step across the token gap between the round and the oblong buildings so that they can watch the play from the gallery above the tiring-house, as in "De Witt" (whereas twelvepenny ones sit on the stage and block the view, Part I, p. 115). Customers can walk on; so it is now plain that the "independent life" *only* meant that the actors are not allowed to walk off. The independent life of a bucketful of scorpions, one must presume. They would think it a peculiarly malignant rule, because there is no possible sale to spectators of the area behind the free-standing building, where actors might dress in daylight and speak aloud. It is hard to imagine what Wickham himself would say to them, if he (instead of Henslowe) had to try to defend to them his savage regulation. They would say they could do the work better if they dressed under tolerable conditions, and daylight was cheaper than candles; true enough, there were sometimes gentlemen knocking about backstage now, but that wouldn't matter; the gentlemen were rather keen to meet the actors (Ben Jonson in *the Poetaster* is nastily suspicious about this). Did Wickham seriously mean that they had to hide in that smelly hen-run till the last drunken spectator had been coaxed off the premises? Henslowe himself said that he could not control them unless he kept them in debt to him; they would be quite willing to speak up to Wickham. I do not believe he could find anything to say. This will be thought a gratuitous fancy, but it really does concern the nature of historical evidence. Pedants may say: "You have no scrap of written evidence to show that actors were allowed backstage"; but in such a case the onus of proof lies on the other side. It would require very strong evidence to prove that they were *not* allowed backstage. Of course, I wish we had more evidence, and am keen to use what we have.

In 1592 Henslowe did a good deal of repair work on the Rose theatre, making a long bill in his *Diary*, and at the end, not adding greatly to the expense, he listed some items which appear to be changes, though he does not say so. "Ceiling the room over the tire-house, 10s, wages for plasterer, 4s, paid for ceilings my lords' room, 14s", and then several items, coming to just over £4, for "making the penthouse shed at the tiring-house door". Wickham makes no comment on the last item, and it is hard to see how he could allow any door to his tiring-house other than the ones on the stage. Henslowe wrote these notes only for himself to read, and is sometimes mildly facetious, as well as careless about grammar, so that he needs interpreting. He speaks of the whole building as "my theatre", so must mean something different by "my lords' room"; probably it is a new venture, a brain-child which is receiving his special care. That is, he has partitioned off the last bay of the ground-floor gallery, on each side, raising the price of a seat there from fourpence to twelvepence, and allowed access only through the stage door; without this last rule, there would be little inducement to pay three times as much for rather bad seats. The gentry no longer have to rub shoulders with the groundlings at the entry, or even be near them during a performance, because the stairs from Hell are what confront the twelvepenny gallery; also they get a civil reception, meeting the actors and allowed the run of the mysteries of the place. I agree that they could not thereafter be kept out of the upper stage, which is given a better ceiling for them; but also they could not prevent its occasional uses in the play (or not without the rest of the audience hooting at them) and they would soon find that it gave a bad view of the play. The reason why a penthouse had to be put over the stage door at the back was that someone had now to sit there all the time, ready to take money and do the honours. This detail comes near to a proof that Henslowe was only now introducing his "lords' rooms" (of course he is making a mild joke about his social aspirations, not really expecting a row of lords paying twelvepence). There would have to be two lords' rooms for symmetry (elegance made a rigid demand here), and besides, among any twenty Elizabethan gentlemen, there would be at least two who needed to be kept apart. This is allowed for by Henslowe's plural S at the ending of *ceilings*. One can also observe from the prices of the plastering that the two lords' rooms did not go all the way back, 12 feet; as the upper stage at the Rose was 16 feet long, and may be supposed 5 feet deep, the twelvepenny galleries (24 feet long in all) would be about 3½ feet deep. They are intended for a front row only, sitting at ease; and this is convenient because behind them the actors can have a proper dressing-room with an outside window.

This coherent interpretation of the details is of course forbidden to my opponent, but he can and does rejoice when Henslowe calls the upper stage "the room above the tire-house", talking as if the inner stage was still the whole of the tire-house. I do not find this puzzling, in a situation of rapid development for theatre design; Henslowe could remember very simple arrange-

ments in earlier times and he was unlikely to be initiating his
lords' rooms – probably the whole company had been urging him
to copy what Burbage's Theatre had been doing. He might well
use a slightly reactionary term, while taking part in the march of
progress rather grudgingly. But of course an actor often *would*
add the last touches to his appearance before bursting through
the curtains; and to call the inner stage *part* of the tiring-house
was merely literal, after the term had come to mean the whole
mass of backstage gadgets. What possible explanation can
Wickham have for the door marked at the south end of the Globe
in Norden's survey of London, except that it was that familiar
institution the stage door (only 3 yards from the inner stage, anyhow)? He seems to me to be arguing against all tradition and
plausibility.

There is a simple answer to the argument that the "De Witt
sketch" must be true, because a very ignorant carpenter could
not guess how to combine a tiring-house with a round gallery, so
he would just lay one against the other. James Burbage had
served his apprenticeship as a carpenter, but had since then
become manager of a successful company of actors, and had
received favours from the Queen. But Van Buchell, the man who
drew the incompetent "De Witt sketch", fits the bill exactly; it is
he who was ignorant, he who could not combine the details in a
picture because he had only heard about them in words, though
what he had been told was often true; and also he who would
assume that the pillars were classical. However, the "De Witt
sketch" may be largely correct; perhaps even as to the tire-house,
if it does not jut out more than a yard. When De Witt saw the
Swan, it had recently been put up by a goldsmith, and would be
the more easy to examine because a troupe of actors for it had not
yet been found. They were found the next year, and demanded
over a hundred pounds for improvements to the building, as it
was not fit for use. (The money was said to be in part for clothes,
but they had had another grant for clothes nine months before.)
The play was the *Isle of Dogs*, which nearly got all the theatres
closed, and a terrifying silence fell upon the Swan. The acting
company would surely have demanded a curtained central aperture on the stage, which would not be very costly; there is no
other reason except this sketch to suppose that the familiar con-
trivance (familiar even at Valladolid, as we learn from Wickham)
had ever been lacking. If the theatre was also planned for baiting
animals, as Wickham believes, then it must have presented a

smooth barrier after the stage had been removed, and the roof with its pillars would have to go too; so they cannot have been massively classical. On any view, some of the evidence has to be rejected. The ill-fated building cannot be treated as a model, even if its first state is depicted correctly.

In Part II of Volume II, published nine years later, Wickham writes that the designers of the Globe *might* have incorporated the tiring-house within the frame, and the same for the Fortune, though speculation here is "dangerous" (p. 189); and as to the Hope, which at the time of the second Globe was to have the cover over the whole stage with no pillars, he says (p. 74):

It is difficult to conceive how this can be done without retracting the tiring-house at least into the frame of the building.

But on the next page he speaks of the nuisance for the Hope of "dismantling and re-erecting the stage and tiring-house" for a bear-baiting, probably one day in four. Presumably, then, he still thought that the monstrous edifice in the yard of the Swan was always removed before the animals were let in. This does seem prudent, as a bull might knock it down, crane and all. Thus the concessions made by Wickham in 1971 are not great, but they do at least prove that he has no fundamental reason for putting the tiring-house in the yard. Perhaps the belief was attractive because he considered carpenters so ignorant; and he was almost startled out of it when confronted by the skill of the carpenters of the Hope and the second Globe.

In Norden's *Map of London*, published in 1593 (Plate III in J. C. Adams), the Bearhouse and the Playhouse are too tiny for much detail, but there is a large black blob for the back door of the Rose Playhouse, whereas the Bearhouse at the same place has only a thin line. No weight could be laid on this, but it may represent the new penthouse at the Rose. The revised map of Norden in 1600 fits in very well with our other scraps of information about the theatres. In 1595, having had a good year after the interruption for plague, Henslowe spent a little over £7 "for carpenters' work and making the throne in the heavens"; presumably it means adding a crane from which a god would descend from the heavens, in a "car". It sounds astonishingly cheap, but Henslowe's accounts are often tricky; maybe most of the expense was covered by repayment of an old debt. At any rate, the revised edition of Norden shows a turret added to the roof of the Swan, and the new Globe has been added to the map in its correct place, with another turret. They both have a door and windows facing south. I do not understand why the Beargarden needed to add a turret too, but perhaps the draughtsman merely felt he was giving good measure. The corroboration from Amsterdam seems to me good evidence that there really was a stage door where one would expect it, behind the stage; this is not surprising, but it is enough to refute the theory of Wickham.

I have next to discuss the report by Wickham on the Boar's Head theatre; there are a good many legal documents about it, which he finds to give strong support for his position. In 1602 a couple of speculators made a theatre in the yard of that inn, and their subsequent lawsuits with one another yield information. For the first year they had genuine theatre-in-the-round, with the stage in the middle of the yard, standers all round it, and galleries with seats all round the oblong perimeter. Next year they built a larger gallery on the south-west side, encroaching upon the yard, and moved the stage a few feet so that it adjoined the gallery there. They quarrelled about which of them should pay for removing the rubbish which was found under the stage, so they were not using that area as a tiring-house. In another lawsuit, one of them said he extended his gallery because people would pay more to sit down; but very likely ambition had been at work in him too; he would want his house to look less obviously inferior to the new Globe and the new Fortune. These galleries were like flights of tall steps, so that you sat between the feet of the people next above (even here, raking the seats was taken for granted). In 1606 the company moved to another theatre.

How then, in the first year, did the actors make their exits and their entrances? They could not have walked in costume through the groundlings, who would pull their clothes about just for fun, even if they were friendly (at least, that was usually supposed). They could not emerge through a trap-door from below, as that area was stuffed with rubbish. Wickham says (Vol. II, p. 187):

The inference to be drawn from this knowledge, so far as the tiring-house is concerned, must be that it was either of the booth kind originally, and remained so, or that it was independent of the stage in the first place and probably continued to be so; otherwise some word about its situation and the requisite structural changes would have been included in the proposed alterations.

I was rather pleased with myself for thinking of a solution, where the great expert had failed. The stage had been 10 feet away from the western gallery, before the change, and this could be bridged by a joy-walk, 5 feet up and 3 feet wide (or 4, lest the groundlings snatch at the ankles); more probably, two joy-walks, at the north and south ends of the stage. The actors emerged, of course, from their dressing-room, and the reason why the carpenters had no orders to alter it, when the stage was moved in, is that there was no need for a change. But then I found Wickham had understood this perfectly well, when he drew the diagram for the earlier arrangement at the Boar's Head (Fig. 11, p. 103). "Tiring-house below gallery" is actually pointed out by an arrow; and he draws two thick lines joining this room to the north and south ends of the stage, never explained in the text, but plainly representing the two joy-walks. A brief sentence actually survives in writing (p. 104) which admits that the tiring-house was at the west side of the yard (and therefore presumably inside the gallery). One often finds, in reading these great monuments of scholarship, that the author leaves lying about the more sensible opinions which he held before his mind set into a grim dogma. For the reset of the book, this section, drawn from the lawsuits about the Boar's Head, is treated as definite proof that the Elizabethan theatre did not have an inner or an upper stage. But how could it prove that? It proves that there were some bad theatres, built for money by men who did not care about the needs of the play-wright and the actor; but we know that Old Burbage was the manager of Leicester's Company, and that the Globe was built by a syndicate of leading actors, including Shakespeare. How can it prove that they built equally badly?

Plays written for the Globe often have sequences which seem to demand an inner or an upper stage; that is why readers came to believe these stages to have been provided. If the plays written for the Boar's Head had passages of the same kind, I confess that the situation would be puzzling; because there the stage adjoined the middle of the long side of an oblong, so that half the audience would not be able to see inside these extra stages at all. One would say, helplessly, that maybe the production was symbolical. But, from what I can learn, no plays survive which were acted at the Boar's Head, at any rate during 1602–6, the time during which the lawsuits give us evidence about the stage architectures. This is probably because they were bad plays. Special reasons there might be, but even so a good play would be likely to get pirated. Wickham has an evasive sentence about this, saying we have no evidence that the Boar's Head was "worse" than its rivals; but no one supposes that it was morally worse, the question is whether other theatres allowed better staging. As we know that the first Globe was an octagon, or at least fairly round, it was inherently able to give a better view of inner stages than the Boar's Head. Why should we suppose that it did not use the opportunity? Here and elsewhere it is hard to see what Wickham can be trying to prove.

He is triumphantly grim when he gets to the Fortune Theatre and its contract (Part II, p. 115):

The stage and tiring-house of the first Fortune were clearly regarded, like those of the earlier Boar's Head and the subsequent Hope, as separate units independent of the frame.

So the tiring-house was somewhere in the yard, but an obscure footnote "assumes" that it was not at the back of the stage, and he uses the whole depth of the stage when he calculates his seating arrangement. The 6-foot ditches at the sides might be curtained over for the purpose, but from his chart (p. 113) he seems to regard them as gangways. Dressing-rooms under the stage he considers to be refuted by the Boar's Head documents (but why need they apply here?). Tents erected in the front seem all he has left, but they would interfere with the sightlines very insolently. He makes no suggestion; we are left to suppose that the actors appeared in the middle of the stage ready dressed, like fairies. I think he has only proved that his treasured principle does not work.

We must learn to control our imaginations, he says, meaning that instead of imagining that the Globe stage had its merits, and might give us some tips, we should recognise that it was very vulgar and sordid. The refusal to imagine any place for the Fortune tiring-house thus becomes a rhetorical device to express his contempt. Anyway, he tells us, the apparently wide stage of the Fortune was actually packed with rows of spectators, 10 feet deep on both sides. The miracle of the actors appearing from nowhere ceases to be oppressive, because hardly anyone in the vast audience could see them at all. This plan might be made less intolerable; raising all the galleries by 1 foot should be enough to prevent a riot from the fourpenny men. But the twelvepenny men, close up at the sides, would feel particularly badly treated, and the ones standing for a penny would presumably see nothing at all. An alliance of these extremes has always made an explosive political mixture, and the magistrates were ready to close the theatres for riot. I doubt whether Wickham could have kept the Fortune open for a week.

The main source of information about sitting on the stage is Dekker's *The Gull's Horn-Book* (1609); but one should realise that he is deliberately confusing together details from the public and private theatres, which had different plans. He describes an audience as getting into a condition which an unfriendly magistrate could easily describe as a riot, shouting and throwing things, because *one* man was sitting on the stage. It is true that he has to slink off because a real gentleman comes, showing, presumably, that several gentlemen could come. We need to imagine an Age of Privilege; some visitors are eminent enough to deserve a seat on the stage, and the crowd decides who can qualify: perhaps a young blood may pass if he lies down on the rushes. Wickham is wrapped in a dream of a nice tidy cinema; "A 7", "F 12" he murmurs to himself, entranced. It is he whose imagination needs to be restrained.

Times when the theatre is packed, and only bribery can get one a seat, for example the performance of the *Game At Chess* with which Hotson opens his book, are not a great comfort to a manager (who seldom even gets the bribe). Crowds come on such occasions because they think the Government is being teased, and very often the Government reacts by closing the theatres. It is hard to guess what Henslowe can be counting, when he lists a sum of money after a dated performance in his *Diary*, but presumably the figures give some indication of the bookings (for example, he cannot just have charged all seats double for a first performance, because the takings for the second and third performances are also high though declining). Taking his entries at face value, his theatre was usually about a third full; getting it half-full every time would have meant riches. And the most we hear of the gentlemen paying is a shilling; if you got 100 of them on the stage, that would not make up for losing 600 groundlings at a penny and 200 fourpenny men from the main gallery. Wickham says that his solid phalanx of stools *must* have been laid out on the stage, because it was the business of the management to make money; a sadly childish line of tough-guy talk which has become common among theorists. Money could best be made by providing tolerable conditions for those who came, and avoiding trouble with the law. However, there is a good deal of excuse for the petulance of Wickham on this occasion. The Fortune Theatre, as the contract is usually interpreted, really does have an intolerably bad stage, almost deserving to be drowned under spectators. But the contract can readily be interpreted to make it a good one.

I need at the end of this desultory first section to give a brief example where the inner stage and its curtain are plainly needed; perhaps I will be told that I describe an amateur production, or a technique which would nowadays only be used in a school, but that does not prove it is historically wrong. What are you to do with the magnificently concentrated sequence in *Macbeth* I.iv? The King in council takes only twelve lines to rejoice at the loyalty of his thanes, announce that his son is to be the next king, and tell Macbeth to prepare for an immediate visit. The play is like a Just-So Story, about "How the Scotch royalty got Primogeniture", so naturally Macbeth has been supposing himself the rightful next king. Hearing his hopes destroyed, he makes a rather stiff speech welcoming the royal visit, and then shouts at the audience: "Well, that settles it. Now I'll have to kill this king." "Exit" is marked for Macbeth, and then the King tells Banquo how wonderfully loyal Macbeth is: "It is a peerless kinsman." Then "Exeunt". Now surely, if they all make these exits from the throne-room, the effect is too near to farce. I do not deny that a skilled and magnetic actor can prevent laughter, but the strain makes the scene too melodramatic for this early stage of the play. The story is that Macbeth damns himself in a hurry, without due consideration, so it ought not to seem plain almost as soon as he appears that he is already damned. Indeed the words of his soliloquy, unlike my summary of their purport, show him hardly able to bear the recognition of his own intention: "let now light see my black and deep desires". He needs urgently to get out of the throne-room, before he can think at all.

Very likely our text has been cut for a shortened Court performance, but the cut version was intended to be effective. There is only one satisfactory way to do it. Macbeth bows himself out of the royal presence, and the back curtain closes, hiding the council scene, so that he is alone. He strides to the front of the apron-stage and hisses his determination at the audience; then he hurries off to a side door, the right perhaps, evidently to get his horse. Duncan appears leaning on Banquo at the left side door, and ambles across the stage, talking over his impressions of the council; they too, in a more leisurely way, are going to the stables. It is now pathetic, not harshly ludicrous, for him to say of the loyalty of his cousin Macbeth: "it is a banquet to me".

(However much you regard the aside as "a convention", it is impossible not to feel that Duncan is a fool if he cannot hear Macbeth standing beside him and shouting out that he intends to murder him. Besides, the Elizabethan audience considered itself ready to laugh at conventions.) Then the back curtain opens upon Lady Macbeth, to whom they are all going; she has not appeared before, but she is surrounded by the Macbeth tartan, so she is easily identified. There have been only eleven lines since the curtain closed on the throne scene, but also a good deal of walking about, so there would be time for a quick change of the inner stage; but in the Globe she probably appeared above, in her boudoir, as the next scene demands the castle-gate set below. Both the "exit" directions in the council scene are literally correct, and to print any fuller directions (meaning what I have just tried to say) would take a considerable number of words.

To bring the audience out of the throne-room suddenly and decisively, so that comments may be made upon what happened there without the throne losing any of its dignity, is one of the major functions of the inner-stage curtain. But there are of course many other occasions when the audience needs to imagine it is *in* a place, with a very specific atmosphere or character, and then to imagine a sudden complete change of place. One of the great merits of the Elizabethan stage is to do this quickly and with very little equipment. To throw away even the possibility of it, by forbidding the use of a curtain, seems to me crazy. Surely the one thing a company could rely upon being able to do, even when on tour, was to rig up a curtain. And the only reasons offered for forbidding it are footling ones.

Wickham does show some awareness that the throne needs to be removed at the end of the throne-scene, and having forbidden himself a curtain he decides to hoist it up on the crane. You could hardly do anything more fatal to the dignity of this throne. It would be a wooden chair on a stand, got up to look bigger and heavier than it was, probably with wings and a top that could be folded back, brightly painted; it was planned for the back centre of the inner stage, to be viewed from the front only. Swinging it about on the crane would be like doing the same thing to the Queen; one would see under her skirts. Cranes were much used for unloading ships, or filling a granary; they were very workaday objects, by no means only connected with descent from heaven. And in the present case, as in many others, Macbeth urgently needs to unbosom himself as soon as he leaves the royal presence; he cannot wait, nor can we, until the sacred object has creaked its way up to the top. Of course, in this case, no throne may be required – Duncan need not have taken his to the battle-field – but the argument would apply in many others; for example, Hamlet cannot wait before saying "O that this too too solid flesh could melt" until the crane has finished its display.

Nor could the throne used in council scenes possibly have gone through the roof, even when folded up. The seat for letting down the god was normally called a "car", and had to be narrow as well as light; it was a minimum object, hidden by draperies. But as a kind of joke it is often called a "throne", because that is what you might expect a god to sit in; this became practically a habit, though without ceasing to be felt as a mild joke. It does not imply any confusion between these two extremely different kinds of chair. I think indeed that such plausibility as my opponents have reached has been won through stubborn misunderstanding of Elizabethan diction, though it had to be combined, of course, with misdirection in other ways.

II

Coriolanus is a test case, because it actually cannot be acted except upon a proper Elizabethan stage. I am sorry if I sound whimsical or paradoxical, but you are not "acting" a play if you leave out its basic event, which explains all the subsequent turns in the drama. Shakespeare is very specific about Coriolanus, making him a man to whom the tragic story would be unlikely to happen, were it not for this initial event. A military hero often becomes a dictator, but Martius (his name till he captures Corioli) is more like a star athlete; indeed, the civil wars between these small towns in Latium, all talking the same language, are presented as rather like football matches, though of course more harmful. He is popular with his brother officers, who are not jealous of his feats, and even the troops put up with his scolding readily enough; but he is not in command of the Roman army, and seems not to expect the position. He has been taught that it is bad form to swank, and he is rigid about preserving his modesty; no doubt he really would lose his popularity if he relaxed the rule. When praised for a particular act of skill or daring he says "Pure fluke, old man", or "Aw, shucks", and if the compliment is repeated, demanding a repetition of the formality, he says something rude, probably "You stink." This makes him incapable of winning a Roman election, but he does not want to go in for politics anyhow. All through the play, one keeps being surprised that Shakespeare knows so much about characters (the Labour leaders, for instance) who don't seem to be Shakespeare characters at all, or Elizabethans either. Somehow, the author has been jolted out of himself and this is also what happens to Coriolanus.

He is a man with very few resources outside the social niche that he has been specially trained for; but when insulted by the mob he walks out of the city insisting upon solitude and saying "I banish you" – he wants to become "like to a lonely dragon, that his fen / Makes feared and talked of more than seen." His misery has made him unrecognisable by the time he offers his services to the enemy. One might think that the whole story had to be accepted because it is in Plutarch and Livy, but they have nothing like it. Neither of them describe him as alone, either when he captures Corioli or when he goes into exile. Plutarch is inclined to think that Titus Lartius was among the few picked men who entered Corioli with him, and that after leaving Rome he entertained his friends at some of his country houses. A Roman visitor to the Volscians spoke to him in his old age, and he said it was rather sad that he couldn't even pay Rome a visit. There is nothing superhuman about his story in Livy either, if Shakespeare went back so far; though he might find a hint at the technique for capturing Corioli.

What the play keeps on saying is that he must be a demi-god, because no human man could capture a walled city singlehanded. We do not know whether he believes this himself, because his rule of politeness keeps him silent, but he appears to accept it when he destroys himself by telling the Volscians "Alone I did it", in Corioli. But we of the Globe audience saw what really happened, so we know that it wasn't superhuman at all, though of course splendidly brave, vigorous, and resourceful, like a coup by Biggles. It is rather shocking that such a good first Act could become forgotten.

I must recall what we are given instead. Two Volscian senators, in Act I scene iv, are summoned by trumpet to the wall of Corioli, and Martius (not yet Coriolanus) asks whether their chief general is in the town:

1st Sen.   No, nor a man that fears you less than he;
         That's lesser than a little. (*Drums afar off.*) Hark, our drums

> Are bringing forth our youth: we'll break our walls,
> Rather than they should pound us up; our gates,
> Which yet seem shut, we have but pinn'd with rushes;
> They'll open of themselves.(*Alarum far off.*) Hark you, far
>   off,
> There is Aufidius. List what work he makes
> Among your cloven army.
> *Mar.*   O, they are at it.
> *Lartius*   Their noise be our instruction. Ladders ho.

By the word *cloven*, the senator tries to delude the besiegers into moving to the main battlefield, about a mile and a half away, so as to unite their army, but the Roman commander says: "Our duty is to fight as they are doing. Bring up the scaling-ladders" (to climb the city walls). While they are awaited, the Volscians come through their gate and drive the Romans back, making Martius angry. They soon withdraw through the gate; he pursues them, and with his usual technique of leadership he yells at his troops that they are stinking cowards but never looks back to see if they are following. Usually they deserve this trust, but when they see the strong gate waiting to shut them in they jib:

> *All*   To the pot, I warrant him.

Lartius returns from the skirmish (if present he would perhaps have restrained Martius) and pronounces a splendid elegy of farewell, taking for granted that the gate cannot be forced, in fact that it is *not* only pinned with rushes; this allows time for something to happen inside. Then, says Dover Wilson's edition for example, "The gates reopen, and Martius . . . is seen within." Dover Wilson does not say that the gates just drifted open, never having been equipped with a fastener anyway, but I do not know what else he can mean. Martius might have done so well that he was at leisure to open the fastening himself, but the Folio stage direction says: "Enter Martius bleeding, assaulted by the enemy"; and surely Lartius must be allowed to imply a touch-and-go situation (of whatever kind) by the brief exultant words:

> O tis Martius
> Let's fetch him off, or make remain alike.

"They fight, and all enter the City", says the Folio, not explaining what route they take. Why were the scaling-ladders mentioned, if they are not to be brought on, or brought on if they are not to be used? Both could only disappoint the audience. Why are all the characters so much impressed by Coriolanus afterwards, if his life merely happened to be saved by a falling open of the ruinous gates?

Plainly, what we have here, as often elsewhere, is a conflated text, which gives the words needed both for a real performance and for the makeshift which might be needed on tour, when there was no balcony. Of course two senators could always appear "above", on a stepladder with a rug round it maybe, but this would not be an area across which actors could present a credible fight. The alternative words are very feeble; why stand on a wall and tell the besieger that he has only to push the gate open? Why have a gate on the stage at all, if it doesn't work? I grant that the senator might be attempting a double bluff; the gates don't work, but he may discourage the Romans from testing them if he talks the language of heroic paradox. They might even suspect a trap. But Romans are too bluff for that; they would test immediately. So the added words are only a makeshift; and they are incompatible with the words *Ladders ho*, which are only said if you have a balcony, and are just going to put the ladders up. No production should use all the printed words. The words offering the excuse (*We'll break . . . of themselves*) can be removed with no break in the verse rhythm, and *Ladders ho* can be removed without causing surprise, though at the cost of a line of poetry.

We are lucky that Hemming and Condell gave the conflation here, as we often only learn of such variants through differences between Quarto and Folio. A great many of these, I think, record arrangements made for performances without the Globe equipment, so they amount to an important support for the belief in such equipment. But we cannot be sure they have that cause; I think it plain that Shakespeare wrote *Hamlet* meaning to have Polonius killed on the upper stage, but maybe it was never done that way even at the Globe, because the other actors did not like it. Even so, the case proves that the alternative was open to them. With *Coriolanus* the matter is much simpler; nobody could ever have preferred the horrible version which was sometimes necessary then, and is always necessary now.

Every gate of a walled city, even small ones with walls only 8 feet high, had a staircase giving access to the wall. (While refugeeing with the Combined North Western Universities of China, I was stationed for a term at Mengtzu, near the border of Annam. That had a city wall 8 feet high, with four city gates in working order; probably very like the walls of Corioli, as the technique went right across the land mass.) Also, the first thing a swordsman does, finding himself alone among enemies, is to get his back to a wall; and he may then, while fighting them off, slide along it. When Martius feels the stairs behind him he will back up them, still defending himself against attacks from in front, and accepting the risk from behind. But we in the audience know he is safe on that count, because we saw how, as soon as he was caught by the closing of the gate, the two sentries on the balcony ran giggling down to see the fun. We next see him emerging on the balcony, fighting every inch of the way, with his back to us. Probably the sentries from the adjacent gates have been alerted, and one from each side should come running along the walls to be stuck by the hero; he also has to deal with men coming up the stair, but they are at a disadvantage. In a way it is a debunking spectacle, because so much less superhuman than we had expected, but by keeping him still at risk (as is demanded by the stage direction) he can be made sufficiently heroic. The effect is that he has cleared a small bit of wall, and the ladders (which had seemed belated) come in at just the right time to take advantage of it. Usually the first man up the ladder faced almost certain death, but not now, and after three or four have got up they might as well be fighting in the open. Marcius therefore did capture the town single-handed, but by accident, and without needing any magical powers. You might think that, if this is so, the dramatist should at least give him a few words to say from the balcony, at his moment of triumph, such as "Come on up, boys"; but nothing needs to be said, and he is never flashy, and at the moment he is a bit puffed, though he soon recovers and walks across to the other battlefield.

Propaganda at once envelopes him. Cominius, the general in command, receives him with religious awe:

> Who's yonder
> That does appear as he were flayed? O Gods . . .   (I.vi)

– and it is Cominius, in his speech to the Senate recommending Martius as consul, who establishes the legend about him.

> His sword, death's stamp
> Where it did mark, it took; from face to foot
> He was a thing of blood, whose every motion
> Was timed with dying cries. Alone he entered
> The mortal gate of the city, which he painted

> With shunless destiny; aidless came off
> And with a sudden reinforcement struck
> Corioli like a planet.   (II.ii)

The *NED* gives this use of *reinforcement* as a separate archaic one, not implying that other troops came and helped him (no doubt Cominius wants to sound oracular); and *aidless came off* has to mean that he was not helped even at the end, but this was not what Lartius thought when he said *let's fetch him off*. He meant "fetch off the city wall", but even after seeing one of the no-balcony versions, with the city gate wobbling open, nobody could believe that Martius had completed the capture of the city single-handed. By the third Act, the Labour-leader Brutus can accuse Coriolanus of acting on the belief that he is a demi-god, and it comes across as a powerful rebuke:

> You speak of the people
> As if you were a god to punish, not
> A man of their infirmity.   (III.i)

Coriolanus does not express this belief, but hearing it so often would make him likely to catch, like an infection, the fatal thought that he has been wronged; he tells Aufidius, after his grizzling in exile, that the other aristocrats ratted on him when he was banished – it was

> Permitted by our dastard nobles, who
> Have all forsook me.   (IV.v)

They backed him as far as they could without bringing on civil war; he should not have expected them to abandon Rome for him. As the play goes on, for other people to call him a demigod becomes almost routine; IV.vi.91, V.iii.11, 150, V.iv.19, 24.[1] He could not say anything that would quiet the process, at least in the earlier stages, because his modesty is well understood as only a clumsy attempt at good manners.

One might think that Shakespeare chose this theme as a kind of farewell to the Globe, regretting that he would henceforth have to write plays also suited to the Blackfriars, or at least that he was using a final opportunity to revive an old technique. But probably he did not know that the Blackfriars would soon

---

[1] New Shakespeare text edited by John Dover Wilson, Cambridge University Press, 1960.

become available, and probably that too had a castle-gate set. I think there was a personal reason for the choice. The belief that one has been wronged, often fatal to the revengers, was also sadly liable to attack playwrights; and he had a breakdown, though a short one, after *King Lear*. (The theory that he had to interrupt writing *Lear* so as to provide *Macbeth* for a royal visit gives a satisfactory solution to their dating problem.) He then wrote *Timon*, but had enough sense to abandon it when almost finished. No one realised his true merits, he felt for a time, in his unique case correctly; but it is worthy of *Nonsense Novels* to describe Timon as burying himself, so as to be beholden to nobody, while writing on his tombstone his curses against all mankind. With the secret intention of curing himself, the playwright next described an absurdly mistaken though worthy man with a fatal belief that he was a god. He was now ready for the sunset glow of *Antony and Cleopatra*, a tragedy where the deaths are a piece of good luck – the lovers only just manage to avoid shame; and then he refused ever to write a tragedy again. This explains, I submit, why *Coriolanus* though so entirely externalised has such a deep ring of experience about it. I wish I could see it produced.

III

For many years, off and on, I have been set to give a lecture course on Shakespeare, and when Coriolanus came round I would explain that he cleared a stretch of the balcony for the siege-ladders, with the city gates below. I would assure my audience that I wasn't being original; what I said was not universally accepted, but other people had said it before me. Of course, a teacher who tells you without warning what nobody else believes is a positive danger, and the doubts of the students ought to be respected there. But, as I happened never to be challenged on this point, I forgot who my authorities had been. At last my colleagues told me that I was quite out of date, and that the Adams theatre had long been exploded; they referred me to Glynne Wickham's book, especially the part about the Boar's Head. I approached the book with alarm, but found it very encouraging about siege-ladders. Before quoting, I should perhaps recall that Old Burbage, the father of Shakespeare's chief actor, built the first public theatre in London in 1576; I had thought nothing was known about the plays performed there for the next ten years, but Wickham undoubtedly knows all the evidence we have (Vol. II, Part I, p. 296):

The play involving battlements, scaling-ladders and cities or towns was evidently much more popular after 1576 than before. There would seem to me therefore to be strong a priori grounds for supposing that professional actors would not deny in their own theatres facilities of a sort demanded at Court and to which provincial audiences were accustomed to be treated at the hands of amateurs.

He then argues in effect that the permanent structure of a public theatre would be too flimsy to be fought over, so that any such fighting would be done across ephemeral bits of carpentry run up overnight. This is obviously absurd; one should realise instead that the theatre in 1576 had already a sturdy balcony, fit for battle. Well then, surely the scaling-ladders must have been old-hat when Shakespeare revived them, not merely in *Coriolanus*, but even in *Henry VI Part I*, and the same for Marlowe? The plays do give rather that impression, when you come back to them.

Marlowe in starting on *Tamburlaine* had intended to rely on his poetry and his world-wide history, not on crude popular gadgets; but his triumph took him by surprise and Part II was rather hard to fill. Besides (he found he could explain) a rousing battle-scene in the last Act of Part II was a good preparation for the impudently philosophical death of the hero. In *I Henry VI* II.i the lords Talbot, Bedford and Burgundy simultaneously ascend three scaling-ladders, which Talbot has sportingly put far apart, so as to make it a competition ("*Bed.* Agreed. I'll to yond corner. *Bur.* And I to this", and Talbot takes the middle). In a real siege, the three ladders would always be close together, because only the leader on the middle one had any chance of staying alive long enough to clear a patch for the supporting troops. The audience have seen this in earlier plays, so they realise that the lords are being wildly aristocratic, or perhaps showing contempt for their opponents. They all succeed, and "The French leap o'er the wall in their shirts", falling into a grave discussion, down below, about what to do next, and trying to blame Joan of Arc. Or rather only the two sentinels actually need to jump over the walls, and all the others may arrive "several ways . . . half unprepared". Probably Joan and the Dauphin come in by a side door, as it is remarked that she has protected him by magic, but probably the three French lords jump, separately. It has been argued that this is a

piece of Leslie-Hotson staging, because we must be seeing events
inside the fortress and outside it both at once; but making the
French jump makes them look ridiculous, which is all that is
required. Nobody regards the jumping as a great feat. Then the
gate opens and an English soldier comes out calling "A Talbot";
this is enough to make the French run away, so that he can take
the grand clothes which they have left scattered. Here again,
there would be little point if the scene were inside, where Talbot
is known to be; what the soldier threatens is that Talbot is coming
out. As to *Henry V*, written just before the Globe was built, the
gates of Harfleur are shown (III.i–iii); scaling-ladders are carried
across the stage to a breach which the guns have made in the wall
further along; and perfunctory fun is extracted from cowardly
troops and pedantic officers. Then the King arrives at the gate to
demand surrender, which is given him; partly no doubt because
of the breach, but it is not mentioned. Shakespeare is concerned
to show Hal as negotiator and morale-builder, and cannot even
be bothered to tell us he invented a trick which won the Battle of
Agincourt, as the older play about him does. All the same, the
Prologues express regret that a theatre cannot show more; he is
in no mood to build a theatre in which the old type of siege-play
could not be performed. In *Coriolanus*, he could allow himself to
revive the traditional heroic siege-incident because, though
hackneyed in itself, it was being used for a special psychological
case.

Thus my military position looked secure; but who had been my
authority for the fight on the balcony? At last I found it, in the old
Variorum edition, under the stage direction *Enter Coriolanus
Bleeding*, a short excerpt from a minor work by a German author
around 1850. I had read the Variorum eagerly as a student, so
this was undoubtedly what I had remembered; and very many
others must have read it too – why had they all rejected it in
silence? The castle-gate set was much easier to trace; it was proposed by Irwin Smith in *Shakespeare Quarterly* for 1956, and in
his book of the same year supporting the Adams Globe; but
Adams in his second edition makes no mention of it. The engrav-
ing which illustrates it is sternly grand, like a Victorian railway
engine, and a severely conscientious stoker stands in front, looking small. I was sorry to find the picture so unwinning, because
the idea is important; *Lear* and *Macbeth* need a castle-gate set,
too. But the artist is not to be blamed for telling the truth; this
gate is much too big. And it is too big because it is planned for the

inner stage of J. C. Adams, which is 12 feet high, whereas 8 feet is quite enough for an actor to jump down. There are many other occasions for thinking so, but this was the first one to penetrate my head. This gate and its frame need to be a single gadget, a little wider than it is high, 9 feet by 8 feet, which locks at all four corners into iron slots above and below the inner stage. (There must be nothing one could trip over, after it is removed.) Each of the two doors should be 4 feet across and 6 feet high, and they shut with a clang; the lock had better be noisy too. However, it need not be very heavy, and anyhow need not be lifted; three or four men should be given practice at moving it into place together. When not in use it is wedged into its nook in a side wall; its only movements are sliding from the one place to the other, about 10 yards each time. When in use it stands a little behind the centre of the inner-stage curtain, which is then opened only enough to show it. With a bit of practice, the movement could be done quite quickly. But all this presumes that the balcony is only 8 feet high; if it is 12 feet, the gate becomes intolerably clumsy to swing about, especially in so confined a space, and no doubt this is why the idea has been rejected.

J. C. Adams of course recognises the need for a large central door in many scenes, but he fits it into the opening at the back of his inner stage. He often prefers to put scenes into the distance, and this is perhaps merely a matter of taste; but in a gate planned for defence it is absurd, as the Elizabethans would realise directly. A city gate was never put at the end of a tunnel through the wall, so that the enemy could walk in underneath the wall and blow it up; that was precisely the situation their engineers were delving for. Sometimes you had a stone tunnel built out, with the gate at the end of it (both at York and Peking), but never the other way round. If the city gate at the Globe was nearly 4 yards behind or inside the city battlements, the audience would not even recognise them as belonging to one structure. In effect, the Adams Globe could no more act *Coriolanus* than a modern theatre can.

Little Arthur in *King John* also jumps from the prison wall, and the rash act cannot always have been fatal to the actor, but it is hard to think of such examples after the building of the Globe, and it occurred to me that a fatal change might have come then; a craving for dignity might have induced a majority of the "sharers" to sacrifice intimacy and humanity. But the death of Antony, when I at last remembered about it, brought complete

reassurance. While dying he has to be lifted to Cleopatra's monument; "help, friends below", she says to the soldiers who lift him
up, and she calls on her women to help in pulling him up the
remaining gap. They can reach down to the point where the
soldiers can reach up; the height is plainly about 8 feet. J. C.
Adams says Antony is pulled up 15 feet on the crane; but why
does she never thank these crane-workers on her monument,
when all the other helpers get thanked? "How heavy weighs my
lord" means that she is pulling with the others, not that they are
merely guiding the crane. Or perhaps the crane is a symbol of
help from the gods; but in that case it is only a painful irony. She
says

> Had I great Juno's power
> The strong-winged Mercury should fetch thee up
> And set thee by Jove's side.

She has no such power, and he dies almost at once. The whole
point of the scene is that they still behave nobly when reduced to
the help of only a few faithful servants. Surely, unless she herself
were pulling hard, it would be unbearable for her to say "Here's
sport indeed." Either 8 feet or very bad taste.

  Such points have long been obvious, but people well-disposed
to the inner stage felt that lowering its ceiling would make it
invisible to the higher galleries. Certainly, its depth must be
greatly reduced, but that is an advantage, because the depth
allowed by Adams distances the action far too much. It can still
be 5½ feet; then, as I do the sum, a man sitting at the middle of
the top gallery can see the head of a man 6 feet high standing at
the back of the inner stage. People at the sides of the top gallery
would not, but then, a man would have no occasion to stand
there. In a council scene the king needs to be well back, but he is
seated, and usually the depth is needed for characteristic objects,
such as rich furniture or shrubs in tubs. Adams gives 3 feet at the
front, never curtained but under the penthouse or "tarrass", then
7 or 8 feet, and then a "central aperture" going back perhaps a
yard, making 14 feet. I retain 2 of the 3 feet jutting out, because
they adjoin the end wall of the window-stage, and a window there
is sometimes used in connection with it; also it is true that you get
action on the terrace, in connection with the lower stage, when
you do not want to open the whole balcony stage; so the curtain
of the balcony stage hangs 2 feet back, and the depth behind it
can only be 3½ feet. The curtain below, covering the inner stage,

has no need to be set back more than 8 inches. Sometimes characters lurk under this penthouse, but they need only pretend to be under cover, or they can push back the curtain. The inner and upper stages both have trap-doors, one just above the other, and the upper one should start just inside its curtain. Of course the actors on the upper stage can come out to the full 5½ feet as soon as the curtain is opened, just as those in an inner-stage scene use the main stage, merely slipping behind the curtain when it closes.

Reducing the height by 4 feet does seem drastic, but I can save one of them at once. Adams makes the brick floor of the yard, trodden by the groundlings, sink 1½ feet in a stretch of almost 30 feet, from the main entrance to the front of the stage; he is very convincing about the need for this. Well then, it would seem fitting, once your eye had noticed it, to have the apron-stage slope down at the same angle the other way, gaining 1 foot from its 20 feet. The space between the big side doors, where a chariot might enter, does not count as apron-stage and remains level. I am told that 1 in 20 is not too much strain for an actor; and if the builders could do the sloping brickwork they could easily do the sloping planks. Of course, all parts of the stage-front are raised together by this 1 foot. Adams gives 8 or 9 feet for the height of a side door, so that the tops of these doors could be level with the floor of the balcony; but there would be no advantage; they had better be impressive, because they are gates to all the world – though they are sometimes used as house-doors, and should then only be half-opened. Nine feet high for the side doors, then, and 5 feet across; this makes a huge door, and to make it secure, built all in wood, takes a fairly large frame, anyway a large lintel is expected. Thus the floor of the window-stage should be 9½ feet high, 1½ below the spectators' gallery, 1½ above the balcony stage. Taking each step as 6 inches high, there are three steps down from the public gallery to a window-stage, and at the other end of it three steps down, curving behind the pillar, to the balcony stage. Taking the drop in two equal jumps, I hope, would make it feel less harsh. Indeed, the whole design should not appear ugly; the basic idea, after all, is that while the spectators are given grandeur the actors are kept on a human scale. One side of the octagon, at the level of the main gallery, as you see it from across the yard, consists of two squares, 12 feet each way; but the main face of the stage, filling another side of the octagon, consists of three squares, 8 feet each way. Or rather, when you look into it, two cubes, 12 feet each way, and three cubes, counting in the central aperture and the half-hidden back stair, 8 feet each way. The galleries for spectators each have a supporting pillar in the middle, but you don't want this arrangement on the inner stage, where it would mean that the king in council (for example); had a pillar just in front of his nose; you have two narrower but brightly painted pillars between the squares. This is a recognised shape for paintings, for example the Leonardo *Last Supper*, and of course you need only open the central square to present a secret intrigue. The balcony stage should help to remove any feeling of oppressiveness, with a ceiling at least 12 feet high. The basic purpose of such a design, I should have said earlier, is to secure continuous performance, as in the cinema; almost any scene can be put on, giving sufficient help to the imagination, but without any interval of time to get it ready. The crouching inner stage may be excused if it gives a muscular impression of this immense capacity.

The two pillars, making you regard the inner stage as three squares, first seemed to me an aesthetic device, to excuse its low ceiling. But they might be necessary; the only other means of carrying the weight would be a tree-trunk 25 feet long, an expensive thing to buy, and it would not have been ferried over the Thames from the theatre, because there the 24-foot side of the octagon had been divided – two side doors, 9 feet high and 4 feet across, between them the inner stage, 8 feet high and 16 feet across. The pillars must not be thick, even if they carry a good deal of weight; an iron strut had better stiffen them behind. After all, if you have all those iron pikes to keep the groundlings out of the gallery, surely you can afford a little iron for aesthetic purposes. Iron is also used for fixing the castle-gate set, which needs to be pressed against these pillars to make it engage with its locks. It should be very firm, and if only held in slots it would tend to wobble. Of course the gate hides the pillars from the audience; you do not want both at once. These various reasons, I submit, make the pillars likely; and besides, they would echo the two pillars that hold up the heavens.

The second edition of J. C. Adams proposes an alteration, not always worked into the body of his text, which I can claim as in favour of my view. He had arranged a staircase for the actors, immediately behind his inner and upper stage, and connecting them; but now he finds that this would not leave enough room, at the back of the building, where of course a passage-way is essential; so he has made the actor's staircase an outside one, like the staircases for the public, in front. He recognises that this does not appear in the survey pictures, and he leaves in his text the evidence that this invisible staircase was a kind of joke readily mentioned to the audience when the door to it is opened; but there is no room for it on his plan. The little sketches in the surveys are only impressionistic, but I think they are strong evidence against this change, because the impression given of the theatre from a distance would become so very different; it would lose all its mystery if this staircase appeared. No doubt the extra time required for using an outside staircase would be trivial. But consider the Queen in *Hamlet*, coming down to her husband's study after the terrible scene with her son; hardly able to speak (though even now she can dismiss the spies with kindness and dignity), but apparently intending to betray her son as soon as she has her voice, and then stubbornly lying to her beloved husband to save the life of her son – this is high drama, and it cannot be interrupted in such a clumsy manner. She needs to be heard stumbling downstairs. Of course the later judgement of Adams is quite right so far as it goes; the very deep inner stage he has proposed does not leave enough passage-way behind.

Another reason for the change must I think have occurred to Adams. He has planned a central aperture at the back of his inner stage, about 6 feet high and 4 across, usually curtained, but needed for special occasions such as the death of Polonius (above), the showing of the eight Kings to Macbeth (below), the revival of Hermione (either). But, on the lower stage, if he has this staircase, it is going to spoil the view every time. With any slope, his symmetrical stair would be 6 feet high halfway across. An Elizabethan actor would probably be only 5 foot 6, but this is too close. Assuming a 1-in-1 slope, as he appears to do (rightly I think), the stair would be 4 feet high at one edge of the aperture. It would be almost impossible to hide by decorations, and what I propose instead would at least be a workable plan. With the same slope of 1-in-1, and only 8 feet to go up, and 24 feet across the inner stage, you can give the stair only half the width; starting 1 foot from the end of the inner stage below, you would arrive a foot short of the middle of the stage above, as you clearly ought to do; Coriolanus can fight his way up to the city wall with the centrality that he deserves. This stair (allowing a foot of it to be visible through the door at the bottom) would not impinge at all upon the central aperture of 4 feet across and 6 feet high; from some of the people at the side it would need disguising, but very much less. Adams, I think, was right to decide that Shakespeare sometimes had a dramatic use for this central aperture, and that only the Globe could give it to him. But Adams cannot combine this insight with his very high and deep inner stage.

I agree that the balcony stage should have a practicable door on the left of its back wall, with a lock and a prominent key, and that it should be presented when convenient as the top of the stairs, since it corresponds with the door on the right below. I agree that a four-poster double bed, when supposed to appear on the upper stage, had better appear only in part, as if behind the central aperture. The rectangle where the stair comes up must have a hinged trap-door, so that it can be closed when some such extra gadget needs to stand there; but the gadget must be removed as soon as possible, because this is the only back stair to the first floor. (The charm of the building, or at least of thinking about it, is that so much had to be packed into the space.) There would be 6 feet left between the stairhead and the back wall, and the next stair up, from the upper stage to the music-room and the crane, had better lie against the middle of that wall, so as not to interfere with the lighting arrangements at the sides. This stair, again taking only a yard, would leave a yard for a passage between. The stair down to the cellar under the stage, only about 5 feet deep, is also at the back of the inner stage; beginning on the left, whereas the stair up to the balcony stage begins on the right. Actors who are going to "pass over the stage" can come there conveniently from their dressing-rooms, but will probably have to stoop, as there is so much danger of flooding. I am trying to fit the various essentials into the space, and it seems possible after the reduction of the inner stage. There are wide trap-doors to storage-spaces, again no more than 5 feet deep, on both sides.

The levels of the ceiling above the ground floor take a bit of thought, but I can see only one solution. Both levels must continue out of sight of the spectator; whatever chariot requires 9 feet must have a stable to receive it; on the upper stage, a soldier must be able to appear running as if from a distance, and the dragon carrying Faustus must fly through on a smooth curve. A perpendicular is drawn from each of the two pillars, at the ends of the back curtain, to the corresponding side wall of the outer octagon. Further from the audience than that line, the ceiling is only 8 feet high, and the dragon of Faustus curves smoothly round above it; but along that line it rises 1½ feet, to fit the great doors. This higher ceiling includes the outside window, which is

4 feet high and 4 feet above the floor. The position of the castle-gate set, while waiting for its next use, now becomes definite. Sliding it out of the inner stage to its usual side, it comes under the higher ceiling at once, so that it is easier to manoeuvre; it is then pushed into prepared slots across one of the back corners of the building, where it just misses obscuring either adjoining window. It takes up 3 feet on the outside back wall, and 6½ on the angled wall, with an external angle of 45 degrees, and this allows it to be 9 feet long. It sticks out a bit from the line where the ceiling goes up, and this makes it easier to handle. The stage door at the back, even with its penthouse, is not very big, but it pushes the windows on that wall to the side, so they may well start 3½ feet from the end pillars. The city gate now lies only 1½ feet from the corner, 1 foot from the surface of the outside pillar, so it wastes very little space, and is securely held. It was much the most cumbrous bit of equipment that this theatre was saddled with, and to show that it could be handled smoothly, without getting in the way, is an important step. The throne, which after being folded up and wrapped was probably hung in the other corner, would be a trifle in comparison.

I can offer four details from the plays to prove the elevation of the window-stage above the balcony stage, and all are familiar in these discussions, so probably more could be found. The first is in *I Henry VI* i.iv, a play that shows a certain boyish readiness to have fun with the details of the stage, so that it is likely to tell truth here. The city of Orleans is besieged by the English, and they have captured a tower in the suburbs. From this they are

> Wont through a secret grate of iron bars
> In yonder tower to over-peer the city
> And thence discover . . .

how best to attack it. A master-gunner is speaking, on the city walls, and he has arranged for an adroit boy to fire a piece of ordnance when any English can be viewed there. With this, he kills Lord Salisbury and Sir Thomas Gargrave, though the window and the balcony were in a flat row against the back wall of the stage. No doubt the window was a bay, pushing out over the side door; but it must also have been noticeably higher than the balcony, or the boy might as well have jabbed at these worthies with a sword. It may seem surprising to meet this refinement of construction so early, but the early plays were the ones that most wanted to play tricks, with Tamburlaine able to enter in his chariot through a high door, and yet with city walls low enough to be jumped off (as they do just afterwards in this play, II.i). Next I can clear up a stage direction in *Romeo and Juliet*, which has been a great bone of contention. When a book of drawings based on the first edition of J. C. Adams came out, C. Walter Hodges reviewed it in *Shakespeare Quarterly* and said that this one stage direction was enough to explode the whole soap-bubble of the Adams theory. It says "She goeth down from the window" (III.v.67), and is found only in the First Quarto, a pirate edition, often said to be a memorial reconstruction. Juliet has just consummated her recent marriage to Romeo, which makes it much harder for her parents to annul, and is letting him down by a rope-ladder from a convenient window when her mother comes upstairs calling her. Hastily tidying the ladder away, she patters across to her bedroom, pretending to feel ill. Her bedroom is the balcony stage, and the characters cannot see through its wall, as we can, though they can see through windows. These literary pirates were presumably interested in the drama, or they would have adopted a more lucrative form of theft; and I expect the comment is heartfelt, though it need only report what the writer had seen on the stage. Juliet is about to make her first false step (accepting the arrangement of the Friar); if she had now told the truth to her parents, she would probably have saved the lives of both herself and Romeo. They might try to kill Romeo, but she has secured his escape for the time, and short of that they can do very little. So she does take a step down when she complicates the position by lying; but her parents might have succeeded in killing him, if she had told the truth, and then it would have felt like betrayal. Be this as it may, there is no reason in the story why she need take a literal step down; it is merely a result of the way the stage is built. If she went right down to the apron-stage to meet her mother, her mother would already have met Romeo there, escaping through the orchard; to make them ignore each other would put an excessive strain on the imagination of the audience.

The other two concern amorous contact between the terrace and a bay-window, and are cited by Adams (p. 250), but I think mistakenly. In Chapman's *May Day*, 1600 (a test case, because it was acted by the children during the War of the Theatres, at the Blackfriars but definitely not at the Globe), the joke lies in the excessive modesty of the two lovers. The girl's father has found a rich husband for her, but she has made a better choice, and explains to her go-between that there is a danger of her being approached through the terrace of the house next door. On this hint the go-between arrives with a rope-ladder and the suitor; the rope-ladder is thrown up to her, and she agrees to "fix it to the terrace". It is an odd form of words, but we may suppose that she regards the outside wall of her bedroom as part of the house next door, since it makes the end of the terrace there. The ladder has sharp hooks, which she pins to her window-sill – there is nothing to show that she gets out of her window, which would be very out of character, so it would be mentioned. The young man is induced to go up the ladder as far as the terrace, where he makes love respectfully. The sardonic go-between shouts up that he is exposing the lady's reputation by standing there talking about her on a "stage". So he is driven, purely out of modesty, to climb further up the rope-ladder into her bedroom. In the Adams model this window is barely a yard above the floor, so that he can step in at once; it needs to be about 1½ feet higher, or he seems excessively feeble. After all, his marriage is part of the happy ending. In Jonson's *The Devil is an Ass* (first acted in 1616, at the Globe) the love is adulterous, and the suitor does not appear timid. He is well received by the lady, and has been assured that her husband is out of the house; but he still does not step through the window. Admittedly, she is now the one on the terrace of the rich house, while he is lurking in a friend's study, but he might at least invite her in. Instead, they behave as if kept apart by some obstacle, and it is just as well, because the husband soon appears behind her. Jonson printed the play in a folio of 1631, and added some marginal notes which have only increased the confusion. "The scene is acted at two windows, out of two continuous buildings", and further down the page, "He grows more familiar in his courtship, plays with her paps, kisseth her hands, etc." There is an air of dotage about this, because he does not alter the earlier passages which make "the window . . . that opens to my gallery" quite definite. But he has a reasonable motive, while collecting his dramas for posterity; he might well reflect that the special arrangement invented by Old Burbage would not last for ever. The point of his note is that the romance of such an an incident, however it is arranged, lies in the difficulty of it, and perhaps danger. There would be none if the man had only to step through the window; indeed, the first audiences would hoot him for a coward. In real life, however crowded the city, such a window into another person's house-room would not be made easy to step through, whereas a window high in the wall would be accepted. The difference is taken for granted at the end of *May Day*, when the modest lover is jollied as one who has used "the help of a ladder to creep in at a wench's chamber window". Probably Old Burbage in 1596 when he designed the Blackfriars had no idea of using this window above the terrace for part of the action; it merely helped to give an impression that all was open and well-lit. The use of it which occurred to two playwrights, probably independently, shows that the terrace was at least 4 feet below the window.

IV

A major piece of equipment, not shown in the Adams plan, needs next to be considered. It is hardly ever essential to a play, which is just as well since it could not be provided at the Blackfriars, but it is very characteristic of the Globe. Allardyce Nicoll, in *Shakespeare Survey* 12, "Passing Over the Stage", listed a number of stage directions which demand it, and reported previous authorities who have believed in it. It is an obvious convenience; two flights of steps, at the opposite sides of the stage, far back but on the apron, rise from the level of the yard; they are generally used for a procession, or for the solitary passing of a character who is only observed by the others, not spoken to. Nicoll expected the procession to cross the yard, emerging from a hole which the "De Witt" sketch calls the Ingressus; it could not come from under the stage, he thought, or the audience would jeer at it as coming from Hell. But the actors would not have crossed the yard dressed up as archbishops and queens and what not; consider, the Fortune contract demands actual fortifications to keep the groundlings out of the spectators' gallery. They would have no special grudge against actors, but to tease and fumble a man dressed like that would be an immediate impulse for them, done for fun (or so many people believed). Nor was there any need for it. The Globe audience, let us grant, would consider anyone who came up through a trap-door as probably emerging from Hell, but not if he emerged from stairs at the side of the stage; after all, he might have come from behind. Anyway, on a Miracle Play wagon even the Lord God had presumably to appear from below, just as he would on Leslie Hotson's stage. There was no need for scruple, and these stairs at the side were probably added from early times.

Leslie Hotson issued a challenge, in *Shakespeare's Wooden O*, saying that a passage from Marlowe's *Massacre at Paris* could not be acted on Adams's stage, and showing how his stage would do it. This is the massacre itself (lines 200ff) and it is certainly a test. Hotson puts up four houses over four trap-doors, filling the apron-stage, and seems here to have no more trap-doors; so far he is not ahead of Adams, who also has four discovery-places. Marlowe allows for some incidental killing of Protestants in the street, but he only has four named people murdered in their houses; and I expect the limitations of the stage were what stayed his hand. Hotson claims to present a fifth place, downstairs at the Admiral's house, and builds an upper storey for his bedroom, but there is no need to show this downstairs room. His bedroom is the upper stage, and people who go to see him just go through the inner-stage curtains. When a soldier is told to see that no one escapes from the house, he just watches the curtain. Then a bell is rung to alert the murderers, and the Duke of Guise leads a mob across the stage, and Seroune is murdered at one of the side doors (his house door, which he opens), then the inner stage is found to be Ramus's study, and he is killed there; enough incident has intervened to make us forget that it was recently (though unseen) the downstairs of the Admiral's house. The other door is knocked at and discovers the King of Navarre and the Prince of Condé, with their "schoolmasters", Protestant theologians who are killed while royalty is spared. All these places can be seen without obstacle, and we do not have to wait while they are built up and taken down. But Hotson does have a clear advantage, on second thoughts, because he can have a mob racing from one trap-door to another, and he sometimes allows the use of two side doors; whereas Adams has no way in and out, because all the apertures are bespoken. Several characters go out during the massacre; to a church service, to become King of Poland, to appear innocent in a rustic seclusion; and obviously there should be more than one exit, as we are supposed to be on a public street.

This proves that there were side stairs on the early stages, but not that they were retained at the Globe. The angled side doors had taken over much of their function, but they were likely to be retained as traditional, and then they could be reserved for processions. The Elizabethans were fond of processions in real life, with a keen eye for correctness in the uniforms, and spent a lot of time waiting for them to pass. On the stage they would expect a thorough parade, coming out to the front of the apron; and yet an obscure obstacle came to be felt here. All ceremony is haunted by the danger of appearing fatuous. To have a row of men walk round three sides of an oblong looks fatuous, because there can be no sensible reason for it – they are merely on show. But if the stage tapers, reducing itself at the front to the old 24 feet, which was still the size of the inner stage at the back, and on its way the procession has to come round the outside of each of the two pillars, well, you can't be sure they aren't up to something. Indeed, the wider stage at the back had been chiefly needed to give this improvement to the processional route. It is not enough to find that high drama gives no evidence for this route; many people in the audience might answer that the drama was just a frill, and what they had come for was the show (for that matter, the crane was also not much used for serious drama).

These considerations explain a rather obtrusive number, which crops up among the very few numbers mentioned in the Fortune contract. That document exasperatingly remarks that a full plan is attached; only the basic essentials, together with some details that are particularly wanted by the buyer, but might not seem important to the builder, rate a mention in the contract itself. (Good windows in the tiring-room, for instance.) Among these we get the figure of 43 feet for the length of the stage – meaning its width from side to side, as the other dimension is to reach the middle of the yard. Our usual picture of the Fortune Theatre (there is a particularly impressive example in the old *Shakespeare Hand-book*), shows a vast blank ploughed field with large drains, 6 feet across, at each side of it. A few depressed groundlings, glared at by the twelvepenny or fourpenny men above them, huddle about in these drains, and the other half of the yard is blank. What on earth can it matter whether the drains are 6 feet or 5 feet wide? Why should that detail be written into the contract? And how could Henslowe make a general demand for a replica of the Globe stage, if the contract was describing an entirely different one?

The Globe is mentioned four times. The first mention says that the "stairs, conveyances, and divisions" of the Fortune must be like those at the Globe, and the last that the new building must have even bigger scantlings. On the second occasion, the stage is to be

paled in below with good, strong and sufficient new oaken boards . . . and the said stage to be in all other proportions contrived and fashioned

like unto the stage on the said playhouse called the Globe; with convenient windows and lights glazed to the said tiring house;

then, after more details, evidently remembered in a random
order:

And the said house and other things before mentioned to be made and
done to be in all other contritions, conveyances, fashions, thing and
things effected, finished and done according to the manner and fashion
of the said house called the Globe.

Presumably a lawyer's clerk took it down from Henslowe's
dictation, and found him so emphatic as to be almost incoherent
here. "Saving only", he went on, "that all the principal and main
posts of the said frame and stage forward shall be square", so he
did at least recognise the squareness, in the decoration.

A beautifully imaginative piece of reconstruction (whether by
J. C. Adams or not) was based on the two main figures of this
contract, that the outer square was 80 feet across and the inner
55. This makes the frame 12½ feet thick. Suppose now that the
Globe, which was two concentric octagons, was 12 feet thick, and
that, taking any side of the inner octagon, the lines of the
adjacent sides met on the corresponding side of the outer octagon. This has extreme elegance; it could readily be noticed in the
open spaces of the main public gallery; and it makes the whole
building feel like a cut stone. All the dimensions of the ground
plan are now defined; the side of the inner octagon is 24 feet, and
the overall breadth of the building is 83. Henslowe of course
could readily treat his square as an octagon; he has only to block
off two small triangles, from the corners of the inner square
adjacent to his stage, and the entire lay-out of the Globe stage
can be reproduced, down the centre of the building. The contract
never says that the stage has to be square, only that it has to be
like the Globe in all its proportions. Blocking off these two bits
would only cost him one-twelfth of the area of the yard, and he
would gain some much-needed storing-space. Presumably he left
the other corners, at the back of the auditorium, to provide extra
seats; and thus the building would be seen as inherently a square,
an idea which was to be recognised in the carving of the main
posts.

However the numbers do not quite fit; not 12 but 12½ is the
thickness that can be deduced from the contract, and Henslowe
had not got 83 feet, only 80. It is usual to have a contract which

repeats the essential parts of what has already been agreed in the plans, but I suspect Henslowe meant to show this contract around as part of his advertising campaign. He would have to reduce the basic measurement, the side of his inner octagon, to 23 feet, and public attention must be distracted from that. The reduction seems right, giving him 6 inches to spare, but these great pillars had to be almost a foot wide, certainly 10 inches. Geometry deals in points, and here, for a ground plan, the point is the centre of the pillar; it looks as if Henslowe's neighbours would find his pillars obtruding upon them for at least a few inches, but he would be likely to succeed in negotiating that. When the contract implies that the frame is 12½ feet thick, he may be allowed to mean from the outside edge of an outer pillar to the yard-side edge of an inner one, which brings down his geometrical thickness to 11½, just right for a modulus of 23; meanwhile he has contrived to insinuate that his frame is a bit thicker than the Globe one, so far from thinner. He could claim to hold more spectators, with his extension round the two sides of the square, even in spite of the overall reduction of 1 in 24; there seems to be an easy margin. Suppose he also built a wider stage; then his talking-points would be impeccable.

The geometry of the two staircases which come up from below, at the Globe, has not yet been considered. Each of them lies in a triangle, with its base at the start of the apron-stage, and the other two sides, angled at 45 degrees, adjoining respectively the twelvepenny seats and the penny standers. The wall for the gentry occupies 12 feet, and so does the wall barring out the groundlings. I had to do the sum first, but the geometry is easy once you know the answer. No doubt we ought to see an extra elegance in it; either side of the tapering apron-stage is parallel to the line joining the centre of the yard to the corresponding back pillar. This wall and its twin on the other side are in line with the two pillars that hold up the heavens, and the main trap-door lies behind them, towards the inner stage; so there had anyway (even if you allowed no stair) to be head-room in this part of the cellar. (The stair might also emerge from the back, but that seems more complicated for no advantage.) The base line of the triangle along the apron-stage is a little over 9 feet, so even with a big central pillar the winding stair can be 4 feet wide at the start. Then the sides close in on it, but it is never less than 3½ feet. The stage here is 5 feet high, and must be reached in one half-turn; a fairly steep climb, but it need never all be taken at a run. Halfway up, the stair is actually 11 feet long (of course the steps ray out across the triangle); and here two or three men can lurk, visible but not obtrusive, till it is time for them to bound onto the stage.

The Theatre of Old Burbage would have needed this convenience, and indeed a bigger one, because at first it concentrated on battle-pieces. The simplest plan would be to erect two walls perpendicular to the sides of the octagon adjoining the back stage, starting from their centres (and only the same height as the stage, perhaps 4½ feet; there is no need to keep the groundlings from looking); these would meet the apron-stage at the same level as the Globe ones, in line with the two pillars. The triangle is now 12 feet by 12 by 17 (very nearly); thus the stair can be 8 feet wide. Just the thing for an invading army, and it makes the old stage look a great deal less pinched. These nooks, adjoining the big side doors, would anyhow be places where you feared that groundlings might make mischief, if they were allowed in there; it would be rational to shut them off. I don't deny that the stairs could be as little as half the size I have given; but why make them small?

In the Globe, the distance across the stage at its widest, just in front of the doors set at an angle, was a bit under 41 feet. At the Fortune, taking off 1 in 24, it would be barely 39. This was the kind of thing that made a talking-point, and the Fortune men thought of an actual slight improvement, adequate to counter it. A small platform was added in front of the halfway pillar, between the twelvepenny seats and the big door, two more feet both forwards and sideways. This would involve removing a few of the twelvepenny seats, but only at the corner which gave the worst view of the stage, so that the gentry could never have wanted them much; whereas they would like having a closer view of the parade. Each actor would pause there, well lit, framing himself against the oak pillar, before going forward in the procession. The dress parade has always been an important part of drama, and this addition would suit Alleyn and his company very well; it was a splendid way to outdo the Globe. And not specially difficult for the actor; taking the climb straight is what makes it steep, but now he had room to move sideways. It may be objected that this is a remote explanation for a number in a legal contract, which would be useless unless intelligible; but the complete plans were available, and the same architect was employed. He was merely being asked to confirm that this small extra thing would be fixed up somehow, whatever obstacles arose. Some reason needs to be offered to explain why the number was mentioned at all.

Our usual theory about the Fortune stage makes it about 1,200 square feet, whereas I reduce it to about 900; though if the Globe additions are all counted in, the inner and upper stages and the two open staircases, it is hardly any smaller. What matters, of course, is that every bit of the Globe stage has possible functions, things it can be used for, making it different from other bits; never can this stage give the impression of a soggy ploughed field, across which an actor must heave laboriously in his gumboots. No wonder Henslowe became excited when dictating his demand for a replica of the Globe; how absurd to suppose he would have been content with our modern barbaric picture of the Fortune instead.

There is of course another way to extract an octagon from a square; you can regard it as a diamond, merely turning the whole plan through an angle of 45 degrees. In the Fortune, the public gate and the stage door are now at opposite *corners* of the square, and Henslowe has only to sacrifice one triangle from his auditorium, instead of two, making only one part in 24 of the area. One would expect him to prefer this, but two big corners would jut out at the sides, as well as the back – perhaps not impossibly to the disadvantage of the spectators, but the effect would be considered very ridiculous, so much so that a mention of it would probably survive. If I thought Henslowe so greedy for large sales as some of my opponents do, I would have to believe he built this diamond; but Alleyn had a keen sense of his dignity, and I cannot see him accepting it. My own proposal, it may be answered, would also look raw and new-fangled; well, it was a bold step within the current mode. Perhaps it is just as well to show that I would draw the line somewhere. On the other hand, it is impossible to suppose that Henslowe accepted a Fortune Theatre, built by the very architect of the Globe, with none of the recent advances in design at all, not even the angled stage doors. Modern pictures of it look like the old Theatre, so magnified in breadth that its crudity becomes obvious, and no longer even permitted the saving broad staircases at the side.

So far from that, the Fortune contract reads to me as if Henslowe believed some magical power to attach to the details of the Globe. I think he really did have in mind something magical, but that needs approaching from another direction.

V

Looking at the photographs of the model of the Adams Globe, in his second edition, my faith in the plan was badly shaken, but I did not know the cause. It looked intolerably twee and like a dolls' house, but why not? It was a dolls' house. The point where the artist might be making a just criticism, I decided, came in the chic little cover over the stage. We are regularly told that this cover both kept the rain off the actors' clothes and also acted as a sounding-board, and so it should; but a parasol held 30 feet up would be useless for both purposes. The contract for the Fortune demands "a shade or cover over the said stage", with no suggestion of a difference from the Globe here. If such an agreement had been made about a farmyard or a Dutch barn, and the case came to court, it would not be judged enough to have covered less than half the area (only the apron-stage is in question, because the main stage, between the slanted doors, is already covered by the crane). I was glad to find that Wickham thinks the same (II.ii.74); he would be sure to know of any evidence to the contrary. He expects that the first Globe was the first building to take the cover over the whole area, and I agree but expect it only came forward a yard or two. The second Globe, in 1613, undoubtedly did have a cover over the whole area, and probably without any supporting pillars (C. Walter Hodges, *Shakespeare's Second Globe*, 1973). Around 1900, as I gather, most experts on this subject expected the cover of the first Globe to be complete, but then the difficulty of lighting the stage occurred to them, so they came to feel that the "De Witt" sketch might be correct. I do not think we need be delayed by Van Buchell, who drew from imagination; he could hardly have chosen a better view-point than the one he did, high above the public entry, and after that choice he was obliged to halve the cover, or he could not have given his other scraps of misinformation about the stage. But the question is otiose, because the second Globe, built with the confidence of experience, presents a far more severe problem. A sheer half is blocked out from the circular opening above the yard, with no side lighting such as the old cover used to permit, and the inner stage has got to be at the far end of the resulting dark hole.

The lighting is a crucial question. The most impressive argument in Leslie Hotson, I thought when first reading him, is that all these open-air theatres, on our usual interpretation, make the audience face the afternoon sun. Consider a bull-fight, he said; only the cheap seats are in the sun, the grandees are in the centre of the shaded area – and so they were at the Globe. But the bull-fighter himself is in sunlight, whereas Hotson's Elizabethan grandees, on a sunny day, would be trying to see actors on a darkened stage while dazzled by the glare from the cheap seats beyond. (This is yet another reason for feeling sure that the balcony would not provide good seats.) Hotson was aware of the difficulty, and he opened his book by describing a production in the second Globe; he proposes a big mirror placed aslant in the "heavens", after first removing the crane no doubt, so as to reflect the sunlight down upon the central stage. Such a reflector would be a remarkable technical achievement for the period, and it is hard to believe that no mention of it would have come down to us, if it had worked. Presumably all the other major theatres would have to have it as well. Hotson has asked a very good question here, but his answer will surely not do; I doubt whether it would even be agreeable, as a method of lighting. What did not occur to either side in the debate, nor to me till long afterwards, is that daylight would come in anyhow unless kept out on purpose – perhaps to gratify these imaginary grandees. Far more probably, the back of the main stage at the second Globe, let alone any inner stages, was lit by daylight on a level, from behind.

But any such light had to satisfy one condition. W. J. Lawrence, in *Elizabethan Playhouse*, Vol. II (1913), remarks that the back window in the upper stage, for which he had been providing evidence from the play-texts, was not much needed for the drama, but "owed its origin to the pressing necessity for light". I am glad to quote an authority who recognises this need, but if an actor is in twilight, a light shining behind him makes him positively harder to see. He needs light from a source which is at the side and also in front, though perhaps not much in front. This might well call for reflectors, or perhaps they should be called "baffles", and I believe Hotson was right so far. But the Globe is so well lit from behind, if one allows a window outside each bay on each floor, that a baffle transferring light from one window (when I try to find a place for it on the chart) is liable to interfere with direct light from another. All the same, the relative amounts of light coming from different windows would vary sharply, and it would be reassuring to have some control over them. Probably the baffles were on stands, ready to be moved about as required. They would be about 6 feet square, thin planks of wood painted white, like the screens used on the edges of cricket grounds; mirrors would not spread the light enough. Thus the reason why the Fortune contract said that the tiring-house must have "convenient windows and lights glazed", as at the Globe, is that the light was needed on the stage; these windows were at the back of the whole building, or in the two furthest sides of the octagon, at the Globe, where they are often shown in the survey pictures. The Fortune is a more difficult question. Of course the whole back-stage area, or at least the ground floor of it, was spoken of as the tiring-house. No doubt the actors demanded light too, but the contract deals with basic requirements. These inlets for light could be curtained off as required, so that, on the frequent occasions when the actors pretend to be in the dark, it really was a bit shadowy; though the front of the stage remained in full daylight. At other times the least well-lit part was around the main trap-door, the centre of the apron-stage, and the action often alternates between front and back.

On the Adams ground-floor chart, there is an outside window in line with the inner stage at either end of it, so lighting it should not be hard; but this window is slightly too far back; two baffles in line with the front of the inner stage, beyond the pillars, and slightly tilted, would give more light from the front. There should be two smaller windows, 3½ feet across perhaps, in the back wall on either side of the stage door, but Adams has now suppressed them because he puts an outside staircase there; they would be a help, using reflectors. The outer octagon has a side of 34 feet, divided by a pillar; each half has a window, which Adams seems to make 4 feet wide, but it had better be 5 feet. It is 4 feet from the floor and 4 feet high, so that all of the light from the window further back is available under the 8-foot ceiling of the inner stage, but both windows are under the 9½-foot ceiling of the slanted side door, so none is cut off from that either. Adams however gives the nearer window to the actors for a dressing-room, decently enclosed; and this means four windows in all, on each side, above and below. Certainly, the actors need dressing-rooms with windows, but they can use the next window along, round the octagon; it means sacrificing some of the fourpenny seats, but these seats would not give a fair view of the stage, and could only cause anger. (Henslowe's *Diary* shows the house nearly full, earning him more than £3, about twice a month; and it is only on these days that such bad seats would be used at all.)

The partition ending the fourpenny gallery needs to go diagonally, from an outside pillar to the next inside pillar along, and behind this comes a queerly shaped but well-lit dressing-room – it is assumed that the twelvepenny galleries were not more than 5 feet deep, being exclusive, so that the actors could pass behind them. To give even the worst-seated twelvepenny spectator at least an illusion of seeing the play (if they ever needed all the seats), the wall ending that gallery also needs to be set at an angle, going on to the outside pillar perhaps, with a door for the actors at the end. Such a wall allows direct entry for light, slightly from in front, to the angled side door, and the same from the outside window in the next storey, to the window-stage. These sources of light would be more important, most of the time, than the inner stages; and there would be no regular need for baffles, so long as the line to both windows (all four windows) could be kept uncluttered.

On the upper storey, the floor of the balcony stage is rather far below its window (I expect that the line of the outside windows went on firmly; if it bobbed down, that did not catch the attention of the survey artists) but diffused daylight works well from above. The balcony could also get reflected light from windows in the back wall. The window-stage needs altering a bit. The audience hardly sees the actors unless they stand at the windows, and then only sees them from the hips upward; the back wall gets little attention, and would look odd if it did, as it slopes away from the bay-window. (It could have a rich object, a bust perhaps, but not a picture or tapestry.) It is dark and firm (the actors must not be lit from behind), and it is parallel to the back of the stage, whereas the bay-windows are set at an angle of 45 degrees. Probably it is in line with the front of the terrace, the outside edge of the balcony stage; this line just misses the outside window, so it cuts off no light from entering the window-stage. But there is a break in the line where the window-stage comes closest to the balcony; a recess 3 feet wide leads back to the three steps down, around the pillar. A window-stage has rather limited uses; a number of attendants may be present, who need not define themselves by coming close to the window, but two or at most three people do the work of the play. They are close to the windows (leaded panes with no glass in them) but they are at this furthest-back part of the window-line, so they are plainly not being lit from behind. The light from the window-stages, of course, normally diffuses over the back of the stage, but it is only when getting near the trap-door that an actor is plainly being lit from behind; by that time he is also being lit from in front.

There is always light from the window-stages, unless it is deliberately stopped; light from the big doors has sometimes to be stopped by the needs of the play, but not for long. In common life, to be sure, doors are usually kept shut; but, as has often been remarked, the Elizabethan stage tended to show a public place, where anyone might walk on; thus it was natural to keep the side doors open, till there was a reason why they should be closed. They are sometimes used as house-doors, and then the light behind them needs to be curtained off; the householder may bring a candle to the half-opened door; but these scenes are commonly brief. This is rather an absurd use of the big door, allowed as an occasional convenience in presenting a story. I think it should be 5 feet wide, as well as 9 feet high, and should be brought forward as far as possible along its bay of 12 feet. The terrace sticks out 2 feet, and this becomes nearly 3 feet where it meets a side wall at an angle of 45 degrees. At the other end, the pillar sticks out nearly 6 inches, and another 6 are needed for the solid framing of such a whopping door. If you put it there, as far out as it could comfortably go, you get it in a direct line with the outside window, and an actor when on the main stage between the two doors (neither apron nor inner) becomes much less liable to appear lit from behind.

I am uneasy about the inner stages, which seem to be losing their claim to act as a kind of spotlight. It seemed fair to say 5½ feet, but with the terrace taking 2 feet and the pillar ½, the aperture at the side reduces to 3. This does not help you to get in light only from the front, and besides, when Faustus and Mephistopholis are riding their dragon over the City of Rome, they need to sweep out on a curve. Perhaps the outside 6 feet on both these long stages should be on a hinge, so that any of the four can be moved back or forward 6 inches or so, and the hidden stair can be moved back 6 inches to allow for it. The whole breadth of the inner stage was only needed for occasions which did not demand very good lighting; a crowd scene, a grand dinner-party, a royal council. A better contrast of lighting could be got by opening the curtains only to two-thirds, or for private interviews one-third, so that the reflectors could be moved in. For such a contrast one would of course close the side doors.

This presents my main theory, but there are some minor

points. Adams while discussing the music-room (second edition, p. 322) remarks that it needed translucent curtains, because:

The light by which the musicians worked was not produced artificially inside the gallery but came through the curtains from the unroofed yard.

"Unroofed" he says; this was the darkest place, just under the centre of the cover. His chart for this level of the building (p. 309) puts a thick line with no windows all round this music-room, and yet the attic as a whole, used only for storage not for acts of skill, is allowed no fewer than six windows to all the winds of heaven. It shows the extraordinary strength of the presumption that no light could be admitted from behind. If the spectators were to admire the constellations on the painted ceiling, there could have been no reason for keeping this high region dark. I agree that the musicians need to have a solid wall behind them, so their shadows do not get thrown upon the curtain; and even here one should be prepared to cut off the light, because there may be dark work among the gods. Our evidence for music up there is nearly all about music made by spirits; such was its status in poetical fantasy, though no doubt musicians really did find the third storey a safe place to store instruments. That was the point of praising Ben Jonson, in a general approval for his sturdy realism, by the line:

Thou layest no sieges to the music-room.

Pedants have claimed eagerly that this proves the balcony stage to have been in regular use as a music-room (whenever the mysterious grandees could be coaxed away). It means that, whereas ordinary sieges on the stage only put up ladders to the balcony, if Jonson had ever permitted himself any such theatrical vanity he would have warred like a Titan with the very gods. He was a classical man. A permanent glow from such a room would be no more than normal.

I have next to defend myself against a rebutting fact which at first seemed to me very strong. The *Long View* of London by Hollar, published in 1647, gives an evidently skilful and careful picture of the second Globe (already destroyed) and it is made to back into a massive clump of trees. This would entirely prevent any such lighting arrangement as I have described. But very luckily we have also his first sketch, in "pencil partly inked over" (Adams, p. 90), and here there are no trees at the back, though there are trees in the neighbourhood. There was an aesthetic reason for the change – the engraver wanted to make the building look rich and plump and contented; various other changes in the detail help to carry out this intention. Other surveys from Amsterdam may gladly be interpreted in the light of this entirely conscientious movement away from literal accuracy. And of course, not showing the back, he cannot prove I am wrong about the windows there.

But the windows at the side which he does show cry out for an interpretation; there are tiny ones close together, stretching in a long line across the round brickwork, halfway up, and then just two of them down below, looking interrupted. We are now too accustomed to modern architecture to realise the impression that this quite elegant arrangement would make on a buyer at the time. It would have said to him "These men reject the decencies of classical architecture; they boast of being grotesquely strange." Of course I welcome this, as refuting any theorist who says that these theatres must necessarily have been "traditional". One must remember that the Globe even in its enlarged form would be very short of storage room, and because the spectators' galleries were raked there would be room underneath the seats for rolled-up tapestries and protected carved-oak chairs and other scenery suited to the upper stage. As one crept along past these archives it would of course be a great help to have small windows, less frequent than in the picture, and there would be another row of them at the lower storey; Hollar began to draw the lower ones, and then found it would be more effective to leave them out. It makes even the first Globe more credible if one realises that life could go on under the public seats. As to shrubs in tubs, I take it that after their stage appearance they were simply rolled out of the stage door, to recover their health. Clearing the decks, for a different play every day, must have been the over-riding necessity.

The piling up of conjecture may rightly irritate a reader, and it caught my own attention as I look back. Practically all this thesis about light from behind depends upon the slanting of the side doors, and what evidence have we for that? Often in this essay I have accepted the evidence given by Adams, for some detail, as it seems to me sufficient and the source is known to the reader; but for the slanting doors he refers us to another author, W. J. Lawrence, *The Physical Conditions of the Elizabethan Public Playhouse*, 1927. If you agree that the old Theatre was an octagon, like the bearpits, and that the Globe had to be built from its basic timbers, it seems plain that any expansion of the stage would have to follow the line of the octagon; but Lawrence maintained that the origin of the sloping doors was something different. (If you think he is a ridiculously archaic author to be cited, you must realise that the later men have simply dropped the line of work he was following.) He collected statistics of stage directions calling for entries from "opposite" sides, and argued that these could not merely mean entries from opposite ends of a flat wall. One must at least agree, I think, that anyone who wrote so felt unsatisfied with the flat wall, and would rather have his piece performed on a different stage. It might be answered that opposition is inherent in drama, and could not need to be discovered there; but Leslie Hotson says a good deal about how his theatre can express opposition, and that of Adams cannot. A truth usually lurks behind a Hotson thesis, and I expect some improvement in the expression of opposition actually did occur in the final development of the Elizabethan stage. Lawrence found from his statistics that the slanted doors developed first in the private theatres, probably in the Blackfriars, but were soon adopted by the public theatres, probably the Globe. Adams, after following the same line of research, agrees with him.

The charm of this deduction is that it gives the whole invention of the Elizabethan theatre to crossgrained Old Burbage, who designed the first public theatre in 1576, and then twenty years later, shortly before his death, adapted the grand hall of the Blackfriars for use as a private one. It was here that he made the crucial innovation which his colleagues adapted triumphantly to the Globe (1599). We need to consider what problems he was trying to solve.

In the easy theatrical life described by Wickham at Valladolid, the actors could emerge already dressed from a curtain onto a square or rectangle, and if the story demanded an event upon an upper stage the spectators in that part of the gallery would readily make room for it. But very few of the audience could see into the inner room below, even if one opened the curtain. Meanwhile the baiting of bulls and bears (and cockfighting) had developed a more circular type of building, of which the octagon was the most convenient type for carpenters. Well then, if you seat the audience of a play round an octagon, it is much more possible for all of them to see just enough of an inner stage. And of course the upper stage too comes nearer. This I think was the first inspiration of Old Burbage, the idea he was struggling for when he built the Theatre, and it was readily enough accepted though he remained in trouble about his money affairs. (Wickham says that he initiated the three storeys of galleries for spectators, which were afterwards imitated by the bearhouse on the Bankside (Vol. II, Part 2, p. 58). But this is not evidence that the Theatre itself was used for bear-baiting.) In the second design by Old Burbage he was trying to attract a more upper-class audience, who would pay more; and the design is not at all remote from his first one; if they pay more, they will be able, so to speak, to get further inside.

The stone walls allowed him a theatre of 66 feet by 46, smaller than the mass theatres but high enough to allow of three storeys. Fairly expensive seats at the sides of the octagonal theatres had already been developing, and he would give more: two lines of boxes at the two sides of the stage, each convenient for two people, with a key behind and a curtain in front; also other boxes above; and on the actual stage in front of his lower storey there would be one or even two rows of stools. Allowing 3½ feet each to a box and the same to the passage behind it, on both sides, the width of the stage is already down to 32 feet, and the side doors have yet to be fitted. Meanwhile, behind the façade of the stage, there is nothing corresponding to box and passage, but ample width. Put the doors at an angle, then, the familiar angle of the octagon, and let the characters come in breezily, as from a larger world. If they march straight ahead they are aiming at the trap-door, but many of them come in sideways, "opposing" one another. A handsome 10 feet for such a doorway, at an angle of 45 degrees, takes only 7 feet of frontage, so 18 are left for the main stage, with its inner stage behind it. Each detail is a bit larger than what he already had at the Theatre, and of course the staircase rising to 8 feet at the back could be fitted in as usual, also the windows over the side doors. The entering actor, if the door is aslant, moves towards the middle of the stage, so the gentry on their stools do not make a serious obstacle for the main audience beyond. The plan was much more natural and dramatic than the flat wall had been, making the situations easier for the spectators to grasp, not only to see. It was exasperating for Old Burbage to be denied the use of his new theatre, after his prolonged struggles, and he is often thought to have died of rage; but the effects were probably good. Having to build the Globe instead, his colleagues applied his new techniques to the mass theatre and the octagon form; and this was just what Shakespeare needed for the next ten years.

C. Walter Hodges, in *The Globe Restored* (1953) and often since, has objected to the Adams plan that such an elaborate device could not have sprung into being without any historical development, or indeed have left no recollection afterwards. The Puritan interruption, and the habitual pert ignorance of the Restoration theatre-men, seems enough to explain the second part; and as to the first, those who appeal to evolution are wrong if they think that all biological events are like the growth of a tree. The birth of a child, or the emergence of an insect from its pupa, must be completed within a fairly brief time, and the only alternative is death. A large-scale human event, such as the French Revolution, is sometimes apparently like that. But a smaller rapid change, such as we are considering here, is almost always due to one man, a "genius", forcing his idea through, suffering great troubles, considered rough and unscrupulous, and then widely imitated as the source of a new tradition. We do not know much about Old Burbage, but everything we do know fits the bill very well.

Some of my opponents say that these boxes and stools were at the back of the scene at the Blackfriars, which had therefore no inner or upper stage. The theory is more plausible here than when applied to the mass theatres, because here there was at least an intention to attract grandees. Here, then, the actors normally had their backs to the great majority of the audience, addressing the grandees. We know about the stools in front of the boxes because there was an Irishman who insisted upon standing up beside his stool, thus interfering with the view; but the account, I confess, never actually quotes anyone saying that the litigants were not at the back of the stage. No one had any occasion for denying an idea which would be so remote and absurd. Ben Jonson scolds his audience, in the prologue to *The Devil Is An Ass*, saying that they crowd in upon actors:

> Who worse than you, the fault endures
> That yourselves make? When you will thrust and spurn,
> And knock us on the elbows; and bid turn;

This sounds bad, and is intended to (whereas Hotson seems to regard it as praise of the system he recommends); but a stool-holder on one side of the stage could hit an actor on the elbow, by way of saying "don't make half-turns to the other side", and this would not be so bad as kicking him on the bottom, by way of saying "turn completely round, and don't address the main audience at all". An auditorium which had reached that extent of disagreement would seem unlikely to stave off riot till the end of the play. And besides, even if Jonson had seen such an incident occur, it would prove that actors often did address the main audience, instead of always turning their backs upon it as Hotson tells us was their settled custom. I cannot deny Hotson's evidence that the Queen sat at the back of the stage in the amateur performances put on for her in Oxford and Cambridge colleges, but here you had an unusual situation, where the main audience was more interested in seeing the grand spectator than the play; surely Hotson does not think this was usual at a Blackfriars performance? There is not a single unequivocal reference to spectators sitting *behind* the actors, or above the stage *at the back*, and surely it would be likely to slip out, if they regularly did?

My argument at least gives a consistent picture. Burbage angled the door-frames at the Blackfriars because (while wanting to make all the details grander) he needed to save breadth; and he needed to save breadth because he had the expensive boxes at the sides. However, we need not doubt that the other advantages of angling the doors became obvious, even if Burbage had not foreseen them, as soon as the Queen's Children began acting in the theatre from which he was excluded. The hall faced north and south, presumably with the stage to the south as was already usual in the theatres, and the improvement in lighting given by the angled doors would be very clear. Probably a large fixed reflector, set at 45 degrees, would be placed across the angle of the wall facing each of the side doors, in the first place to provide something harmless to look at for a box-holder who could see through the door. It would be natural for the Company, when forced to build the Globe because they were excluded from the Blackfriars, to incorporate its main technical improvements. When they had the use of both theatres they transferred plays readily from one to another. Thus the invention quite probably dates back to Burbage, though it is not essential at any building before the second Globe. There, I do submit, a play could not have been put on without it, any more than at a modern theatre without electric light.

Very likely Henslowe did not realise how much difficulty he was running into, with that easy demand in his contract for "con-

venient windows" in the square building. The diamond plan
would at once have given him the convenient lighting arrangement of the Globe, and would also have let his theatre face south-
west, directly towards the afternoon sun, instead of the west.
(Probably the sight-lines were found too bad.) With the square
form, the crucial outside windows are further away; still, the
forward ones, supplying the side door and window-stage, are
only 2 yards further away, and the inner stages could be lit with
reflectors, from windows in the back wall. He would have to
allow 4 or 5 feet of run-off at each end of his upper stage, and then
presumably take the boundary of the 8-foot ceiling direct to the
back wall; this would be an obstacle to lighting the side doors
from the back wall, but I expect he would try to do that. Around
the stage door you expect a fair amount of gangway, but a stretch
holding nothing but light to the far wall on each side would be a
waste of space for storage. Perhaps (on each side at the back) a
window of 4 by 4, reaching up to the 8-foot ceiling; then, a little
beyond it, a bigger window, 6 by 6 perhaps (in small leaded
panes), reaching up to the 9½-foot one. But then again, we do
not know whether his neighbours confronted him with solid high
walls at his boundary; it has been suggested that the reason why
he could build the Fortune so cheaply was that the neighbours'
walls propped it up. He had bought more land than he was
allowed to build on – clearly, the occupiers had their rights. At
the start, he had some difficulty even in getting adequate access
to the site for the builders; but later on the Company could entertain Ambassador Gondomar and his suite in the garden of the
theatre. No doubt the neighbours were willing to be bought out,
but took their time; even so, it looks as if Henslowe would have
to provide alternative means of lighting at the start, to be sure of
getting enough. No doubt he felt that, even if the actual effect of
his lighting was inferior to the Globe's, no one could prove that,
and his windows at least made a handsome show. When he prepared the contract for the Hope, in 1613, he made no demand for
tiring-house windows, and they cannot be seen on Hollar's
sketch of the Hope, which soon had to stop showing plays
because the actors' companies, for one reason or another,
rejected it (Wickham, Vol. II, Part 2, p. 76); but these hints are
by no means decisive. He may have left out mention of the tiring-
house windows because they had become the usual thing, or
because he had given up the struggle. He was not far from his
death.

VI

None of this explains why Henslowe was keen to have the Fortune copy the Globe as closely as possible, and hired the same architect to make sure of the likeness. One would expect the reason to be something plain but impressive, a triumph for Henslowe, and there are not many plausible candidates. I suggest that it was another result from the extension of the "heavens".

There was always an engineering reason for taking the cover some way out. Adams well remarks that the two pillars holding it up should not be thick, like the structural pillars, or they would interfere with the view; they should be like the masts of small ships, which could well be 30 feet high. Such a support, though it can carry a good deal of direct thrust, is liable to yield when pulled sideways; so it could not be put at a corner of the roof, as our modern pictures assume – unless the roof was powerfully stiff. Adams puts these pillars just on the spectators' side of the main trap-door, not quite halfway out on the apron-stage, and this does seem the best position for not getting in the way. Then the cover would need to go most of the way out, to make it balance.

It may be objected that these pillars needed to be massive, and their balance could not be affected by an extra bit of roof, because they were carrying half the weight of the crane. Probably not; I take Adams to mean, by his chart on p. 375 of the second edition, that a sheer tree-trunk 42 feet long and 33 feet up crossed the stage at its widest point, with the crane just behind it, so no weight from the crane would fall on the outside pillars. This trunk would be a valuable object, but it probably did not need buying, having been inherited from the old Theatre. At what date the descent of a classical *deus ex machina* became a need for a public theatre I am not sure; Henslowe seems to have installed the equipment in 1595; but surely the Theatre would have got it soon after, if they hadn't had it from the start. Another objection comes from Hodges, and adherents of the "De Witt sketch"; that the pillars must have been classical pillars, or they would have been considered untraditional, so they must have been massive, and also cannot have gone higher than two storeys. Badly though the top gallery was treated, it cannot have been excluded from almost all sight of the stage, so this is enough to refute the position; the idea of classical pillars comes only from the "De

Witt" sketch, and De Witt himself had written that he was interested in this theatre because it was so like a classical one, so the mistake of the disciple who drew the picture is understandable. This detail seems enough to prove that the Globe did not ape classical architecture, which would have made it ridiculous. The Company got rid of the pillars as soon as possible, in the second Globe, when they were rich enough to buy the expertise for covering the whole stage without them; but meanwhile they had attracted a kind of affection as quaint obstacles.

Adams thinks that a second crane was added in the Globe, to work far out, over the trap-door (p. 368); it was not meant to carry a man, but even so it would add to the strain of the roof. The "blazing star" in the *Revenger's Tragedy* (Globe Theatre, 1606) must have been lowered in a chair from this device, just after its fuse was lit, or it would be too dangerous. Anyway, the three large huts shown at the top of the Globe prove that the technicians had been up to something. This further inward drag on the pillars would need to be balanced by an extension of the cover outwards; so probably, when the Globe was built, it did get pushed out to the end of the apron-stage and perhaps 2 feet further. Peter Street might also reflect that the Company could afford to have a proper cover, with the improved lighting at the back.

This could easily produce a magical effect. The mid-point of the front of the apron-stage was the exact centre of the octagon, and when an actor spoke just there, after the sounding-board had been brought well over it, he resounded. They found they had got a microphone. (I owe this idea, and most of the following details, to Francis Berry.) *Julius Caesar* is believed to be the first play by Shakespeare introduced at the Globe, and here he can be found testing the new equipment, as if uncertain how far it can be relied on. There is little intimacy in the play, and the complexity of character of Brutus is little more than a set of debating points against Stoics; probably the Company had asked for a Roman tragedy, to open the building with proper grandeur. Maybe Shakespeare had drafted the scene with the Ghost of Caesar before the special trick of the new stage had been discovered. Plutarch says that everyone else was asleep, whereas Brutus was thinking of weighty matters, when the Ghost came; in the play he has just had the quarrel with Cassius, which ends with making friends again, and he is feeling almost placid, though he will need to read himself to sleep. Behind him, on the inner stage, with

only the middle third uncurtained, we see one of the standard
sets, "the tent of a general in the field"; it could be set up quickly
and was immediately recognisable. Of course the actors did not
lurk there all through the long scene – the quarrel particularly
needs the front stage, and Brutus has his cushions brought out
afterwards to enjoy the cool of the night. This might seem too
absurd, on the night before the battle, or you might feel that
Shakespeare is wriggling out of the proper use of the inner stage.
But no; we have been told of elaborate precautions to guard the
secrecy of the conference, which of course a tent cannot provide;
it is a good bit of Roman grandeur to have an invisible ring of
sentries patrolling all night. Besides, nothing less would make
him feel certain that the Ghost is not a human intruder. It may
therefore be at the front of the apron-stage, with candles, that a
drowsy servant sings the restless general a lullaby but is put to
sleep by it himself:

> Gentle knave, good night;
> I would not do thee so much wrong to wake thee;
> If thou dost nod, thou break'st thy instrument;
> I'll take it from thee; and, good boy, good night;
> Let me see,let me see; is not the leaf turned down
> Where I left reading? Here it is, I think.
> How ill this taper burns . . .

and he turns to look at it, only to meet the glaring eyes of the
Ghost (it was usual for ghosts to have this effect upon tapers).
Here the words labour to explain that he is talking *so quietly as
not to wake* the page, and yet he can be heard by an audience of
one or two thousand. Probably he declaims in the old style when
he tells the Ghost to speak:

> Art thou some god, some angel, or some devil
> That mak'st my blood cold and my hair to stare?

– but when it answers trivially he too adopts an everyday tone:

> Why, I will see thee at Philippi, then.

He hurries back to his tent, wakes the servants and questions
them (though without real hope that it was an intruder) and starts
announcing new plans. Cassius must be told to hurry on the
engagement ("bid him set on his powers before and we will
follow"). The producer should make him write feverishly at his
desk, preparing for the battle, with torches held up for him. What

the Ghost says is nothing – Caesar finds it absurd to be a ghost; but after hearing him Brutus always presses too hard, and it is suggested that he loses the battle in consequence. So here the swing from front to back of the stage makes a dramatic point, or at least prepares us for one. The Ghost had better emerge and return through the main trap-door, which needs to close before Brutus makes his rush across it, carrying a book and a few cushions; this is arranged for by ten lines with the servant, before telling him to sleep again.

Having thus tested the technique and found it workable, Shakespeare made it practically the subject of his next play. Hamlet regularly walks out to the front of the apron-stage and talks to himself, confident that he is keeping his secret, and yet heard by all. He will sometimes "rant" at the audience too, but it is part of his function to make them despise the old-style manner, so he despises himself when he uses it. He has become *above* being theatrical, because he can speak to the audience as if in private, and yet this makes him the first character in drama who is uneasy about whether he is theatrical. The quarter-century during which Shakespeare was concerned with the theatre, 1588–1613, moved steadily towards a less formal style, as is most evident in the loosening of the end-stopped line till it could hardly be told from prose; and Shakespeare's Company was a leader in this shift of fashion, so that it could laugh at the theatricality of the Admiral's Men. The good fairy could not have tossed to the Globe a more welcome christening-present. It seems likely that the passionate demand by Henslowe for an imitation never taught the Fortune to play the same trick. He had not got a symmetrical enough design.

VII

Lastly, the evidence from contemporary pictures should be given its due. We have a number of "surveys" of London, describing what you would see from a balloon at a specific point above the town; the Dutch seem to have invented the technique, a display of skill with perspective. Some modern experts have discounted such evidence, especially when the engravings are made by foreigners, who are unlikely to have seen what they drew, but surely a survey of London was intended chiefly for sale in London, even if it was made in Amsterdam; and the theatres received plenty of attention – most Londoners would at least

know what they looked like from outside. One could not maintain that the sketches are accurate – they are impressionistic; but
they were planned to satisfy informed persons, even if only as
caricatures. If we can decide on the purpose of the distortions,
they become a source of information.

The earliest surveys show the theatres and bear-pits as round,
(e.g. Adams, Plates 3 and 4), and it has been argued that even
this was literally true; but it would have been absurdly expensive,
as they were made of wood. The sketches are very small, and
vertical lines making them polygons would only look fussy.
Besides, they aspired to being round, like a Roman arena or
amphitheatre; indeed, they became so when the owners could
afford to build in brick; to describe them as round was a deserved
compliment. Even when the vertical lines begin to be provided,
there seems to be a formula for showing two vertical lines only,
which make three divisions of almost equal width. This would fit
an octagon seen quite symmetrically, but has sometimes been
interpreted as a hexagon. The height is now shown as just about
equal to the breadth. The break-through comes with Visscher's
View of London (Plate 8), published in Amsterdam; the surviving copy is dated 1616, three years after the first Globe had
burned down, but this need not be the earliest edition. It cannot
mean the second Globe, a round brick building which was
slightly broader than the first and is always drawn as much
broader, cosy and triumphant. Visscher's Globe nearly keeps to
the formula of two equally spaced verticals, but the shadowed
side, on the right, has another vertical marked, thus making it
definite that there are more than six sides. The building is now
taller than it is wide, and it tapers; the bottom looks wider than
the top by about one part in six, but maybe less. The height is
perhaps equal to the width at the bottom, but definitely more
than the width at the top. The sketch is bigger and more detailed
than the previous ones. Just the same proportions are given to
the nearby bear-pit, so this formula is not a special compliment to
the Globe. However, it came to be accepted as one; J. C. Adams
says:

Visscher's delineation of the first Globe was copied in a number of subsequent views purporting to illustrate London in the same period,
among them the undated revision of Visscher; the Merian, 1638; the
Profile de la ville de Londres, 1643; the anonymous view in Howell's
Londinopolis, 1657; and the King-Loggan, 1658. All these derivative

views indicate that for many years Visscher's representation of the first Globe was highly regarded.

He only shows us one of these, the French version of 1643. The theoretical French have made the Globe startlingly high and tapering, like a lighthouse, with a flagpole almost as tall as itself; but a distinction is made; the despised Swan, far to the left, is not allowed to taper at all, though it is even more of a skyscraper. J. C. Adams does not tell us whether the other imitations of Visscher's Globe also taper; indeed he never mentions this peculiar feature, no doubt finding it too absurd for comment.

He is already fretful at the earlier surveys for making the theatres as high as they are broad; this was done merely to make them noticeable on the map, he says, though actually they were quite well lit from above:

It is too often forgotten that the Globe Playhouse was twice as wide as it was high and similarly that the width of the unroofed yard was almost twice the height of the encircling galleries, measured to the eaves. (p. 45)

Still, as this pictorial formula was accepted and progressively exaggerated, it probably had some merit; I think it conveyed the impression one got when one was inside the theatre, as a spectator. Anyhow, Adams rather overstates his case here. The Globe, on his view, was 58 feet across the interior yard and 34 feet high to the eaves-lines. But above that you saw the thatched roof, which needs a fairly steep run-off, probably 60 degrees; rising to the middle of a stretch of 12 feet, it would add about 10. Then the yard needed to slope down from the galleries to the edge of the apron-stage, by nearly 2 feet; Adams's argument seems to me convincing there. Thus the visible height, of the actual pit that contains you, is 46 feet. We must next remember that each gallery advanced inwards 10 inches beyond the one below, to keep the drip of the rain from rotting the wood, and the thatch may be expected to overhang an inch or two, making 2 feet at each end of the open space; thus the width at the level of the eaves is 54. If you took off a sixth part of that, the width at the level of the eaves would be *less* than the height. Also, you still have towering above you the huts where the cranes live, and above them again the flagpole with the white silk flag, big enough to be seen easily across the river; another 15 feet at least, making the visible height considerably more than the visible width. The audience would feel very piled up and enclosed in such a theatre.

You may feel that, inherently, there can be no corroboration of such a fancy. But the development of the pictures might have been invented for the purpose. The tapering cannot be real, and its only possible use (in the sketch) is a "subjective" one; spectators at the Globe felt that the building tapered, because the two upper galleries progressively closed in. Only to a slight degree, indeed, but it is a thing the eye readily picks up, and any more of it would be oppressive. Clearly, the chief merit of such a theatre is its concentration; a large audience is made to feel extremely close to the turns of an action or the feelings of an actor. The acoustics are inherently likely to be good, and any improvement in them will be recognised thankfully. But one can have too much of this, especially in a long performance with no intervals; the two inner stages, increasing in size till the Globe was built, were chiefly needed for occasional relief, distancing the actors from the audience, though not for long periods. Adams made this relief-hatch the chief feature of his Globe, thus letting the pressure out of it; no wonder so many people have felt his thesis to be inherently wrong. But a reduction of his distant stages, together with a reason for concentrating on the very front of the apron (so that the action often swings between these two well-lit areas), is enough to restore the balance. No one else, in this field, has achieved so much.

Most of our information about the theatres, apart from legal documents, comes from foreign visitors, whose enthusiasm makes the sullen dullness of the natives look all the more odd. But the English at the time do frequently mention the stage, in their surviving letters; they just assume that what we want to know is already known. The acceptance by later English artists of the Visscher formula for the outside of the first Globe does tell us something. They agreed that it had looked very odd and new, and were ready to accept that. To have visited the Visscher Globe, unassuming though it looks, would clearly have been a memorable experience; for one thing, it has no links with the past. Surely this is enough to disprove the argument from "evolution", nowadays so frequent, that Old Burbage must have felt obliged to copy the wagon-stage of the old Miracle Plays, or the layout of the screens of college dining-halls, or the pillared approach to the front door of a country mansion (the castle dungeons, come to think of it, might well be the model for the stage front of "De Witt"). Old Burbage was an originator, with the typical struggles of one; but he had the advantage that the public theatres were expected to be low-class, and did not have to worry about design. It does seem notable, I admit, that the first Globe received hardly any praise till after it had burned down; even Jonson's phrase "the glory of the Bank" was only struck out in his *Execration of Vulcan*. But one can understand that the class situation, made so evident, produced a certain shyness among the literati, so that the building was praised more readily after having become an ideal which could no longer be attained.

We need not think it unattainable now. The long struggle, necessitated by the extraordinary lack of information, is nearing a successful conclusion; and it is time to think of a modern replica. "Replica" is the term, as the commercial success of such a building would largely turn on whether it was recognised as authentic. This reputation could survive a certain amount of vulgarising in the decoration, to make it "period" at first glance, which would probably be needed. The pillars that hold up the heavens should be plainly second-hand ship's masts, and if they are painted to look like marble, as De Witt reports about some parts of the Swan, that will add to their period charm. In general, it would be fair to make the decorations a bit rougher and more primitive than they really were, raw wood and coarse plaster, though contrasting with occasional outbreaks of flamboyant intricately patterned ornament. On second thoughts, what I have proposed would be far too expensive; a great many massive oak beams can certainly not be procured; but surely they could be faked (thin slivers of real wood). The overall dimensions really must not be faked; the public interest in the building would depend upon acceptance of them as right. We could not pack in so many as the Elizabethans, but even with all modern con-veniences we could seat around 1,000. Matinees billed as reproducing the original lighting should occur regularly, and if the day is too dark and wet a change-over should always be announced beforehand. Probably it would be sufficient to have a canvas Big Top, which can be slid rapidly across the whole build-ing, above the Heavens, and side walls of canvas which run up to meet it. Electric lights are then used, as Shakespeare would cer-tainly have done if they had been available, but the experience of returning to the lighting at the time should also be available. Of course there would be regular night performances with the theatre shut in and lit.

It is upon a sociological ground that a literal replica is inherently impossible. If 600 men are to stand in the yard

throughout the performance they will have to be hired, at considerable expense, and they would not produce the right atmosphere. The audience in the yard must be allowed seats; benches
covered in leather (and padded under the leather) would make
the best impression. This in itself would make little difference,
merely raising the floor. But also, iron pikes would not be needed
to keep them from invading the first gallery; and the need for
some escape from their stench, which is frequently mentioned,
would no longer make it necessary to have the first gallery well
above them and 12 feet high (for air). Many changes in the proportions might follow from this; and also, the modern audience,
accustomed to wilder spectacles, cannot feel any magic in a door
9 feet high, so the window-stages could be made level with the
balcony. I feel that the queerness of the old arrangement might
excite a dislike, now that the reason for it has become invisible;
and I would not want to retain it merely as a curiosity, if that
meant losing an audience for more important things. On the
other hand the queerness of it might be found a positive attrac-
tion. (There will never be a control experiment on this point.)
One can be sure at least that the top gallery needs treating less
badly, the floor of the first gallery could be put at least a foot
below the stage, and 11 feet would be ample height for it, so the
top gallery could be higher.

There would have to be some concessions like that, but the
main equipment is so very good, and so much better than what
we now use instead, that it would make its own way.

6 Fairy flight in *A Midsummer Night's Dream*

This is the new Arden edition of *A Midsummer Night's Dream*, and it is splendid to have the old series still coming out. Full information, and a proper apparatus at the foot of the page: where else would you find that? It has got a bit stiff in the joints; the Introduction is so long and so full of standard doctrine that it is hard to pick out the plums; but the sobriety itself is a comfort. One major new emendation is proposed – that Theseus said: "Now is the mure rased between the two neighbours." Harold Brooks admits that this is bad, and agrees that Shakespeare may have agreed to have it changed on the prompt-book, but is certain he wrote it at first, because of the rules invented by Dover Wilson for the misinterpretation of his handwriting. Surely anyone used to correcting proofs knows that all kinds of mistakes may occur, whereas this bit of pedantry would be quite out of key for Theseus. "Mural down" (Pope) goes quite far enough.

As part of a general process of soothing, he speaks warmly of the merits of Bottom, but adds that "he is quite unsusceptible to the romance of fairyland", and will soon have forgotten his meeting with Titania. What on earth can the weasel-word "romance" be doing here? As a Greek of the age of myth, he simply worships the goddess. As a man who is driven by his vanity, he finds her love for him immensely gratifying, but not really surprising, so that he can keep his cool. When we see him return to his friends he has urgent news: they may collect their theatrical props and go to the palace at once, but he is bursting to tell them his dream as soon as there is time. When Oberon remarks that he and the lovers will remember the night as "but the fierce vexation of a dream", he is not giving an order, and some fierce dreams do get remembered long and vividly (or at least you can remember your reconstruction of them). The real feeling of Brooks, I submit, is: thank God we don't have to watch a lady actually giving herself to a stinking hairy worker. "Even a controlled suggestion of carnal bestiality is surely impossible", he remarks.

These cloudy but provocative phrases conceal a struggle which had better have been brought into the open. The opponent is Jan Kott, who wrote *Shakespeare Our Contemporary* (1964), and the Peter Brook production (1970) which dramatised his findings. I take my stand beside the other old buffers here. Kott is ridiculously indifferent to the letter of the play and labours to befoul its spirit. And yet the Victorian attitude to it also feels oppressively false, and has a widespread influence. We need here to consider Madeline Bassett, who figures decisively in the plot of a number of stories by P. G. Wodehouse. This unfortunate girl, though rich, young, handsome and tolerably good-tempered, has a habit of saying, for example, that a dear little baby is born every time a wee fairy blows its nose. She never repeats herself but keeps steadily within this range. It excites nausea and horror in almost all the young men who have become entangled with her, and their only hope of escape without rudeness is to marry her to the sub-human Augustus Fink-Nottle. Such is the mainspring for a series of farces. However remotely, her fancies are clearly derived from Shakespeare's *Dream*, and Wodehouse was a very understanding, well-read man, with a thorough grasp of this general revulsion. Such is the strength of our opponents. It is no use for the present editor to complain in a footnote that the Brook production lacked "charm": a too-determined pursuit of charm was what spelt doom for poor Madeline Bassett.

What a production needs to do is to make clear that Oberon and Titania are global powers, impressive when in action. There is nothing to grumble about in the tenderness of the fairy scenes towards small wild flowers and young children, but it needs balancing. Many thinkers, summarised by Cornelius Agrippa, had believed in these Spirits of Nature, neither angels nor devils, in the first part of the sixteenth century, but Luther and Calvin denounced the belief, and the Counter-Reformation largely agreed, so further discussion in print was prevented by censorship. But ten of the Cambridge colleges, at the time of the play, had Agrippa's treatise in their libraries. So the dons were not hiding it from the children, and it gives you positively encouraging advice about how to raise nymphs from water-meadows. The New Astronomy was in the same position: learned books arguing in its favour could not get a licence, though a mere expression of agreement with it was not penalised. And Copernicus in his

Introduction had actually claimed support from Hermes Trismegistus, who was considered the ancient source of the belief in Middle Spirits.

The fairy scenes here say a good deal about astronomy, though none of it further out than the Moon; and there are other reasons for thinking that the public had largely accepted the daily rotation of the Earth, but thought its yearly orbit to be supported by obscure arguments and probably dangerous.

If these spirits control Nature over the whole globe, they need to move about it at a tolerable speed. When the audience is first confronted by the magic wood, at the start of Act II a fairy tells Puck, "I am going everywhere, faster than the moon's sphere", because she has been given the job of putting the smell into the cowslips. As they all come out at about the same time, this requires enormously rapid movement, continually changing in direction. She should be found panting against a tree-trunk, having a short rest at human size, but when in action her body must be like a bullet. It seems tiresome to have human-sized spirits described as very tiny, but it is standard doctrine that they could make themselves so, and we find that they could also make themselves very heavy. It is an old textual crux that Puck speaks to Oberon of "our stamp", but immediately after this warning we see him do their magic stamp, which should be echoed tersely by a deep-voiced drum under the stage. Thus we are prepared for Oberon and Titania to "shake the ground" when they dance good fortune to the lovers: the drums now become a form of music, echoing each step (there is a very faint repetition of it when they are dancing off-stage in the palace bedroom). Then, immediately after shaking the ground, they go up on the crane, apparently weightless. Oberon remarks:

> We the globe can compass soon,
> Swifter than the wandering moon.

He is thus recalling what the fairy said at the start. He does not say they will do it now, only that they can do what is needed with a comfortable margin, if they are to dance again in the palace soon after midnight.

At the end, after the fifth Act, in the palace, Puck says again that fairies prefer to live permanently in the dawn: they run

> From the presence of the sun,
> Following darkness like a dream.

At the equator they would need to go 1,000 miles an hour, nearer a quarter than a third of a mile a second, but probably they stick to the latitude of Athens, at about 800 miles an hour. Titania, for one, does not seem a very athletic type, and the idea is more plausible if they merely rise above the air resistance, afterwards remaining at rest and observing the Earth as it parades beneath. For so long as they can be bothered, the lords of Nature hold a continual durbar.

To explain this might offend the censor or part of the audience, and anyhow would hardly fit the style. But the words assume it without any room for compromise. The distance to the Moon is about 60 times the radius of the Earth, as was already known in Classical times, and the Moon goes round the Earth in about thirty days, so the speed of the middle of the Moon's sphere, the part which carries the Moon, is about twice the speed of the equator, which revolves in a day. So the working fairy does at least half a mile a second, probably two-thirds, and the cruising royalties can in effect go as fast as her, if they need to. Puck claims to go at 5 miles a second, perhaps seven times what the working fairy does. This seems a working social arrangement. But if all the stars go round the Earth every day, with the Moon and planets lagging only slightly behind, the speed of the Moon's sphere is about sixty times the speed of Oberon when he remains in the dawn, and the working fairy is going very much faster than the boast of Puck. I agree that the phrases are meant to sound rather mysterious – probably Shakespeare asked the advice of Hariot, who was certainly a friend of Marlowe – but they would not be meant to be sheer nonsense, as has for so long been assumed.

Coming now to the flights of Puck, I am sorry that I must just assert conclusions, but the evidence is rather lengthy. Puck really did fly – that is, get jerked aside on a rope. This was easy in the hall of a mansion, where he could be caught by three strong men behind a curtain, but it was an achievement of the Globe Theatre to make him do it in public, flying into one of the upper lords' rooms. The trick was dangerous and impressive, and quite enough to prevent you from regarding the fairies as footling. Also it was a challenge to a third act of censorship, as would be obvious if this hush-up (unlike the other two) had not triumphed. Puck says he can go anywhere, as far as possible on the round earth, in 40 minutes. Now this is just the speed that Major Gagarin was going at, when he took the first trip in space round the world. Or rather, he took 42 or 43, but the accepted radius of the Earth then was too small by about a seventh, and this makes the answer a bit too small, but it is right if you let the astronaut get above the air – say, 30 miles high.

Hariot had arrived at this important result in 1592 or so, and was refused publication: probably it was the university dons rather than the clerical censorship who said (with some excuse) that his proof was riddled with ignorant fallacies. He was furious, and refused to print anything ever again, though warned that he was losing all his priorities. There must have been some major early incident to make him sulk like this, and his indignant supporters would need a slogan. Hariot would insist upon "Forty for Half-Way" because the figure really was nearer 40 than 39 or 41, whereas to be correct one would have to say "79 to go all round" – a less ringing slogan. Shakespeare, of course, would not use it in a play unless a number of people in the audience would know what it meant, but perhaps he had used it first in a satirical piece to entertain Southampton, in 1592, and merely retained it in the greatly enlarged play for the wedding in 1596. A number of people in that distinguished audience would remember what it meant, though perhaps very few in the Globe of 1600. It is to the credit of Harold Brooks, by the way, that he does not copy out the note: "*Forty*: Used frequently as an indefinite number." I should add that the idea of an astronaut, with only enough power to start and stop, would not trouble the mind of Hariot, or indeed of Puck. Opponents of the daily rotation always said that it would throw us off into space, as from a spinning top, and Copernicus had had no answer except that this movement was a natural one and would therefore do no harm. Hariot found the real answer: no one would be thrown off the Earth, even at the equator, unless the Earth went round eighteen times faster than it does, which allows a comfortable margin. Five miles a second is the speed at which you have no weight, and if Puck had gone twice as fast he would be struggling all the time not to fly up to Heaven.

Brooks quotes someone who remarked it was "boyish" of Puck, before his second flight, to say:

> I go, I go, look how I go!
> Swifter than an arrow from the Tartar's bow.

It is hardly a point of character: surely, if he had said this and then merely scampered off, the Globe audience would have hooted him. This is the strongest bit of evidence that he really flew. It looks as if the second flight was added for the Globe production: partly to give more length, partly because it seemed wasteful not to use the machinery twice, and partly to give each side of the theatre a good view of the trick. Puck is offended at being told he chose the wrong man, and insists that he can clear it up at his immense speed: but it does not really need using at all, to look round the wood. The third Act is now well over 600 lines, far longer than the others, because to excuse the flight Shakespeare added there an extra complication for the lovers, which I have to feel makes them a bore, undeservedly. Several critics have felt this, and Brooks does not really refute them by showing that the boys and girls argue according to the correct rules of rhetoric. It is a comfort to observe that Puck is so unshaken by his flight as to return after only eight lines: but they are solemn lines, restoring Demetrius to his true love, from whom he switched by no fault of the fairies. The grand smash of the second flight is followed by this priestlike behaviour from Oberon.

A different type of care is taken over the first flight. In Act II, scene i, as the audience first sees the magic wood, Puck meets the working fairy and shows how jolly he is in rhymed couplets. Then Titania and Oberon enter from the two sides and quarrel, and Puck says nothing. Then his master calls him up to receive orders, and he behaves like the traditional Scotch head-gardener, respectful but curt, plainly an expert. Of course he talks prose. He says only, "I remember", before he says: "I'll put a girdle round about the earth in forty minutes." He must be presumed to fly off at once, and Oberon, absorbed in passion, says: "Having once this juice . . . " It is a rather life-like feature that he presumes Puck to have talked blank verse, as *he* does. Then, when Puck comes back, impossibly quickly, he says:

Oberon: Hast thou the flower there?
          Welcome, wanderer.
Puck: Ay, there it is.

For the last line of the scene, when Puck has learnt the intention of the plot is to make Titania "full of hateful fantasies", he is pleased, and rhymes with an approving leer as he leaves his master.

Oberon: And look thou meet me ere the first cock crow.
Puck: Fear not, my lord, your servant shall do so.

He has got back to rhyming, but he has never once used blank verse so far.

We have here a familiar type of textual problem. The First Quarto inserts the word "round", thus making the lines scan:

Puck: I'll put a girdle round about the earth
            In forty minutes.
Oberon: Having once this juice . . .

As to the choice between 5 and 10 miles a second, I doubt whether the word "round" makes much difference. The familiar dressing-gown has a girdle held up on slots, and most of the time it goes half-way round, with the ends hanging from the slots. Puck has only in mind going to a far place, not going all round. But it makes a great difference whether he is singing in opera or talking like a Scotch gardener. The Second Quarto is only a pirate edition, but it is described by the *Riverside*, for example, as "a reprint of Q1, with a few added stage directions, and an occasional correction of obvious errors". The intrusive "round" seems to me an obvious error, which might well have been corrected on the text of Q1 available to the pirate. It is still excluded by the Folio, which is admitted to have had further sources of evidence. Even so Brooks might feel that Q1 is impregnable: but then, why does he not print it? It gives the remark of Puck as prose, even while adding the word which excuses printing it as verse. Both other sources also give it as prose. Granting that he was determined to print it as verse, his apparatus ought to have admitted that it always comes in prose. But he was determined to make the fairy sound "charming".

As to whether it is "bestiality" to love Bottom, many a young girl on the sands at Margate has said to her donkey, unblamed: "I kiss thy fair large ears, my gentle joy." If the genital action is in view, nobody denies that the genitals of Bottom remained human. The first audience would not have admired Bottom, and nor would I, for letting the thing go so far if unwilling to respond. The sequence is sadly short. After their first contact, she leads him to her bower, and a scowling husband holds them up. They arrive, and he speaks charmingly to a few babies, but then says: "I have an exposition of sleep come upon me." He often gets words wrong, but you can never be sure, and if he means a pretence of sleep it is greeted by immediate connivance. Titania orders her fays to explode like shrapnel ("be all ways away") and hugs him saying: "how I dote on thee". He is still quiet and cautious, but this is the time for exploring fingers to enquire whether she is solid enough for the purpose, and also whether he is genuinely welcome. This groping process could be made obvious and entertaining, but then the lurking husband comes forward and performs an act of magic. Probably it sounded like a pistol going off, and the audience wondered whether he had killed them, but no, they are only in deep sleep. He at once speaks confidently to Puck, having got what he wanted and settled all the other troubles. Soon after he wakes up, and they are ready to do their tremendous dance.

Kott says that the four lovers, or the six including Titania and Bottom, all wake up in an agony of shame, determined to forget what has happened, because they have had an orgy. It is a wild degree of misreading. No act of sex takes place on the fierce Night, and there is never anything to drink. Bottom really would have felt shame if he had heard what Titania said about him after she woke, but he has been carefully spared from it. He proposes to boast about his memory for the rest of his life. The others all wake up awed, rather exalted, wanting to explain themselves to each other, and we are soon told they had decided they had been teased by spirits. Harold Brooks says archly that of course Shakespeare would add any lie for a dramatic effect: but this only occurs to him because he does not believe in Middle Spirits at all. Among people who did, such as the lovers, it would only be a matter of checking up on the details.

The sex life of the spirits needs also to be considered, but this review is already too long. The book is an excellent one, and the points where it is too much within the tradition can easily be recognised.

Harold Brooks' edition J A MND

7   Hunt the symbol

We are told in a biography of Hugh Kingsmill, whose Shake-speare criticism, I think, has been underrated, that he was once walking through Blackwall Tunnel under the Thames, and became overtaken by laughter. This rather old piece of engineer-ing, narrow, straight and white-tiled, has an echo, so that he was making a titanic noise. A sympathetic pedestrian behind him was heard to say: "Jesus, that must have been a stinking one", think-ing that only some comment upon our sexual nature could have caused such intense happiness. But no, the following passage from *The Winter's Tale* was what had crossed his mind:

Cleomenes: The climate's delicate, the air most sweet:
        Fertile the isle: the temple much surpassing
        The common praise it bears.
    Dion: I shall report.
        For most it caught me, the celestial habits –
        Methinks I should so term them – and the reverence
        Of the grave wearers. Oh, the sacrifice!
        How ceremonious, solemn and unearthly
        It was i' the offering!
Cleomenes: But of all, the burst
        And the ear-deafening voice of the oracle,
        Kin to Jove's thunder, so surprised my sense
        That I was nothing.

I suppose Kingsmill felt that the middle-aged Shakespeare had become pompous and respectable, prepared to pull a long face about any accepted solemnity, but also endearingly unbothered at having to turn on the tap of this pretence. I can't say I laugh heartily at the passage myself, but I have more respect for the reaction of Kingsmill than I have for the standard one of modern analytical criticism, such as this by S. L. Bethell, in his book *The Winter's Tale*:

231

Here we have a number of epithets evocative of religious awe: "celestial", "grave" and especially "ceremonious, solemn and unearthly". The whole speech with its reference to priestly garments and the offering of a sacrifice, together with the epithets just quoted, sounds almost like a description of the Mass. Power is expressed in "the ear-deafening voice of the oracle, Kin to love's Thunder", which Cleomenes says "so surprised my sense that I was nothing" – the familiar mystical annihilation of sense in the presence of God.

No parody could invent anything better than the word "familiar" at the end; the gross impudence of it is so perfectly in keeping.

In a reaction against the "character-mongering" of A. C. Bradley, and his habit of treating a play as the historical evidence for biographies of the characters, it came to be thought that reiteration and coherence of imagery are what matter in a poetic drama. They do matter of course, but to give them this unique position leaves your judgement with no dramatic situation to work upon. A particularly good field for the Neo-Imagist Movement was found in Shakespeare's last plays, because there the story is often so fantastic that one is driven to look for some other support. I will take examples of the results from *Shakespeare: The Last Phase* by D. Traversi (1954); not as particularly bad, but as a striking representative of its kind.

Traversi says that the symbolism is somehow inherent in the poetry and the story; he does not mean anything crude; but the effect is that, in the last plays, "Shakespeare's power of uniting poetry and drama is now such that the plot has become simply an extension, an extra vehicle, of the poetry." The plot thus appears subordinate, while both of course have the "symbolic" purpose of expressing something about redemption and the unity of death and rebirth. He praises the long row of denouements at the end of *Cymbeline* because "the scene, in fact, uses the familiar mechanism of romantic reconciliation for symbolic ends of its own, working up through successive stages to a final inclusive effect" – meaning I suppose that, when each member of the cast gets a different happy ending, it feels as if we are all in Heaven.

Even with an absurd plot, the effects of ignoring it in favour of the symbolism are bad; this is particularly clear, I think, about the flowers at the sheep-shearing festival. Perdita has been made "Queen" of this village do, as one might be Queen of the May; she explains to her guests that she is only talking poetry to go with her fancy dress. A slight difference of opinion arises with an elder guest, when she regrets that she cannot provide him with streaked gillyflowers. Their piedness is made by art, because to produce them we marry a gentler scion to the wildest stock, therefore they are bastards and she will not have them in her garden:

> No more than, were I painted, I would wish
> This youth should say, twere well, and only therefore
> Desire to breed by me.

She points out her lover as "this youth"; unknown to her, she is speaking to the disguised King, who is determined to prevent him from marrying her; but he finds himself speaking in favour of the cross-breeding of gillyflowers. It is summertime, and she goes on to wish that she could give the visitor the flowers of the spring, such as the pale primroses which die unmarried (meaning apparently before the sun gets hot). Traversi remarks, "the beauty of these lines is devoid of strength, even clings pathetically to its own lack of vigour", but all the same "it is full of meaning in view of the intense reaction against passion which preceded it". I think he means that her answer about the gillyflower was the reaction against passion, but perhaps he meant her line about the marigold, suited to middle age because flowering in middle summer; it goes to bed with the sun and with him rises weeping. The whole sequence, says Traversi, proves that "her innocence is still unprepared to come to terms with certain necessary aspects of mature experience":

Her youth rejects an attitude which is essentially that of "men of middle age", and indeed her own marriage will eventually and naturally be with youth, from which the stresses and egotisms present in Polixenes will be precluded; but it also, at this stage, suggests an exclusion of passion, "blood", which is itself incompatible with maturity.

The idea that young people can't have stresses and egotisms like middle-aged people is surely too absurd to discuss. It may well be that Perdita fears pain and disgust from the first act of sex, even while longing, as she says she does, to have her lover "quick, and in her arms". But a critic could not imagine her to be worrying about that just now unless he had refused to attend to the story. She is saying that if she is separated from her lover she will die of despair; it seems almost a natural process, like the withering of the flowers: and the critic explains that she is frightened of copulation.

But Perdita's fierce and scrupulous intelligence is working differently from this. Believing that she is a peasant, and that peasants and princes are different breeds, she is proud of her breed and thinks it should be kept unmixed. Whether or not she disapproves of aristocrats, she disapproves of their interbreeding with peasants; that they might do it without marrying does not even occur to her. Maybe she is only playing with these theories, while certain that the King will forbid the marriage; but such is what her words mean. Not to see it is to ignore her heroic courage, while she expects to die a virgin in despair; and to suppose that she "reacts against passion" is a comic irrelevance. Also it does not even fit the idea that Shakespeare had become religious. As a Puritan he would wish to dramatise a temptation; she is behaving with a wild, as she believes a suicidal, degree of virtue, though she does not seem to realise that she is refusing the usual kind of love with a prince; how could the author want to weaken the effect by insinuating that she has no desire?

There is yet a third reason why it is out of place, though I grant that the story is so absurd, and the learned notes about "conventions" are so muddling, that which bits the Elizabethans took seriously is rather hard to grasp. They thought it very important to be well born, but having got yourself well born they thought the next important thing was to be brought up away from luxury on a farm. For one thing, this put you above squeamishness or false sexual shame; and Perdita gives a rather terrifying illustration of the belief. All the talk about the flowers, which Traversi finds symbolic, was unlikely to hit an audience with any shock. What did do that was the word *breed* used coolly by a young virgin. It would sound shameless if she were no less fiercely virtuous; but somehow the effect of being so farmyard is to appear very aristocratic. Having now got a certain amount of life into the character, we may be encouraged to escape from the tacit assumption that the Symbolist Poetry is just an interior monologue. The suggestions in the flower-poetry are intended by Perdita, and she is using them to needle her lover; she will die unless he marries her, and in the answer about the gillyflowers the analogy means that she will refuse his offer if he makes it; but she is not bound by that, and the only meaning she expands is that she disapproves of false seeming. Unreasonably perhaps, she is

not wholly in despair if only Florizel can be kept up to the mark.
The scene is very fine if you let the character and the situation be
real; but if you think of nothing but the symbolism, you are
bound to get into a muddle, since it is not her policy to make her
words express her meaning completely. Her character is very
unlike what Traversi deduced from her imagery, and his criticism
there would seriously mislead a producer or an actress, if they
ever believed him.

   A great deal more has been said about maturity, of course. My
students at Sheffield continually bring it up, from finding it in
books no doubt, but even so it seems rather sweet of them to have
so much reverence for old men. It seems to me that old men often
get sillier and sillier, and that Shakespeare in his last plays had no
plan to praise maturity. His sentiment is just the opposite: "Well,
the kids will have to take over soon, and I expect they'll make less
of a mess of it than we've done." A noble end, though an
unassuming one, and it makes the plays feel much better.

   Derek Traversi, in his turn, approaches with farcical solemnity
the passage that made Kingsmill laugh in Blackwall Tunnel:

In *The Winter's Tale*, tragedy and reconciliation, death and rebirth are
closely bound together into a single process. That is why now . . . the
action shifts for a moment to an entirely different place, indicates in
pressing the positive spiritual forces which are already, at this
apparently unpropitious moment, in charge of the action. Such is the
meaning of the dialogue . . . This is poetry, indeed, in which the delicacy
of exquisite sensual refinement appears as the tangible manifestation of
a hallowed state. Associated in Dion's reply with the "celestial habits"
and "reverence" of the priests, and the spiritual quality, "ceremonious,
solemn and unearthly", of the offering of the sacrifice, it becomes the
prelude to a return journey which is "rare, pleasant, and speedy", filled
to the brim with a pervading impression of the supernatural (an
impression, however, which is itself conveyed through the continuous,
intense operation of the senses) and leads finally to a taking-up of the
keyword of the play, in the final prayer "*gracious* be the issue".

We have heard about this key word before:

Value and spiritual perfection are, indeed, closely associated in the
queen's reply: "Grace to boot."

I seriously recommend to Traversi that he should get hold of the
text of a pantomime and make a study of its ample symbolism.
What Shakespeare was providing was very like a pantomime,
and the symbolism though genuine and wholesome need not be

made much of in either case. I recognise that this passage is felt to need special treatment, because it might tell us about the religious position of the final Shakespeare. But the audience for whom it was written did not expect to take pagan gods seriously; or rather, the gods would only stand for something serious in an evasive way. They let you be grave enough for a dramatic effect without the appalling gravity which might follow from real religion. Traversi does his best to find any expression of "religion", feeling that it could not be worse than atheism, whereas Shakespeare was accustomed to listeners who had one specific religion and thought others bad. The first audiences, surely, need only have felt that the passage was well enough suited to the tinsel god; and was he going to descend again, as he had done in *Cymbeline*?

The pantomime tradition, I think, has a bearing on the vexed question whether Shakespeare wrote the words for these descents of gods. It was long considered impossible because they are so frightfully bad; but G. Wilson Knight has found decisive evidence that he did (*The Crown of Life*, 1947). To put the matter in less splendid language than that of Knight, who seems rather indifferent to literary style as long as he can find a noble meaning, Shakespeare simply thought that gods in plays ought to talk in bad rhymes, like the fairy queen in the panto.

I have no wish to deny that there is a good deal of religious or mystical feeling in the last plays; I think, indeed, that while he wrote them he was preparing his soul for death, but also that he would not regard the plays as a means of doing it. To continue turning them out had evidently become an unwelcome duty, though he carried on for three or four years. In the year that the Company got the use of the indoor Blackfriars Theatre Shakespeare somehow did not want to write another tragedy. Turning over a bad play by someone else, he felt that this kind of stuff would do; and during his subsequent years in harness he in effect just went on using that story again. *Pericles* did not pass without notice; terribly short of audience-gossip though we are, we find Shakespeare being jeered at for putting on such a salacious and catch-penny play. Some of it is, indeed, very peculiar, but not for being salacious.

The gallants leaving the brothel, for example (IV.iv):

> *First Gentleman:* But to have divinity preached there! did you ever dream of such a thing?

Second Gentleman: No, no. Come, I am for no more bawdy-houses: shall's go hear the vestals sing?

Here we meet a thrilling extremity of bad taste; plainly it was screwed up by the hand of the master. Probably (if I may return to a question which really puzzles me) the passage was within reach of the mind of Kingsmill in Blackwall Tunnel. Or the delicious heroine herself, protesting her innocence (IV.i):

> I never spoke bad word, nor did ill turn
> To any living creature: believe me, la,
> I never killed a mouse; nor hurt a fly:
> I trod upon a worm once, 'gainst my will.
> But I wept for it.

The narrator Esther in *Bleak House* arouses the same electric nausea; it is done by implying "I'm such a good girl that I don't even *know* how good I am." In short, this is tear-jerks at their most reeking; Dickens is the only other prominent author who can go so far too far. (A tiny amelioration in the text has been found, but even that is doubtful.)

Here then is something for critics to explain, when Shakespeare writes like this immediately after the great tragic period. One needs to consider whether the false sentiment comes from a new mood of Puritanism; and we do seem to find him telling lies, which is so often a mark of moral earnestness (IV.ii):

> *Bawd:* The stuff we have, a strong wind will blow it to pieces, they are so pitifully sodden.
> *Pandar:* Thou sayest true: they're too unwholesome, o'conscience. The poor Transylvanian is dead, that lay with the little baggage.
> *Boult:* Ay, she quickly pooped him; she made him roast-meat for worms. But I'll so search the market.

Syphilis was reported as a galloping disease when it first hit Europe, but within twenty years it had settled down to be gradual. My headmaster was accustomed to tell boys anecdotes of rapid death after enjoyment of a bad woman; very likely he was handing on an unbroken tradition. But in these passages by Shakespeare I seem to get a reassuring echo of the poet Auden; a glaring eye, or I delude myself, peeps through the mask. He is not inviting the audience to join the fun; a situation of greater strain must be imputed. To start with, he feels: "Why should I tear myself to pieces for them? I *won't* write still another tragedy; they don't know what it costs. Just for this one year, only once, I shall fob them off." Later, when he finds that dickering with *Pericles* has produced a triumphant money-getter, his spirits revive and he begins actually to enjoy the appalling character of his nursling; his additions to it become a parody of it, and his prophetic genius foreshadows Dickens. This is conjecture; but I think it closer to the texts than the opposing conjecture which I take now to be our current orthodoxy: that he had suddenly been converted to Christianity, and was struggling to recommend that religion to his audience, by secret means, as was necessary since they were Mohammedans. I agree that he was thinking about his latter end, but I think that the reason for his reticence was a more refined one; just as the reason for turning out such a coarse play was more refined than Ben Jonson supposed.

As to the moralising which these religious critics naturally insert as part of their programme, I have a different objection: I think their morals are bad. Just as there isn't only one "religion", but a lot of religions, so there are many different ethical beliefs and a man who is simply in favour of "religion and morality" is pretty sure to include bad ones. The instincts of Derek Traversi keep him fairly straight, but his principles might land him anywhere.

In *The Tempest*, Traversi invents a startling punishment for the clowns: "Stephano and Trinculo will be, in turn, left by Prospero on the island which he himself abandons to return to the fullness of civilised life." Prospero says to his guests, when the two sinful comics and Caliban shamble in at the end:

> two of these fellows you
> Must know and own; this thing of darkness I
> Acknowledge mine.

The "cell" needs getting ready to lodge the guests, and almost all Prospero says to Caliban is:

> Go, sirrah, to my cell:
> Take with you your companions: as you look
> To have my pardon, trim it handsomely.

The "owners" of the fellows are responsible for looking after them, and Caliban is given a strong hint that he will be pardoned. Marooning was naturally thought a terrible punishment, and the only drama in the play is that Prospero has brought himself to forgive his enemies. Traversi had no reason to expect marooning,

except that he felt spiteful, and believed that this was a moral way
to feel.

Caliban has also to be viewed gravely because in his case there
is Symbolism at work. Sentimental critics have given Caliban
credit for a poetical nature, but Traversi has an answer: "the
poetry which we admire in Caliban was given him, at least in part,
by Prospero" ("You taught me language; and my profit on 't / Is,
I know how to curse"). We know that Caliban is beyond redemption because when boasting he threatens to inflict on Prospero
"unrestrained physical cruelty"; whereas when Prospero makes
Caliban scream with pain all night that is spiritual power. Indeed
"Caliban is bound by his nature to service"; please notice that
Traversi is expressing here the pure milk of the master-race doctrine, and it is presented with the usual glum sanctimoniousness
as a traditional Christian moral, with no sign that it has ever been
questioned. Before the first entry of Caliban, Miranda expresses
distaste for him and Prospero answers:

> But, as 'tis,
> We cannot miss him: he does make our fire,
> Fetch in our wood; and serves in offices
> That profit us.

The kind of life that Prospero has established in his retreat assumes, in
fact, the submission of Caliban as a necessary condition. That this submission requires an effort, indicates once more that the island is a reflection of the outer world.

It appears that, if you have to pinch Caliban black and blue as
soon as he stops chopping wood, that is rather like keeping a vow
of chastity. I must say, I wouldn't like to run into a Moral Critic
on a dark night; there is something very shambling and sub-
human about the whole movement.

Frank Kermode, whose edition of *The Tempest* came out the
same year as *The Last Phase* (1954), realises that the tradition of
"the Savage" was a very contradictory one: he appreciates the
paradoxes of *The Faerie Queene* Book VI, and denies that the
utopian fancy of Gonzalo is meant as satire upon the reflections
in favour of savages by Montaigne. But he maintains that the
description of Caliban in the List of Names as "a savage and
deformed slave" means that Shakespeare considered him
inherently a slave, much as Aristotle would have done. Well,
Caliban simply *is* a slave of Prospero, who first addresses him as
"slave!"; this is not in itself proof that Shakespeare approved of

slavery. You might as well say that to write "a prostitute" in the dramatis personae would mean approval of prostitution. When Kermode assumes it he is accepting a formula: "Way back in early times they didn't have advanced ideas, like we have; they just had moral ideas, and that was much better." His own mind does not stop there, and I was not struck with the praise of slavery in reading the introduction to his edition; but then a student at Sheffield wrote an essay on it for me, and it was plain that her natural earnestness had been gravely misled. How *could* a prince be wicked, she wondered, when he has royal blood and a first class education too; it seemed to her a more painful difficulty than it does to Kermode; though she too brightened up at the thought that it illustrates the doctrine of Free Will. The first audiences of course could hardly feel the same surprise, because they seldom saw any play without a wicked prince in it. Surely it is an absurdly deluding education for the modern world, when it reaches the peak of this exquisite flowering confusion – how *can* a royal prince be bad at all? I don't think there can be much future in it.

When Prospero says "they are in my power" Traversi explains: "The power is, of course, magic, symbolical in quality, and not therefore to be realistically judged." Symbolists no doubt regularly do think in this childish way, assuming that bad motives may be indulged if the method is artistic; Elizabethans thought that magic was quite practical and certainly ought to be "realistically judged", all the more as it was usually Black. Belief in the possibility of white magic was no doubt a support for the rising impulse to develop the sciences, but two acts against sorcery were passed in the reign of Elizabeth (*Shakespeare Quarterly*, W. D. Smith, 1958), and the groundlings were so unenlightened as to burn the house and the curios of her astrologer Dee. When Paulina at the end of *The Winter's Tale* insists that her magic is "lawful" this doesn't prove that the play symbolises Christianity, as Traversi thinks; it merely staves off the obvious suspicion that she is working for the Devil. Cerimon in *Pericles*, at the start of the series, excuses himself to the audience in the same way. You could call any pantomime "religious", as there are magical events in the story, but for the playwright to be so very non-denominational here was rather a feat of engineering; he was more concerned to remove the suspicion of religion than to drive it home.

As a magician, then, Prospero did not have to symbolise perfection, when viewed in the light of history; we may next consider him as a coloniser. Here it is a surprise to find so little historical obstacle or need to despise our ancestors; at the end of their period of expansion, the English regard imperialism much as they did just before it started. The reason is that the Spaniards were doing the colonising, and they were the enemy; it was common form or official propaganda to say that they treated the natives very wickedly. That indeed was why it was not wicked for privateers to rob the Spanish treasure-ships, so the belief that one ought not to torture natives for their gold had a fair chance to take root in England. The Life of Drake, for instance, reports that the natives would gladly supply his ships when they realised that he, too, hated the Spaniards. After the failure at Roanoke, blamed upon the Spanish Armada, we planted no colony till 1606. The supporting fleet of 1609, which only just managed to make Jamestown survive, was more costly and widely advertised than the founding one; most people in London with spare capital then invested in The Virginia Company and none of them got anything back – it soon became the stock example of a false offer.

The excitement was at an early peak when *The Tempest* was written; we may praise Shakespeare, as Kermode did, for "his rejection of the merely topical" because the references leave doubt whether the island is in the Mediterranean; but he has given it almost every possible topical interest. Scholars agree that he had read William Strachey's account of the Bermuda wreck, before publication, so he is likely to have read the abortive *History of Virginia* too. This was intended to be a strong defence of the colonists, but it was not printed till 1849, I suspect because it was thought bad propaganda. The introduction feels like an indignant Kenya settler writing to the *New Statesman* – what gross injustice for stay-at-homes to say we cheat the natives; they cheat us, all the time; and so the familiar argument goes on. Evidently the home public, adjured to finance the venture, had been saying: "I bet they'll behave pretty wickedly if they ever get there. Bad as the Spaniards, we've got to be now, have we?" The Sermons to the Virginia Company, I understand, give evidence of the same feeling. They find plenty of arguments against the view that we ought not to take land from the natives, but they recognise that arguments were required. Now Prospero is described as a South-European coloniser, so the first audiences would not find him obviously a forerunner of the British Empire. To this extent he was not "merely topical"; and the effect was simply that Shakespeare was free to put in the jokes against the colonists.

The play gives a very clear-eyed though grim picture of the

process of colonisation, which the first audiences would be bound to find interesting; though I would agree that Shakespeare need not have been very interested in these parts, which are a condiment giving the needed flavour of reality to the romantic play. What they do prove is that Prospero was not designed to symbolise the White Man's Burden, or to support what Macaulay called the nigger-driving interest; when Traversi argues for this symbolism in his high manner, taking for granted that it is very "religious", he does a moral injustice to Shakespeare and his audiences. They were not so bad as Traversi, who I take it was struggling to be as bad as God meant us to be, as bad as we were before the free-thinking Enlightenment.

The book does not set out to express actual religious beliefs, but perhaps comes nearest to them in some remarks on Destiny. Ariel carries away the dinner of the villains while dressed as a harpy, and tells them in a set speech that he is a "minister of Fate", in that "the powers" have stirred up Nature to punish their sins. Traversi enlarges upon the point for several pages:

perhaps for the first time in his work, the voice of Destiny delivers itself directly in judgement . . . This affirmation (of Destiny) is, in its unequivocal expression, unique in Shakespeare's work . . . All Shakespeare's symbolism, with the harmonizing purpose which underlies it, moves towards a presentation of the problems, moral and artistic, involved in the final acceptance of the reality of Destiny.

Any tolerably cool-headed member of the audience knows at once that Ariel is lying. It isn't true that God (who must be meant by "the powers") has made Nature revolt against the villains, because Prospero boasts of doing it himself. But we are not meant to blame Ariel for telling a lie either (the trouble about Symbolism is that, while claiming to be very refined, it promotes such infantile crudity). The pretence might shock the villains into repentance just as Edgar's lies to Gloucester in *King Lear* persuade him to stop blaspheming. After recalling some of the dreadful events in the tragedies, Traversi says that:

The Tempest, with its insistence on ideas of penance and amendment that can only follow from acceptance of a personal, spiritual conception of Destiny, is conceived as nothing less than a counterpoise to this tragic process of ruin.

It does seem clear that Shakespeare felt he had done enough tragedies and wanted to present reconciliations. But "a personal conception of Destiny" can only be God; why is this confusing phrase required? Jupiter was thought to be one of a series of Supreme Gods, none of whom had created the world; his power was limited by the Nature of Things. The Absolute of Hinduism, the neuter Brahma, is a similar conception. But the Christian God does not accept this belittling; Fate has to be his own Predestination. It so happens that we can compare two groups of people specially addicted to this belief. At one extreme (they say) you cannot induce an Arab villager to sweep away the flies on his son's eyes which he knows will blind him, because of the belief in Kismet; if the child is going to go blind, that is God's will. The Calvinist Roundheads were equally convinced of predestination, and it made them astoundingly determined men, forever forcing something through by an act of sheer will. This proves that the doctrine is only a verbal delusion; from knowing that a man believes in it you cannot predict his behaviour. Shakespeare can be observed to see through Fate; he regularly makes it the excuse of weak men, such as Gloucester, or strong men while pitying themselves, such as Othello, or while boasting, such as Julius Caesar. The reference to Fate by Ariel is again somehow verbal; and perhaps, like other references to classical religion, it was a way of sketching a grave reflection in the theatre without the risk of blasphemy. Shakespeare might well combine it with taking Christianity more seriously; but to say that he had at last yielded to the delusion of Fate is something like libel. I am not sure why Traversi wants it; but one can see that a totally meaningless belief is particularly convenient for Symbolism.

The history of the drive against character-mongering in Shakespeare criticism, personality in actors and actresses, and eventually against any indulgence in human interest while art-work is in progress, is complex but is evidently intertwined with the anti-humanist movement of Pound, Wyndham Lewis, Eliot, etc. My impression is that good local uses for the principle, to brush off some unduly greasy piece of habitual sentiment, were often found; but that the inhumanity and wrongheadedness of the principle was bound to shine through in the end.

Select bibliography

Adams, J. C., *The Globe Playhouse*, London, Constable, revised edn 1961.

Berry, Francis, *The Shakespeare Inset: Word and Picture*, London, Routledge and Kegan Paul, 1965.

Bethell, S. L., *The Winter's Tale: A Study*, London, Staples Press, 1947.
   Shakespeare and the Popular Dramatic Tradition, London, Staples Press, 1948.

Bradley, A. C., *Shakespearean Tragedy*, London, Macmillan, 1904.
   "The Rejection of Falstaff", *Oxford Lectures on Poetry*, 2nd edn, London, Macmillan, 1950, pp. 247–73.

Bridges, Robert, "The Influence of the Audience on Shakespeare's Drama", *Collected Essays*, Oxford University Press, 1927–36, no. 1.

Brooks, Cleanth, *The Well-Wrought Urn*, London, Denis Dobson, 1949.

Brown, Carleton (editor), *Poems by Sir John Salusbury and Robert Chester*, Early English Text Society, Extra Series No. 113, London, 1914.

Chambers, E. K., *The Elizabethan Stage*, 4 vols., Oxford University Press, 1923.
   William Shakespeare, 2 vols., Clarendon Press, 1930.
   The Shakespeare First Folio, Oxford University Press, 1955.

Duthie, George I., *The "bad" Quarto of "Hamlet": A Critical Study*, Cambridge University Press, 1941.

Eliot, T. S., *The Sacred Wood*, London, Methuen, 1920.

Empson, William, *Some Versions of Pastoral*, London, Chatto and Windus, 1935.

Flatter, Richard, *Hamlet's Father*, London, Heinemann, 1949.

Gollancz, Israel (editor), *The sources of "Hamlet": with Essay on the Legend*, Oxford University Press, 1926.

Harbage, Alfred, *As They Liked It: An Essay on Shakespeare and Morality*, New York, 1947.

Harrison, G. B., *Shakespeare's Tragedies*, London, Routledge and Kegan Paul, 1951.

Hodges, C. Walter, *The Globe Restored*, London, Benn, 1953.

244

Review of *Shakespeare's Globe Playhouse. A Modern Reconstruction with Scale Drawings* by Irwin Smith (New York, Charles Scribner's Sons, 1956), *Shakespeare Quarterly* 9 (1958), pp. 194–7.

Shakespeare's Second Globe, London, Oxford University Press, 1973.

Hotson, Leslie, *Shakespeare's Wooden O*, Hart-Davis, 1959.

Mr. W. H., London, Hart-Davis, 1964.

Huxley, Julian, *Essays of a Biologist*, London, Chatto and Windus, 1923.

Jack, A. A., *Young Hamlet*, Aberdeen University Press, 1950.

Jones, Ernest, *Hamlet and Oedipus*, London, Victor Gollancz Ltd, 1949.

Kermode, Frank (editor), *The Tempest*, Arden Shakespeare, Methuen, 1954.

Kingsmill, Hugh, *The Return of William Shakespeare*, London, 1929.

Knight, G. Wilson, *The Wheel of Fire*, Oxford University Press, 1930.

The Crown of Life, Oxford University Press, 1947.

The Mutual Flame, London, Methuen, 1955.

Kott, Jan, *Shakespeare Our Contemporary*, London, Methuen, 1964.

Lawrence, W. J., *Elizabethan Playhouse*, Stratford-upon-Avon, Shakespeare Head Press, 2 vols., 1912–13.

The Physical Conditions of the Elizabethan Public Playhouse, Cambridge, Mass., Harvard University Press, 1927.

Leech, Clifford, *Shakespeare's Tragedies*, London, Chatto and Windus, 1950.

Lewis, C. S., *English Literature in the Sixteenth Century*, Oxford University Press, 1954.

Lewis, Wyndham, *The Lion and the Fox: The role of the hero in the plays of Shakespeare*, London, Grant Richards Ltd, 1927.

Madariaga, Don Salvador de, *On Hamlet*, London, Hollis and Carter, 1948.

Matchett, William H., *The Phoenix and the Turtle: Shakespeare's Poem and Chester's Loves Martyr*, The Hague, Mouton, 1965.

Maxwell, J. C. (editor), *The Poems*, Cambridge New Shakespeare, Cambridge University Press, 1966.

Muir, Kenneth, " 'A Lover's Complaint': A Reconsideration", *Shakespeare 1564–1964*, edited by E. A. Bloom, Providence, Rhode Island, Brown University Press, 1964.

Nicoll, Allardyce, "Passing Over the Stage", *Shakespeare Survey* 12 (1959).

Nosworthy, J. M., "A Reading of the Play-Scene in *Hamlet*", *English Studies* 22 (1940), pp. 161–70.

Robertson, J. M., *The Problem of Hamlet*, London, Allen and Unwin, 1919.

An Introduction to the Study of the Shakespeare Canon, New York, E. P. Dutton, 1924.

Literary Detection: A Symposium on "Macbeth", George Allen and Unwin Ltd, 1931.

Rowse, A. L., *William Shakespeare: A Biography*, London, Macmillan, 1963.

Smith, Irwin, " 'Gates' on Shakespeare's Stage", *Shakespeare Quarterly* 7 (1956), pp. 159–76.

Smith, Warren D., "The Elizabethan Rejection of Judicial Astrology and Shakespeare's Practise", *Shakespeare Quarterly* 9 (1958), pp. 159–76.

Spurgeon, C. F. E., *Shakespeare's Imagery and What It Tells Us*, Cambridge University Press, 1936.

Stewart, J. I. M., *Character and Motive in Shakespeare*, London, Longmans, 1949.

Stoll, E. E., *Hamlet, an Historical and Comparative Study*, Minneapolis, University of Minnesota Studies in Language and Literature, 1919.

Art and Artifice in Shakespeare, Cambridge University Press, 1933.

Stopes, C. C., *The Life of Henry, Third Earl of Southampton*, Cambridge University Press, 1922.

Tillyard, E. M. W., *Shakespeare's History Plays*, London, Chatto and Windus, 1944.

Traversi, Derek, *Shakespeare: The Last Phase*, London, Hollis and Carter, 1954.

Walter, J. H., "With Sir John in it", *Modern Language Review* 61, no. 3 (July 1946), pp. 237–45.

Wickham, Glynne, *Early English Stages*, London, Routledge and Kegan Paul, Vol. I *1300–1576*, 1959; Vol. II *1576–1660*; Part 1, 1963; Part 2, 1972.

Wilson, J. Dover, *The Manuscripts of Shakespeare's Hamlet*, Cambridge University Press, 1934.

The Fortunes of Falstaff, Cambridge University Press, 1943.

An Introduction to the Sonnets of Shakespeare, Cambridge University Press, 1963.

(editor), *Hamlet*, Cambridge University Press, 1934.

(editor), *Henry IV Parts I and II*, Cambridge University Press, 1946.

(editor), *Macbeth*, Cambridge University Press, 1947.

(editor), *Coriolanus*, Cambridge University Press, 1960.

Wylie, J. H., *The Reign of Henry the Fifth*, 3 vols., Cambridge University Press, 1914–29.